Read *The Wheel and I* and you'll know why I'm proud to
call John Crean a good friend. In these pages you'll meet
a man who is a brilliant entrepreneur, a rambunctious
adventurer, an amusing television personality and, now, an
excellent author.
— Milton Berle

The Wheel and I is terrific!
— Steve Allen

John Crean has excelled at so many things in the life he
writes about here—from mischief to race car driving to
creating Fleetwood Enterprises—that I think everyone
should read this book.
— Buzz Aldrin

The Wheel and I by John Crean is a priceless document,
the story of one man's redemption that enabled him to
climb from the bottom to the top, through his inherent
character. A classic American success story!
— Buddy Ebsen

If you created John Crean as a fictional character in a
book, people would say, "Too unbelievable. Get real."
Well, John is real. I can attest to that. He has been my
friend for over thirty years now, and *still* seems like a
character in a book. Now that I think of it, he is. *This* book.
— Stan Freberg,
from his introduction.

The Wheel and I

My Life Driving Fleetwood Enterprises to the Top

By John Crean,
with Jim Washburn

The authors wish to thank the following for their kind assistance in the completion of this book: Martha Barrett, Johnnie Caruthers, Donna, Andy and Johnnie Crean, Marge Freeman, Marc Goldin, Ken Hoffman, Glenn Kummer, Leonard "Speed" Merrifield, Larry Miller, Manuel Najar, Dr. Robert Roper, Dave Russell, Elden Smith, Barbara Venezia and a very special thanks extended to Thomas Fuentes for his gracious editing assistance.

Library of Congress Catalog No. 00-191382
Printed in the USA
ISBN 0-9700945-0-7

Authors' Limited Preview Edition
Available postpaid for $30 from:
John C. Crean
PO Box 8449
Newport Beach, CA
92658-7452

To Donna

* JOHN CREAN

TABLE OF CONTENTS

PREFACE

This is my life as I remember it. Some of you may, however, recall that Lerner and Loewe song from *Gigi*, "I Remember It Well":

He: We dined with friends. *She:* We dined alone.

He: A tenor sang. *She:* A Baritone. *He:* Ah yes, I remember it well."

My wife Donna and I will sometimes sit around talking about events in our lives, and find that, even though we were at the same place at the same time, Donna has an entirely different recollection than I do. So, while the words herein are the truth as I saw it, I'm not saying everybody saw it that way.

I've been pressured for years by friends, family and colleagues to get my life story down on paper. Maybe they thought I'd use up all my anecdotes and finally shut up at the dining table, but they're wrong.

FORWARD, BY STAN FREBERG

If you created John Crean as a fictional character in a book, people would say, "Too unbelievable. Get Real." Well, John *is* real. I can attest to that. He has been my friend for over thirty years now, and *still* seems like a character in a book. Now that I think of it, he is. *This* book.

John goes through life playing the role of John Crean, a part he has—by now—mastered to perfection. The John Crean I knew 30 years ago is the John Crean I know today—or tonight—so little does he vary in his portrayal of himself. As actors say, "He's got the role down cold."

As such, John continues to be one of the most interesting characters I have ever known. He is eccentric, ultra-conservative, ultra kind-hearted, ultra-rich and a Freberg fan—qualities I try to look for in a friend.

In the decades that my wife Donna and I have known John and *his* endearing wife Donna, our close friendship has been bound together with—among other things—our identical senses of humor. This is a forward to a great book by the one-of-a-kind Master Wood-worker, Carpenter & Inventor/ RV Pioneer & self-made Captain of the Recreational Vehicle Industry/ hilarious syndicated TV Chef/ closet philanthropist and now Author, John Crean. His book traces his quirky life from a World War II Merchant Marine, to hand-crafting a better Venetian blind for house trailers in his father-in-law's garage, which led to his hand-building his first trailer—and creating Fleetwood Enterprises (and, decades along, hand-building its flagship RV the Bounder), which John proceeded to build into a multi-billion dollar Fortune 500 public company—the most successful manufacturer of RVs and alternative housing in America.

Since John never went to college, let alone the Harvard Business School, this remarkable feat remains one of the industrial wonders of the business world. And he did it all in his eccentric, non-Harvard Business School way—as you will discover in this book. Being a non-conformist, non-Harvard, somewhat eccentric person myself, it's no wonder John and I would gravitate toward each other. He first sought me out in the late sixties, to help him with an advertising campaign for his brief excursion into the motion picture business, producing the Elizabeth Taylor, Richard Burton semi-epic *Hammersmith is Out,* directed by Peter Ustinov. If John and I survived that colorful experience and are still the best of friends, we can survive anything. No wonder it took this thick a book to cover his many careers, not least of which is his starring as a non-conformist chef on his successful syndicated TV show, *At Home on the Range*. Come to think of it, that *is* the least of his careers—albeit a runaway hit. After building his Fleetwood Enterprises into an RV icon and American institution, it would be bizarre indeed if John Crean were mostly remembered as that funny guy in the chef's hat doing all the oddball cooking in the world's most unorthodox cooking show. Ah well. Such is life.

   With its voluminous number of pages, this book now takes its place—pound-wise—alongside the Random House Encyclopedia and Winston Churchill's History of World War Two. After reading it, you may want to use it as a doorstop. You may wish to use it as a doorstop *before* you read it… but don't. You're in for an exciting adventure in reading—just like John's colorful and non-conformist life.

   When you're a house guest of John's and this lovable millionaire calls you on your guest room intercom at the crack of dawn to say "Now here this: we're going out to breakfast! The bus is leaving in one hour! Over and out!" – you may expect to be taken to the Four Seasons. Don't. John will most likely head for his favorite dining experience: *Denny's*! And when he says "the bus is leaving" he doesn't mean one of his top of the line Mercedes or BMWs, he means his Volkswagen bus is leaving—with him at the driver's seat honking. I am the official Crean Footman, who puts the step-stool down and assists everyone on and off the bus.

John still works every day in his huge wood-working shop on his estate which he and his wife call "The Village Crean." The shop is the size of an airplane hanger (behind the mansion which John built himself in the likeness of Twelve Oaks in *Gone With the Wind*) and has every industrial saw and tool known to man. In his shop he has hand-built everything from RV prototypes to his exquisite San Simeon-sized cherrywood dining room table. Like William Randolph Hearst's table, it often sports a ketchup bottle and mustard jar. John being the patriot that he is, I figure he must have chosen cherrywood because of its connection to our first president, George Washington.

In his shop he also fashioned the three-story mansion's entry hall centerpiece; a set of enormous eight inch thick cherrywood banisters curving upward, which John carved himself. I once participated in a roast honoring John, which took place in his huge and elegant living room. Along with me on the dias were John's son Andy, and his friends Joey Bishop, Buzz Aldrin, Mr. Blackwell and Milton Berle. When it was my turn, I looked around at the inlaid Parquet floor, wooden walls, wooden pillars and wooden beams overhead. I said, "You like this house? John *whittled* it!"

Same with this book: John whittled it, out of his marvelous memory. My friend John Crean—born on the 4th of July—is an American original and one of a kind.

—Stan Freberg

SOMEWHAT LESS FORWARD, BY TOM FUENTES

The Twentieth Century has been the American Century. This book is the story of one dynamic, lucky American experiencing that era.

From the Great Depression through World War II, to the boom years of prosperity of Post-War California, John Crean has enjoyed a great life amid the ordinary. He filled his life with extraordinary accomplishments. Along the way, he achieved the wisdom shared in these pages.

His trust in family, faith and freedom sustained him. Alcohol challenged him. Bankruptcy threatened him. But, an honest and straightforward character has guided him through every danger and landed him on top.

From his start in a Compton, California garage, he built a unique company, Fleetwood Enterprises, that has provided shelter for millions of Americans and offered recreation for millions more. Along the way, he crafted a set of business policies that guided his manufacturing company in becoming a giant publicly-owned, multi-billion dollar success. He did it all by playing square with his customers, his employees and his stockholders.

Now, late in life, John has come into an era of corporate manipulation in which the attitude of big business has all-too frequently become one of the customer be damned, the employee be damned and the stockholder be damned. From my vantage point as a colleague on the company's board of directors, I saw firsthand how the treachery and greed of others have tossed John, and the business policies he established, out in the street.

John's story is one of life-long friendships, as well as of dynamic business relationships. While he has spent three quarters of a century as a keen observer of all shades of the human character, he has always chosen to see their better nature. The trust, responsibility and opportunity he has given to thousands of Fleetwood employees has sadly been rewarded by betrayal by a few in their quest for power. Because of John's character, their actions against him wounded him less than their betrayal of the philosophy and ideals he taught them. As you'll read here, John has moved on and is applying his philosophy to bold new horizons.

This book was written by a man who is full of hope and who is constantly looking for the good in others. There is much to learn from these remembrances, the lessons from which, I trust, will well serve the reader into the Twenty-first Century.

— Thomas A. Fuentes,
Chairman of the Republican Party of Orange County

So Little Forward It's Nearly An Afterward, by Jim Washburn

If you want to know what a person is really like, it is said, go to sea with him. There is something to being confined on the vast ocean that reveals one's true nature in a way rarely approached by land life.

Well into the process of writing this book with John Crean, he invited me along on a two-week cruise aboard the Donna C, which is pretty much your average $7 million, 113-foot luxury yacht.

And what did the trip reveal about John? Not a damn thing. All I saw in those weeks was the same man you'll find on these pages: honest, funny, compassionate, original, annoyingly right most of the time, and never so at home as when he's up to his elbows in engine grease.

Most rich folk don't pilot their own yachts—don't know how and can't be bothered. Crean does, along with being the chief mechanic and chef, and for his trouble he routinely gets mistaken for hired help by the swells in the yachts docked near him in port. He does nothing to disabuse them of that notion. John has no use for airs, and is generally more happy shooting the breeze with a poor Mexican ponga fisherman than he is in the company of congressmen and corporate bigwigs.

Docked in Cabo San Lucas, we found ourselves adjacent to a yacht packed with young fellows, drunk on self-congratulations (among other things) for having been the support crew for a team that had just run the Baja 1000.

They partied on, unaware that their Baja 1000 race only exists because of the initial speed record set in 1967 by the "old hired hand" next door, who, on a lark, had driven his kids' toy-like VW dune buggy on the then nearly untrod non-route from Tijuana to La Paz (These days, participants drive tricked-out road fortresses worth $250,000 or more). That jaunt resulted in the inaugural Baja 1000 race later that year, in which Crean's wife, Donna, was the first woman ever to compete.

Though it's impossible to write a book of your life without blowing your own horn a bit, John otherwise isn't one to trumpet his accomplishments. When the Creans travel in one of the RVs John manufactured, they rarely let on to their campground neighbors that his Fleetwood Enterprises made the motor homes and trailers in which the majority of them are sleeping. Fleetwood for years has been the world leader in recreational vehicles and manufactured housing. John, who grew up poor in the Depression, the son of an Irish immigrant, is the largest home builder in America, having built enough homes to house the entire 3.5 million-plus population of Ireland.

Nearly as many people in thong bikinis and such were crowding into the hot tub on the boat next to the Donna C, to pick up that thread for a moment. Meanwhile, Crean, his 22 year old grandson Billy and I were on our hands and knees on the Donna C's clammy-moist top deck, underneath a precariously-balanced jet-ski, crawling through splooshes of marine cement, aluminum slivers and splinters, helping John to make new mounting blocks for the jet-ski.

Billy and I occasionally took note of the thong bikinis, etc. next door, and asked ourselves, "Are we on the wrong goddamn boat or what?"

The honest answer, though, was, "Of course not." You can always frolic with a bunch of women in a hot tub (I can't, exactly, but I'm supposing you can), but how many opportunities do you have to see one of this nation's most creative manufacturing minds at work?

Crean is an anomaly in this gray corporate era: a man whose company and products bore his indelible individual stamp. He started a business in a Compton garage, steered it into a $3 billion dollar a year Fortune 500 company, and based his success on the all-too-rare notion that you should put your customers and employees first.

His employee profit-sharing plan and other company policies were pioneering, but they pale beside his visionary inventiveness. Fleetwood's greatest product successes sprang from John's mind and hands.

On the Donna C, I saw the same absurdly practical mind that revolutionized the motor home industry with the best-selling Bounder applied to a variety of problems. When the steering system gave out on the ship's tender boat, John simply cut the cables free and bolted a two-by-four to the outboard motor. One afternoon at sea, when he had a chunk of frozen meat far too thick to thaw in time for dinner, John took it down to his tool room, introduced it to his band saw, and voila!

The late physicist Richard Feynman, whom John is not unlike in his storytelling ability, once theorized that the entire universe might simply be composed of one very busy particle. Some people seem to get around nearly as much. The same race car driver who was the original customer for the James Dean death car is the guy who produced the ultra-trashy Liz Taylor-Richard Burton flick *Hammersmith is Out*, as well as being the star of an oddball cult-fave cooking show that turns up on TV as far away as Australia, while also finding the time to fund seemingly every charity within a hundred miles of him. That's all John, and that's just the tip of it.

He loves mischief. Sober for 50 years, he still revels in telling tales of his drinking days. He enjoys swearing so much that Donna calls it "just John speaking his native language." I've never met a person who talks less about being a Christian, or who acts more like one. Ask him about the compassion, forgiveness and charity he and Donna practice and he'll only say they live that way because it's more fun.

There's a lot of advice in this volume on how to be successful, but even more, it is a treatise on how to *be*. The raw joy John finds in living is contagious.

One has reason to be suspicious of "as told to" books,

since you rarely know if it is the celebrity or the scribe who is actually doing the telling. But if this book were a mosaic, the tiles would be virtually all John's. All I did was help arrange the tiles and trowel some mortar between them. He's a natural storyteller, and most attempts to improve upon his delivery nearly always resulted in my going back to his original prose.

John probably has a few more books in him. Along with the still-untold anecdotes—after nearly two years of working on this tome, he was still remembering different times he was arrested—he is starting anew in business. He turns 75 this year, 2000, but I won't be at all surprised if he makes as big a mark in this new century as he did in this past one.

— Jim Washburn, co-author

THANKS FOR THE FIREWORKS

I was born on the Fourth of July, which can give you a pretty warped idea of your own importance when you're a kid. My earliest solid memory is of my fourth birthday, at Banning Park in Wilmington on the Fourth of July in 1929. The sky overhead filled with blossoming fireworks, everyone was waving flags and whooping it up, and I was pretty sure that they were all celebrating my birthday.

The other special things about that day were that I had never before seen a dragonfly and I had never before had all the fried chicken I could eat. I gorged myself on the chicken and got heartburn. Somehow, I connected that with the dragonflies, and for nearly two decades every time I saw a dragonfly I got heartburn. That's how strangely the old gourd atop your neck can work. Hell, I still kinda think everyone's celebrating my birthday on the Fourth.

When I turned four, my family had just spent a whole year on the road, migrating from North Dakota to Southern California, by way of Texas, Washington and a six-pack of other states, in two Model T trucks my dad had made into primitive RVs. That whole year, the bed my sister and I shared doubled as the driver's seat. I don't remember any of that nomadic existence, but maybe the highway hum got to me subliminally, because I wound up spending my life making houses that rolled, and my favorite thing still is to take off in one with my wife, Donna.

Though I'm not associated with the company I founded anymore, we like to count the Fleetwoods in the camp grounds where we stay. Maybe 35 percent of the RVs on the road are ones I've made, and about 73,000 families a year have been buying a Fleetwood manufactured home to live in. I'm proud of that. If Donna and I go for any period of time without seeing one when we're traveling, we get depressed.

I don't strut around the RV parks telling people who I am. Sometimes people have spotted the manufacturers' plate on my rig and asked about it, and I'd say, "Yeah, I'm with the company." If they questioned me further, some of them figured out who I am. But just by talking to people incognito, you get a lot of ideas for designing the RVs. And sometimes you'll get someone telling you what a piece of crap they think it is. That goes with the territory, but I'm usually given a pretty good feeling about the business I built.

I think if I'd been born in the Soviet Union, I'd still have ended up as a boss. Even when I was running around with my little buddies when I was six, somehow I'd get them to push the wagon while I rode. I was just a shrimp—the other kids were bigger than I was—but I was able to get them to do things my way.

Later, I really had no choice but to be my own boss, because I was no goddamn good working for anyone else. Once I became my own boss, I was able to take my business from my father-in-law's garage to the Fortune 500, and I had a hell of a lot of fun along the way.

The farm where my father was born in County Cork, Ireland.
It was unchanged when we visited it in the 1960s.

My father, Andrew Crean,
shortly after his arrival in
New York at the
turn of the century.

My mother, Marie Skjold,
in her confirmation
photo.

The farm house where I was born, outside
Bowdon, North Dakota. Character building, isn't it?

The family in 1924; my father, sister Mary,
brothers Speed, Kenny and Gerald, and my mom,
with me in the oven.

THINGS I DON'T REMEMBER

I was born in 1925 in Bowdon, North Dakota, in the middle of the state, 20 miles west of Carrington, which is pretty much 20 miles west of nowhere. Bowdon had 500 people, a Catholic church, a Lutheran church and some nondenominational whorehouses. The James River—they call it the Jim River—has its beginning right on my family's farm, where an old swamp trickled out into a stream. Boy, did they have mosquitoes. I visited there years later and the population was about the same, just with more mosquitoes.

I'm almost positive I had to have been an accident. My mother already had three boys around from a previous marriage, and probably only wanted a girl before she stopped. She'd had that in my sister, Mary. My parents were both getting up in years, so when I came along three years after my sister, I'm pretty sure that was an "oops."

Mom was the oldest of five siblings. Her four brothers were all born in the US, but she had come here from Norway with her parents when she was three. Her maiden name was Marie Gunhilda Skjold. I never met my grandfather, and my grandmother never did learn English. She spoke Norwegian all her life. She could have been speaking Martian for all I could tell.

Mom married a guy who was a revenuer for the Federal government, Gilford Merrifield. They had my brothers, Speed, Jerry and Kenny, and lived near Terry, Montana. They were twelve miles out of town, with no automobile and no phone. That wasn't the handiest place to be during the influenza bout in 1918, and that's where and how Gilford died.

My father, Andrew Crean, grew up on a farm in County Cork, Ireland. He'd been schooled by nuns who beat the tar out of him, and he'd become super anti-Catholic, which didn't present much of a future in a country where the Church controlled everything.

So he came to New York City when he was 19 years old, by way of Havana, where he learned the cigar business. He had what they called a cigar factory then, which was just a small shop where they made cigars in the back. I have photos in which he is a tall, gangling young man, well-dressed and evidently prosperous, but it's possible he was only borrowing the photo studio's clothes.

His health was bad. Though they didn't know what to call it then, he had emphysema. His doctor told him he needed to move to the country, so he bought a 320-acre farm in North Dakota, sight unseen. Somebody must have really sold him a bill of goods, because you don't go to North Dakota for your health. If he'd come to Southern California then, his health might have ended up as a different story.

His house on the farm was actually made from a kit you could order from Sears-Roebuck, that was shipped with all the lumber cut to size and a set of "tab A goes in slot C" type instructions.

After living on this mosquito farm all by himself for a while, he ran an ad for a housekeeper. My mom, who had moved to Fargo after her husband's death, answered the ad and went to work for him, moving in on the farm with my three brothers.

They got married in 1921, but I think it was mainly a marriage of convenience. It was a sad situation with my mom because she never buried her first husband. The older she got, the more wonderful Gilford became. From what I could tell, he really wasn't wonderful at all. As a revenuer, he was on the road a lot, and he never came home with any money. The excuse he gave her was that he spent it all on magazines, and she believed that. You can only read so many magazines! But she was really in love with him, and when he died it just never quit for her.

I knew she felt that way because she'd always talk to

me about him when I was little. I imagine most kids would feel uneasy about that, but it didn't bother me, because the way she described Gilford, he seemed more like Mr. Good Guy in a movie than a real person. With his work taking him away from home so much, I don't think she even knew him that well.

She was always comparing him with my dad, and it's hard to compete with a ghost. So my parents weren't that happy, although they were very loyal to each other, no question about that. When she died in 1973, though, she wanted to be buried in Fargo, next to her first husband, instead of with my dad in California.

Around the time I came along, my brothers were all teenagers. The two oldest helped on the farm while my mother and Speed did the housework and gardening. It's hard to say exactly what my dad did. I don't think he did a day's work in his life that I know of. He couldn't really, with his health. But he was a resourceful guy, and really good with mechanical things. I heard about a guy who had come by the farm with his Model T, with his rods knocking so bad he was about to knock the bottom out of the engine. My dad dropped the pan, wrapped some bacon rind around the rods, tightened the rod caps up against the rind and the knocking vanished. It was enough to get the guy home.

He was always hustling some sort of business. When he first got to the farm, it was just mud all over the place. Of course, being from New York City, he wanted some pavement around, so the first thing he did was get some concrete. People around there didn't even know what concrete was, so he had to have a freight car load of Portland cement shipped in to Carrington. He rented a warehouse and became the concrete distributor for the area, and also became a Briggs & Stratton representative. He went to an industrial fair in St. Paul and saw a device called a fresno, a dirt-scooping gadget that did a lot of work. He bought a couple of fresnos and put in the low bids to do road repairs in two counties.

He never worked the farm himself—my brothers or

hired help did that—but he and my mom managed it pretty wisely. They grew wheat, corn, oats, beans and other crops. One year they lost an 80-acre bean crop to an early frost. My brother Speed remembers another year when, instead of planting what everyone else was, they put about 40 acres in potatoes and made some good money. The next year they planted nearly the whole farm in potatoes, but everyone else had followed their lead, and the price went *pfft*. So Dad had all the potatoes put in a big ditch and covered them with straw and tree limbs, then buried them so the frost couldn't get to them. They left an opening and dug potatoes out of there all winter to feed to the hogs and cattle. They raised some fat hogs during that winter, which is usually tough to do. As far as Speed knows, some of those potatoes are still buried there.

The Depression hit the farm states long before it hit the cities. After a while, no one could afford cement anymore and the counties couldn't collect enough taxes to pay for the road repairs my dad had been doing. There was no market for his crops. Things really went to hell in a hand-basket, and in 1926 the bank foreclosed on the farm and we moved into a little house Dad bought in Fargo.

Eventually he decided he'd had enough of North Dakota. He bought two Model T truck chassis, designed camper houses to put on them and had my brothers build them. They even had wood stoves with stovepipes coming out of the roofs. We left as soon as the vehicles were ready, in the middle of winter, on January 5, 1928.

My dad had already been down to Texas one winter to scout the place out. So we headed to West Texas, to a one-horse town near Lubbock where we camped while my brothers got work on a road construction crew. But it snowed there, and my dad had seen enough of that, so we kept moving. My mother's brothers were in Seattle, and we aimed in that general direction.

Along the way, my brothers got work building a dude ranch near Carlsbad, New Mexico, then on a road crew near Roswell. The family continued up through Colorado, then

Wyoming. There was one day on the road when there were seven flat tires, and they had to pack one tire with rope so they could straggle into the next town. My mom started keeping a diary of the trip, but after a couple of months it tailed off. I'm sure it was all she could do to keep us clean and fed while we were camping along the roadsides. The family did harvesting in Idaho, and then dam-building in eastern Oregon.

Mom's brothers had become pretty successful running bus lines in Seattle. Somehow the sight of all of us pulling up in these road-kill Model Ts must have given them the idea that we meant to freeload off them. All I know is they initially gave us the cold shoulder, and my dad didn't wait around for it to thaw. He was too proud, and he had his sights on Southern California anyway. It had been my mom's idea to go to Seattle, while Dad had been keen on California ever since one of his Bowdon neighbors had moved there and written back about how swell it was.

We headed south, until my brothers found work on the Tagus ranch near Tulare in central California. It was one of those company store situations. You'd get in debt to the company store and couldn't move on until you got out of debt, and they would never pay you enough to let you get out of debt. We were stuck there, broke, like in *The Grapes of Wrath.*

This whole time, though, my folks had our house in Fargo on the market, and it finally sold. The day they got the proceeds from that, we paid our bill and headed for Southern California. We arrived in Long Beach—initially sleeping on the beach at Terminal Island—exactly one year after we left North Dakota, on January 5, 1929.

That year on the road was quite an odyssey, and I wish I could say that my character was formed by the experience. But all I got from it was one disjointed memory, of fish flopping around in tubs at some roadside fishing spot. That's a kid for you: You can take him to the rim of the Grand Canyon and instead he'll be fascinated watching some stink bug crawling in the dirt.

The house my dad built in Compton.

The family in 1933, around the time of the Long Beach
Earthquake. Gerry, Speed and Kenny (top row), Gerry's wife Teddy
holding my neice Linda, my sister Mary, my dad, my mom,
and me.

Downtown Compton, obviously also around the time
of the Long Beach earthquake.

STRAIGHT OUTTA COMPTON

My parents rented a house in Compton, which wasn't what you'd call the inner-city then. The town was mostly chicken ranches, open fields and truck farms. "Downtown" Compton was just two long blocks, between Alameda Street and the Pacific Electric rail tracks. There were two markets—a Smith's and a Safeway—along with a J.C. Penney's, a Woolworth's, a Newberry's, two drugstores and a couple of barber shops. The shops would stay open late Saturday evenings, because that was everybody's big shopping day. It was a terrific little town.

The city limits measured maybe a mile by a mile-and-a-half, and most of what constituted the "city" was fields overgrown with yellow mustard, dotted with farms and dairies and the occasional housing tract. Then you were in the boonies until you came to Lynwood or Long Beach, each about eight miles away.

Most housing tracts such as the one we soon moved into didn't actually include the housing back then. The developer would only scrape some land clear and put in streets. You'd buy a lot and get your own house put up somehow. My family built a little three-bedroom stucco house in a tract that used to be a fruit orchard two miles east of downtown. Like just about every house built in California in the '20s and '30s, it was Spanish style, white with red tile trim.

It was only a three-street tract, with more vacant lots than houses. It looked great compared to the next tract to the east of us. There, most of the people had bought their lots right before the Depression hit. Then they had no money to build, so they slapped up little garage houses with studs and tarpaper. The tract was nicknamed Hooverville, because everyone blamed Herbert Hoover for the Depression.

There was no smog to speak of then. I could climb up

on the garage roof, look north and see the Los Angeles City Hall and oranges on the trees to the north-east around Pasadena, then turn south and see the smoke stacks on the steamers in San Pedro harbor.

I wasn't really old enough to get in any good trouble my first couple of years in Compton. The only thing I remember my mom getting upset about was that she expected me to come home to go to the bathroom, but I'd just take a crap out wherever I was and keep on playing.

One of the Model T's was parked behind the house and that's where Kenny and Speed slept. Before too long, Jerry and Speed got married and moved out, and Kenny moved into the house. My dad sold that Model T to a neighbor on the next block who took the camper off the chassis and used it for a chicken coop. Our remaining camper was by the garage and that became my hideout.

By the time we arrived in California, my dad was pretty much an invalid. Along with the emphysema, he had a bad case of rheumatism. He'd been bucked off a horse in North Dakota and injured his back. When cold weather set in he could hardly move.

My dad was tall and thin, with high cheek bones. When I was growing up he mostly wore bib overalls, and a hat he only took off when he was in bed. He had a real farmer tan, brown to where his neck ended. He never had any gray hair; it stayed coal black his whole life.

Maybe that's because he never seemed to worry any more than he had to. Several times, when people were bitching about the Depression and not having jobs, I remember him saying, "I don't know what you're complaining about. You're not *cold*."

He'd been cold all his life. Having been born in Ireland, and then living in New York City and North Dakota—when he got to Southern California he thought he'd died and gone to heaven.

He'd do what he could, whatever could be done sitting in his chair. He'd buy leather and make our shoes. He was really handy with things like that.

My mom got work in the sewing rooms in LA, making maybe $1.50 or $2 a day, and spending 40 cents of that on bus fare. She had to walk the two miles into town to catch the bus. Even so, she was always very prim, always well dressed, very careful about her appearance.

Mom and Dad never displayed much affection toward each other, but you rarely saw adults showing affection then. Mom didn't show me a lot of affection either.

My sister and I shared a room. We cared a lot for each other, when we weren't killing each other. I really had a no-win situation with Mary because if I didn't do exactly what she wanted me to, she'd slap me hard. I'd scream and holler and run to Mom about it, then Mary would tell mom I'd done some horrible thing and Mom would always believe her. I just had it coming.

But in between that, Mary could be really nice. We shared a bed when we were little, and we'd lay there and talk about all the things we were going to do in our lives and how much we liked each other. But Mary had very poor eyesight and as we grew up she kept to herself a lot, curled up in her room with a book. She was a loner and didn't volunteer to do much around the house, or even show herself much to get volunteered.

With my mom working and my dad laid-up so often, I was kind of a latch key kid. I spent a lot of time by myself in the vacant lot behind our house. I rigged up a bit of a fireplace with a piece of stove-pipe on top, because I loved making fires, throwing wood in there and getting it roaring. I'd heard that if you could make a fire hot enough, you could make a diamond, so I'd be pouring motor oil and everything else I could lay hold of down that smoke stack.

The primer gray Model T we'd kept was sitting up on

blocks, and I'd use an apple crate as a step to get in the door. It wasn't much to look at, but it was sort of mine.

I kept the Model T pretty much to myself, as my secret refuge, but I'd range over the whole neighborhood playing with other kids. We'd scramble around doing the "Bang, bang, bang, you're dead" bit. Some of the other kids had real cap pistols, but my gun was the door handle off an old car, and that was as good as anything to me.

Later, we figured how to make rubber band guns out of slats from apple crates, clothes pins and a cut-up inner tube. We'd also play a game we called Real Estate, which was basically mumblety-peg, where you divide up each other's property by taking turns chucking a pocket knife into the dirt. We'd also get milk bottle caps from the dairy and play what the kids now call Pogs.

I was never very good at softball or the organized sports, but I was real good at playing hide-and-seek with the rubber band guns and things like that, because you had to be tricky. It was every man for himself.

I was a happy kid, having a good time. Life was a circus and I didn't really think much about anything. I'd hear about the Depression, but I didn't know what they were talking about, because we had plenty to eat, and I'd never been anywhere or done anything else. You don't miss things if you don't know you're missing them.

When I was eight something happened that changed my happy-go-lucky attitude. 1933 was the year of the Long Beach earthquake, and, despite the name, it just about leveled Compton. I'd been very comfortable up to that point because I had it in my head that adults had everything under control and nothing bad was ever going to happen to me.

But this one night I was by the kitchen sink fixing myself a sandwich. I was hungry, and dinner wasn't going to be served for another five minutes, because my dad always listened to some radio show until six o'clock. Suddenly, though, at five minutes to six, all this home brew my dad had in bottles under the sink started flying out of the cabinet, and the whole house was shaking. My first thought was that it was the home brew exploding, because it could do that.

I headed for the front door, but was knocked on my ass three times before I made it there, the floor was shaking so bad. We had an upright piano against one wall, and it got knocked over to the opposite wall.

No one knew what was going on, because all the radio stations were knocked off the air. Then some official came through the neighborhood telling everyone to stay out of their houses because most of the gas pipes had probably broken, and you could asphyxiate or go up in flames. In our yard, my dad pitched the tent we'd used on our trip to California. We pulled mattresses out from the house and slept in the yard for the next week while the aftershocks continued.

All through that first night it kept rocking, and sometimes I couldn't tell if it was the ground or me, I was shook so bad. My mom was a nervous wreck, and she wasn't alone. All night long you could hear women in the neighborhood screaming or praying in hysterical voices. And the out-of-control sound in their voices really scared me, because these were the adults who were supposed to be keeping my world in order.

I kept shaking until the middle of the next day. I was really a case. Then my dad said, "I heard the street down there broke in two. You want to come along to see?" I walked with him, and that calmed me down. Down on Rosecrans Avenue, the asphalt had split apart and one side had been pushed up five inches above the other, and that was pretty neat.

All of downtown Compton was built of just brick and mortar, and the whole place had come down. You could stand on Main Street, look in any direction, and have an unobstructed view over the roofs of the collapsed buildings. The schools were gone too. It was six weeks before they got temporary classrooms made up from two-by-fours and wood-chip boards. The schools weren't rebuilt until the next year.

When they were rebuilding the town, we kids were getting paid 1/4-penny a brick to knock the old mortar off, so they could use them again. It was a good time. Everybody was helping everybody else fix up their houses. People weren't griping and complaining like they had been about the Depression—they were busy putting things back together. As the merchants got their places rebuilt, they'd each have a big celebration, with free balloons and country and western bands.

The center of activity in Compton was the Pacific Electric depot on the west side of town, where the Red Car line came in from Los Angeles. The shoeshine stand was there, and that's where the only black people in Compton were then. They'd come in on the PE streetcar from Watts to run the stand. That was a great place to hang out because of the hilarious jokes and antics those guys would come up with. To me, they were easily the most interesting and talented people in town.

I've always loved humor. I'd be glued to the radio most evenings, listening to Fred Allen, Amos and Andy, Jack Benny and the other comedians. My dad had a good sense of humor, too, and my mother didn't like it at all. He was always clowning around, and she'd get terribly embarrassed. I took after him, and it got me in a lot of trouble at school.

I never felt deprived that my dad wasn't healthy like other kids' dads. I was crazy about him, and one of the reasons was that he was always there. If I had a question, there he'd be, and he was always very patient, taking the time to explain things to me. Other kids' dads usually weren't working, but they'd be out looking for work or doing whatever. So I felt very fortunate to have my dad at home.

He didn't require a lot of looking after, and I took care of him during the day when I wasn't in school. There was an old doctor in town who would come by and see Dad. They'd just sit there and talk politics because there really wasn't anything the doctor could do for him.

My sixth grade class. That's me distinguishing myself in the back row, second from the left.

With Mary

With my dad, model airplanes were one of my loves, then and now.

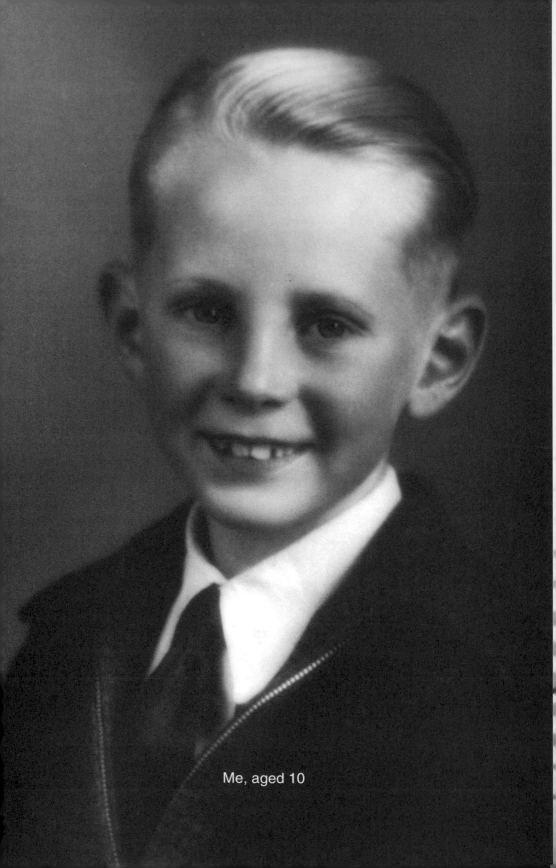
Me, aged 10

My dad was a Democrat. Everybody was a Democrat then, where we lived, thanks to Hoover. For a time my dad was very active in politics. He convinced one guy to run for the State Assembly and helped campaign for him. The guy won, so in January, off he went in his Model A to Sacramento, to serve in the Assembly for six weeks, and then he'd come back home. That's all there was to running the state in those days, as opposed to the year-round conniving that goes on now.

Having been poor in Ireland and living through the Depression here, my dad always felt there must be a more equitable way of distributing wealth. He explored Marxism, but he never adopted it, because it conflicted with his strong notions of individual responsibility. He would swing back and forth on that. For a while, he thought Joe Stalin was the greatest. Then, when more of the truth came out about him, he decided he was a bum.

When Upton Sinclair, who was an out-and-out communist, ran for governor in 1934, my dad supported his campaign and I passed out literature for him. Sinclair had a program called EPIC, which stood for End Poverty in California. He proposed that everybody over 60 years old get $100 a month, and that they had to spend the $100 in that month. That was supposed to pump enough money into the system to bring us out of the Depression. He damn nearly got elected, and at the time I thought it was really a bummer that he lost.

We never had much money, and we had even less after my brothers moved out and had households of their own to support. My parents had financed building our house with a mortgage that was held by a Mr. Stakemiller in Long Beach. He was a reasonably wealthy man because in the 1920s he had invested in real estate on a knob of dirt east of Long Beach called Signal Hill.

There wasn't much high ground in the greater Los Angeles area, so the view from this 500-foot hill made it a prime real estate prospect. But then an oil exploration company punched a hole in one of Mr. Stakemiller's lots. Oil has been squirting out of the hill ever since, and it never did get developed for homes. Today the hill looks like a tired old place that never had a chance. It's now dotted with injection wells, pumping salt water into the ground because it's been sinking as the oil was pumped out.

None of which is part of my family's story, except that Mr. Stakemiller's good fortune made him better disposed to hear my dad's tale of woe when we couldn't afford our mortgage payments. As the Depression worsened, my parents simply didn't have the money.

My dad took me with him on the bus to Long Beach when he met with Mr. Stakemiller. He was anything but the stereotypical mortgage holder anxious to throw poor people out on the street. Rather, he listened sympathetically to my dad, and then asked if we could at least afford to pay the interest on the loan. They shook hands on that.

A year or two later, when my parents couldn't even afford that, I went with my dad to see Mr. Stakemiller again. This time, he suggested that we just pay the minuscule taxes on the property and keep on living there. That situation obviously worked for us, and it was also in Mr. Stakemiller's best interest. By then, the Depression was so bad there was no real estate market at all, and our living on the property at least kept the place maintained and safe from vandals.

In my younger years, Dad was still fairly active. Eventually, it got to where he could hardly breathe. I spent a lot of time with him when he was that way, and it got pretty sad.

I'd do the cooking for the two of us. I baked a lot of angel food cake, because it isn't anything but egg whites, sugar and a little flour. We had tons of eggs, because everybody had chickens.

We had all the vegetables we wanted to eat, basically for nothing, because the little farms and dairies nearby just couldn't sell their product in the Depression, and they didn't want it to go to waste. Hardly anybody had refrigerators then. My main memory of visiting my brothers' grandparents—who lived in Los Angeles—was that I got to suck on ice cubes from their fridge. That qualified as a special event then.

When I started kindergarten, the first day I took it in and told two of my buddies, "I don't like the looks of this whole layout." So the first time the teacher went out of the room, I got those two buddies and hightailed it out of there. We were on our way home, crossing a big field, when one of the kid's moms saw us and herded us back to the school. That was the beginning of my academic career, and it didn't get any better.

Actually, I did pretty well in the first through third grades. Then, because I did so well, they skipped me from the third to the fifth grade, and it was really downhill from there. I'd skipped over too much and was never a good student after that. I learned more from my dad, who taught me my multiplication tables, drilling me over and over.

Though I liked to clown around in grammar school, I really looked up to all the teachers I had. They were a cut above everybody else to me. For starters, unlike most of the people around, they were working steady. And they all seemed like model citizens, never using profanity or letting their tempers show.

I'd had skin problems with eczema since I was a baby, and I was very sensitive about it as a kid. My neck and the insides of my arms would get all red, so I'd wear collars and scarves to try to hide it, which I'm sure looked even dumber. Sometimes my face would break out.

I think my skin condition may have contributed to me doing as poorly as I did in junior high, because, whenever I was broken out, I simply didn't show myself at school. The other kids didn't give me as bad a time as I gave myself. I think that's because a lot of them had impetigo, which was a skin condition you got just from being dirty.

Up through the sixth grade, I pretty well toed the mark,

never playing hooky or acting up. But junior high was a whole different routine, where you had a different teacher for every class, and you got the feeling you were on your own. I was always in hot water there, missing classes and smarting off to teachers. The first semester of seventh grade, someone nominated me for student council, and I was elected. I don't think I was on that council for three months before I got in so much mischief that I was tossed off it.

Then I got thrown out of school. I wish I still had my dismissal notice: I was "insolent," "incorrigible" and all manner of things, though chiefly I just wasn't doing my homework and was giving them lip over it.

I had to switch from attending Lynwood Junior High to Roosevelt Junior High. Then I got tossed out of there and *back* to Lynwood.

During that time at Roosevelt, I met a guy who became my best friend for years after that, Red Caruthers. He'd been one of maybe half a dozen guys in the eighth grade who smoked. I'd hang out with them when they'd duck out behind the baseball backstop, even though I didn't smoke then. I'd tried, but when I inhaled, I got dizzy and fell down, and that scared the daylights out of me.

Like you might guess, Red had freckles everywhere. He had thin, sharp features and was short and wiry. His right arm had a deformity, where he couldn't turn his hand over. He carried that arm funny, out from his body, so you could spot him from a mile away. He also always wore a dumb little motorcycle cap with a leather bill.

I didn't have many friends then. After the sixth grade, I hadn't been getting along with my schoolmates. It's hard for me to recall what it all was about now, but I was just a nasty kid. It wasn't until the tenth grade, when I had a mechanical drawing teacher who took me under his wing, that I calmed down a bit.

In history and English, I didn't know what the hell they

were talking about, because I'd missed so much when I was skipped past the 4th grade. But I was good at mechanical drawing, print shop, wood shop and electrical shop, all things, curiously enough, that came in handy later in life.

My mechanical drawing teacher was a fairly young guy, with a wife he'd only recently married. One Saturday, he took me with them in their new Plymouth coupe to March Field, because we were both crazy about airplanes.

That was one of the first times I'd been anywhere, because we usually didn't have a car in my family. Growing up, I think I got to go to the LA County Fair once and to Catalina on the steamer once. And that was it, except for one time when my brother Speed drove us out to Hemet to see a Russian airplane that had flown clear over the North Pole and had landed out there in a farmer's field. The old farmer was holding it captive and charging people a dollar a carload to look at it.

It seemed like I was always anxious to make a buck, and I had some sort of hustle going from the time I was seven years old. We had a big blackberry bramble in a vacant lot off the backyard. It was pretty picked over, but I tunneled under the thing and got inside where nobody had picked, so I got a lot of berries quick. I was selling them for a nickel a quart.

I would go through the trash in backyards looking for aluminum pans and bottles that could be sold to the junkman. I'd make a couple of pennies and go buy some candy. I'd typically bounce into the little neighborhood market a few times a day anyway, to see if they needed my services. The store had a wooden board floor. When change fell between the boards, the owner would mark the spot on the floor where it had fallen, and I had the job of crawling under the store and finding it. If I retrieved a quarter, I might get a nickel. Sometimes I'd find some change under there that they didn't know about, and I'd just pocket that.

Starting when I was about 12, I'd hang out at the Compton Airport. Every time an old plane came in, it would have oil all over the fuselage. I'd bring rags and wipe them down, not for pay, but for rides, which I really loved. Looking down on the countryside—and it was mostly all countryside then in Los Angeles County—was thrilling. Almost all the planes had open cockpits, and you sure knew you were somewhere special, with the wind pouring by, the motors roaring, and you up in the sky where thousands and thousands of years of mankind hadn't been. It was like an E-ticket ride at Disneyland, except there was nothing like Disneyland then to compare it to.

On Sundays people would drive out and park just to watch the planes take off and land, because there wasn't anything else to do. I got the idea that I could sell some candy bars there. I'd ride my bike down to Smith's Market and buy candy bars three for a dime, put them on a little tray with a string around my neck and run around hustling them at the parked cars. I sold just piles of candy bars, for a nickel apiece. I'd run out of them, bicycle back to the market and start in again.

I did that for a month or so. Then the man who owned the airport got on my case about selling the candy. He wanted me, a 13-year-old kid, to give him a cut. I went home and talked to my dad about that, and he said, "You tell him to go right to hell." And that was the end of that.

About that time, I also started selling the *Herald Express* on the streets in Compton. It was just like in the movies, where you'd stand on the corner and holler. You'd sell it for a nickel, and get to keep two cents from that.

You'd pick up the papers at the Pacific Electric station, where they'd been sent down from LA. Then, you'd start in the afternoon, hawking the sports edition, which was pretty much the morning paper warmed over. Then you'd carry the night edition, which would arrive after 5:30. That's the edition that sold the best. Then there was the night final, which had the race results, and a lot of people played the horses so they bought

Lynwood Junior High School

While the Japanese were flying over Pearl Harbor, I was flying model airplanes over L.A. (ribbon)

ELEVENTH
SEMI - ANNUAL
CONTEST
Sponsored by the
GAS MODEL
AIRPLANE
ASS'N.
of Southern Calif.
December 7th - 1941

PLACE WINNER
22
CLASS A

This is one of the planes at Compton Airport in which I'd get to ride in exchange for wiping it down.

that. It arrived at the station after eight, so I'd get home from my work around nine.

My location for selling newspapers was in front of the Mid-City Drug Store, which was the new game in town, a big drug store with a soda fountain. Every time I got seven cents, I'd get a banana split there. The soda jerk, Don Klosterman, wound up being the manager of the LA Rams.

It wasn't a bad corner. But there were about a half a dozen neer-do-wells—not much older than I was—who were always loitering about town and stealing stuff. A couple of times they beat the bejesus out of me and took my money. One time, though, they were starting to work me over and an adult, a good friend of my brother Kenny, came by, pulled them off of me, thumped their heads together and kicked them in the ass for good measure. You didn't call the police on a thing like that.

There was one patrolman who walked the two blocks downtown, but he went off-duty around 5 o'clock at night. One of his big chores was running kids with bicycles off the sidewalk. That's how tough a town Compton was then.

What I really wanted was a paper route, but they weren't easy to get. You had to be 14 to get a route of your own, but I did everything I could to prepare myself. I started hanging out where they folded papers and got to know the paper bosses. I learned some of the routes other kids had and worked as a substitute for them. By doing that, I was given a route of my own as soon as I turned 14.

I threw the *Long Beach Press Telegram* for 13 months, never missing a day. Every afternoon I'd get out of school, ride my bike downtown, fold the papers and do my route. As spread out as homes were then, I rode 13 miles to throw 60 newspapers, for $3.50 a week. I built the route up to 85 customers before I quit.

$3.50 was a lot of money then, but the money wasn't as important as the satisfaction of having a job. It made you feel as if you were something special because everybody was looking for a job then.

It was 1939, and the war in Europe broke out that year. Like my parents, nearly everybody around wasn't far from being an immigrant, so they were all anxious to get their papers every day to read about the war boiling over there. Meanwhile, there was such a terrible heat wave in Southern California that people were sleeping in their yards at night just to be a little less hot. So I was really sweating and straining on my route.

Kenny was living at home then. He was my drinking brother and never could get two bucks ahead for anything. He was an alright older brother, though. He had an old Model A, and he took me out a couple of times to show me how to work the gears. Kenny didn't know that I was mostly self-taught, though. I did a morning paper delivery on the weekends, and sometimes I'd borrow his Model A. I figured he'd worry about it a lot less if he didn't know about it. So at 3:30 a.m., I'd push that Model A into the street and down the block a little before I'd start it up. I'd do my route and be back by 5:30, killing the motor and coasting in onto the front lawn. Kenny would usually park it drunk, so he had no idea where he'd left it.

I quit the paper route because I got a job with Western Union delivering telegrams for 25 cents an hour, and a lot of the time you got paid for was just sitting on a bench. The exciting thing about that job was that the Depression was just coming to an end, and a lot of the telegrams I delivered were from the shipyards and aircraft companies telling people they had a job. As I was walking away, I'd hear everyone in the house whooping it up.

There were two depressing things about that job. One was delivering the death notices, which you could identify because they came in a special black-bordered envelope. The other bummer was that in movies you'd always see the Western Union kids getting a tip, and I never got one, ever.

By this time we had moved into town, near Compton College. My mother had gone to a trade school in LA to learn the custodial arts, and in 1937 she became custodian of the new women's gymnasium, a WPA project, at the college. The school district was paying her a hundred a month, which was great money. With that coming in, I didn't have to contribute to the household, so everything I made I kept or spent.

When I got the paper route the first thing I bought was a little bedside radio—$13.50, on time payments of 50 cents a week—so I could listen to the Lone Ranger and Amos and Andy. Then I bought a new bicycle, a top of the line Schwinn with twin headlights, for about $65. One day I left it parked in front of the theater, and somebody stole it. My mother really chewed me out for that, saying that anybody who left a bike lying around like that deserved to have it stolen.

But all that lecture did was give me that idea that if there was anything laying around, maybe I should steal it, because the stupid guy shouldn't have left it there. That's kind of like the connection I made between the dragonflies and the fried chicken. As a result, I did a lot of stealing.

I loved stealing stuff, but I didn't start in seriously until my drinking years, which weren't so far away at that point. As a kid, I still scared pretty easily. I got caught stealing at the dime store and was terrified they'd tell my mom. Fortunately, the kid with me was the assistant manager's girlfriend's brother, so he just chewed us out and let us go.

A guy named Bob Paustell and I discovered we could steal the padlocks off garage doors, using filed-down beer can openers as keys. People would assume they'd been burglarized and report it to the cops. We'd get the biggest kick out of finding our latest crime in the police blotter in the newspaper. People who set forest fires probably do it for the same reason: they just want to read about themselves.

We were getting a hell of a collection of padlocks, which Bob latched together in a chain and draped across the rafters in his garage. One day his dad came out there and saw those locks, and that was the end of that.

Another time, I was passing another kid's garage and saw a set of pneumatic wheels laying there that would have been really neat for making a soapbox racer, so I stole them. Not long after that the kid, Lane Schultz, built a wagon and told me he'd lost the wheels he was going to use.

So I said, "I've got some wheels that might fit that I'll sell ya." He bought his own wheels back for two dollars. It was only a few years ago now that I got a phone call from Lane, and, in the course of things, he asked, "Are you sure those wheels I bought from you weren't the ones from my garage?"

"Hell yes, I stole them, buddy." 50 years had gone by before he caught on.

I used to steal stuff out of glove compartments, but it was nothing I ever wanted. In fact, one time after I stole a camera, I noticed how nice it was, realized I didn't know the first thing about it, and felt bad about taking it from someone who did. The next night I went and put it back in the glove compartment. I don't know if the owner ever even missed it.

Even later, when I was drinking heavy and stealing, my mother never believed it. She was in total denial that her son could do that. That was good, because she could do some disciplining. When I was a kid she'd catch me at something—like once when she caught me stealing money out of her purse—she'd make me take my pants down and take a razor strop to me but good. I got off light; my older brothers had gotten similar whippings, but first she'd made them wait with their pants down for half an hour, anticipating it.

The few times I got whacked I really did deserve it, but I got away with things a lot more than I ever got caught. My dad never did any of the disciplining. Even verbally he wouldn't get on me. And I'd talk a lot more with my dad. I wouldn't tell my mom anything.

There's a strange thing I've only thought about in recent years. My dad and I spent two summers, in 1940 and 1941, on the Kern River at a place called Hobo Hot Springs, just the two of us in a tent. He'd go up there for his health, and take me with him. We'd have apple boxes nailed up on a tree for shelves and our little Coleman stove, a nice rustic setup. I did the cooking and washed the clothes and dishes in the river.

There was a bunch of kids up there, and I got along with everybody just beautifully. I evidently had a totally different personality there. Then I'd get home with my mom, and I couldn't get along with anybody. She was always on my case about everything, while my dad never was. If I did something wrong, he was never critical of it, but if I did something good, he'd praise me. He was just easy to get along with.

At the Kern River, Dad would tell people what a good boy I was and how I took care of him. When he'd praise me in front of other people like that, it was a real turn-on. I wish he could have lived to see how I turned out, though I'm not sure he would have believed it. I know my brothers are still incredulous.

I think Dad also liked getting out of the house. He was a lot more comfortable away from my mom. When he'd get away from her, his asthma would always get better. I think a lot of your health is influenced by your emotions like that.

Once, when he was doing our monthly grocery shopping, my dad bought a sack of groceries that didn't fit what we usually got. I didn't know what he was up to, until he set the bag inside the tent of a poor old Swiss woman near us. I asked my dad, "Aren't you going to leave a note telling who it's from?" He said, "No, that's not the way you do it." That really influenced me in the years to come.

Hobo Hot Springs was a great place for a kid. You'd go swimming in the river every day, and at night there'd be a zillion bats out. Up a switchback trail on a cliff above the river there was a hotel and spa that people from all over would visit for their health. The restaurant had a back room where kids would hang out at night. Nobody hassled us about it, which was neat, considering they never made any money off us aside from an occasional nickel in the jukebox.

My dad and I camped by the river, in a US Forestry Service campground where you could stay for free. The next year we stayed in the adjacent private camp. It was $3 or $4 a month to stay there, and it had flush toilets and electric lights.

I completed my driver's education at Hobo Hot Springs. An older couple was camped next to us, and whenever the husband got his pension check, they'd drive in to Bakersfield to do their shopping for the month. They had a fairly recent Chevrolet, a little one-seat coupe that would hold three, and they asked me to go with them once.

In Bakersfield, we parked the car at a market, and while the wife shopped, the old guy and I walked down the street. We passed a saloon, and he said, "I used to come in here years ago. Let's see if the same guys are here."

Of course, he didn't know anybody in there, but he proceeded to sit at the bar and get drunker than a four-peckered goat. He was *slopped*. I guess we were there a couple of hours, and I didn't know what was going on. Finally his wife came storming in and she was furious. She'd been waiting all that time in the car with the groceries.

She didn't drive and he was in no shape to. She asked if I could drive, and I said, "Oh sure, yeah."

I'd had that little experience in the Model A, but from Bakersfield to Hobo Hot Springs was 40 miles, and 20 of that was really nasty mountain road. I was too little to see over the dash, so she propped me up behind the wheel with a Kotex box under my butt. That's how I drove all the way to camp. Boy, I felt proud of myself.

When my mom heard later that I'd driven all the way from Bakersfield, she figured maybe it was OK for me to drive. I lied about my age, and I got a learner's permit when I was 14. Mom had a little Studebacker Champion by then, and on Sunday mornings we'd drive all over the place.

My first day of leave after Navy boot camp. I
visited my mom. Then I got drunk.

WORLD WAR BOOZE

One night in the summer of 1941, a bunch of us teens decided to steal watermelons from a Japanese farm in South Compton. The watermelon patch was right by the farm house, which had a big short-wave radio antenna, so they were spies, no question about it, right?

We were thumping the watermelons deciding which ones to steal, when they flipped on the headlights of their produce truck and caught us right in the beam. They'd been laying in wait for us. We all took off running, and they were right on our ass blazing away with shotguns. *Tik, tik, tik*—we could hear the pellets hitting all around us. Man, we were running full bore, and we dove into a drainage ditch and got away.

That's the closest I ever came to a foxhole, but I do like to claim that we were some of the first people the Japanese shot at in World War II.

I was 16 when they bombed Pearl Harbor. Coincidentally, I have a ribbon with that date on it, December 7, 1941, because I was nuts about building and flying model airplanes—still am—and won the ribbon that day at a model plane contest at a field at Western and Rosecrans.

When the news hit about the bombing, everyone was wondering where the hell Pearl Harbor was. No one even seemed to have a good idea of where Hawaii was. The next thing I felt was indignation: Who was this chicken-shit little country that made ticky-tacky wind-up toys to be attacking the United States?

Compton was mostly WASPs then. There were a few Mexican-Americans, but most of the non-WASPs were Japanese truck farmers. As kids do, we made fun of the Japanese, maintaining that they were all primitive and backward. But even then their kids kicked our asses with their school grades. The Japanese worshipped at shrines in their homes and the whole family would take a bath every day. I had a friend named Snau Hiroshi, and his family had a huge bathtub, heated by a fire underneath it. Meanwhile, we were all running around shoeless, maybe taking a bath once a week and calling them dirty.

Another family, the Kitanos, had the nursery in town, and they were real Americans, tried and true. But after the war, the word around town was that their oldest daughter turned out to be Tokyo Rose. I'm not sure where that rumor started. There were indeed several US-raised women broadcasting for the Japanese during the war, but only one was prosecuted for it, and it wasn't the Kitano girl.

By the time the war broke out, a lot of the Japanese families had already moved back to Japan. Many of them had only come here to make a stake and then go back home, and had been sending money back to Japan all along. Their kids attended Japanese school on Saturdays and the families only listened to Japanese programs on their short-wave radios. They weren't too impressed with the US.

I went to the going away party for one of my classmates, Tony Yoshahara, when we were both 13 in 1938. I was still making balsa-wood model planes, while he was going back to Japan to begin training for the Japanese air force. I never saw him again, unless that was his plane buzzing my ship later when I was in the Merchant Marine.

Snau was one of my favorite playmates, and I spent a lot of time running around with him. His old man had money. One day, he walked into the Chevrolet dealership in his overalls and he couldn't get anybody to talk to him, so he walked down the street two blocks to the Buick agency and bought a brand new Buick, for cash. That story sure went around town. (The same thing happened to Donna and me years later when we went shopping for a Rolls Royce at a dealership in Pasadena. We were dressed like we worked for a living, and they wouldn't even unlock the car door for us.)

When the war started, all the Japanese who hadn't already gone back to Japan were rounded up and sent to relocation camps. I missed Snau, but otherwise didn't really question it. That's just the way it was.

I was in the 12th grade when the war broke out, but was mainly still doing makeup work from the 11th grade. I recently came across a letter I wrote to my dad (he was away somewhere for his health) when I was in the 11th grade: "I got my report card last week. I got an F in English, a D in typing, a B in printing, an F in gym and a B in Spanish. This next semester, I'm going to do a lot better."

I did do a lot better, at building model airplanes and screwing off, but I was still failing most of my classes in the 12th grade. Then the military came up with a program where your high school would issue you a diploma if you'd enlist. I was never going to graduate at the rate I was going, so I jumped at that, signing up in May of '42. You could join the Navy when you were 17 years old. I was actually still 16, but got in thanks to the driving learner's permit on which I'd lied about my age.

I chose the Navy because I'd heard all the stories of Army guys slogging through the mud in World War I. On a ship, I figured, you'd have something to eat and a warm place to sleep. Pearl Harbor may have been a disinducement to living on a ship, but, to my way of thinking, until the sailors got killed, at least they were comfortable.

When I first went down to the Huntington Park Post Office to sign up, I was rejected because I didn't weigh the minimum 115 pounds. I was always skinny. At 15 I had been 5'2" tall and weighed 85 pounds. At 16, I was 5'10" and had gained some weight. I gorged myself on bananas for a week, and then drank as much water as I could right before I went back to the enrollment office. I was 114 on their scale. That was close enough for them to let me slide, and I was soon on my way to the naval training station in San Diego.

Boot camp made a big change in me. Growing up, my mom had convinced me that I wasn't strong enough and in good enough health to do the kinds of things the other kids did. I had bought into that. But in boot camp, they didn't care if you weighed 115 pounds or 200—they were going to grind you. And I found myself doing just as well as the others, and better than a lot. I felt good about that, very grown up.

The first morning, they took us into the mess hall right after daylight, and fed us beans and a lot of crap I wasn't used to eating, and I turned my nose up at it. But after they take you out and march you for five hours, they could serve you the spots off a Dalmatian and you'd eat it.

We had to march with a rifle and do the manual of arms, and take a swimming test, which was a joke. Hardly anybody could swim, but they'd cram you all into the pool, and the guys that could swim would drag those who couldn't across, en mass. Once, they bussed us up to Camp Pendleton, and we had to crawl across a field while Marines were shooting machine gun rounds right above us. That was exciting, feeling them whiz by.

I was a quick learner in the Navy, but mostly what I learned was how to drink. After we'd been in boot camp for three weeks we had a 12-hour liberty. All that everybody ever talked about in the barracks was getting drunk, so another 16-year-old kid and I got an older sailor to buy us a pint of whiskey, and I drank most of it. I just barely got back to barracks at midnight, got in a beef with some guy and got the shit beat out of me.

I woke up the next morning with lumps on my head and a hangover, and couldn't wait to go out and do it again, and I did.

After boot camp, I got assigned to aircraft ordnance school over on North Island Air Station. I was really thrilled about that, because maybe I could end up as a tail gunner on a dive bomber. When you're that age, that's great news.

When we arrived at the air station, we mustered up,

waiting for roll call to ship out. But the ship's service—the Navy version of the Army canteen—was right near where we were standing. I said to another kid, "Hell, let's go in and get a malt while we're waiting." We did, and when we came sauntering out we'd missed roll call. The old Chief said, "Well, this makes it easy. Out of every class we need two people to stay back and do mess duty for thirty days, and then you start with the next class. Guess who those two are?"

So, instead of being in a gun turret, I was in the mess hall, washing dishes, serving food, swabbing floors and the like. But the neat thing about it was you got a liberty card to go ashore every night. After a few weeks they put me on barracks detail, where, when we got done, we could just leave.

Downtown San Diego was a bore, just a sea of white hats, sailors shoulder-to-shoulder looking for something to do. Instead, after winding up the barracks detail at about two in the afternoon, I'd stand on the Coast Highway and hitchhike home to Compton, meet with my old buddies and party it up until two in the morning. By then, I'd be totally blitzed and they'd take me down to Long Beach and pour me on a bus. It would arrive in San Diego a little before seven in the morning and I'd catch the ferry to the air station just in time for muster, do the barracks detail until two and hitch back to Compton again.

Actually, the very first time I had gone up to Compton I got thrown in jail, drunk, until the shore patrol came to collect me. That was the first time I'd been arrested, and I learned what not to do on my future arrests. I was kicking and screaming and trying to get away and they tossed me in a padded cell. I didn't like that one bit, so every time after that it was "yessir" and "nosir."

That arrest got me kicked out of the air school. Instead, I was assigned to ship's service, with a job breaking up cardboard boxes and putting them in bundles. I was restricted to the base for 30 days, but they forgot to take my liberty card from me. So, I was back out there right away, going to Compton every night.

Sometimes if I missed the bus back to San Diego, I'd steal a car, drive it down and abandon it at the ferry landing. In those days people didn't take their keys out of their cars like they do now.

One night I was nearly halfway to San Diego in one of these borrowed cars and was so sleepy I could barely see. But I did see another sailor hitchhiking, so I picked him up and got him to drive. Before long he was conking out too, so he woke me up to drive and fell asleep on the back seat. When I got to San Diego, I just jumped out, caught the ferry and didn't give the sleeping sailor another thought until I heard later on the grapevine that he got hauled in by the San Diego PD for car theft. Oh well.

This was long before there was a freeway between LA and San Diego. You'd take the coast road down. Officials were worried about Japanese submarine attacks, so you couldn't drive with your headlights on. Instead, they had little sawhorses by the side of the road with red lanterns that barely gave off enough light to guide you. There were two or three occasions when I'd wake up driving a stolen car and these goddamn red lanterns and sawhorses were flying over the top of the car, followed by a brilliant spume of burning kerosene. It was a hell of a show to wake up to.

Usually, though, my friends would just get me onto the bus. After a few weeks of this routine, I was a total wreck. I broke out with a really bad skin condition. I'm pretty sure that was caused by me climbing up in the filthy, dirty baggage racks of the buses to sleep on the way back to base. I was sent to the infirmary until it cleared up, and I couldn't drink in there. But as soon as I got out it was back to the same routine.

A few weeks later it came up that they were going to transfer me to the destroyer base for a six-week course to learn to operate small craft, and then I'd be out in the war. I was really thrilled about that, but before I could start school, my skin broke out again and I was sent to the skin ward of the hospital.

One night they brought a patient in and put him in the bed next to me. This is when they were bringing the injured back from Guadalcanal, and this fellow—his name was Al Schmid—had a hand grenade go off right in front of him and was blinded. He had a little bit of vision out of one eye, but that was all. The other eye looked pretty weird, and he was quiet and surly as a result of it.

People would come to see Al, but he wouldn't talk to anybody. He was just really nasty about the whole thing. But late at night, in the beds next to each other, he'd get to talking with me.

He was 19. After boot camp he'd been sent straight to the invasion of Guadalcanal. They made a landing without much resistance, and soon had fortified a line facing the direction from which they thought a Japanese attack might come. On the other side of camp, where there was supposed to be little chance of attack, Al and two buddies were positioned in a machine gun nest overlooking a river. There came a bright moonlit night, and all of a sudden the Japanese were coming across, pushing logs in front of them. The three of them opened up with the machine gun but hundreds more kept coming.

Later Al got a commendation stating he'd heroically killed 200 of the enemy, but he told me all he was thinking at the time was, "What's the matter with these crazy bastards? Don't they got no sense?"

The barrel of Al's water-cooled machine gun overheated from being fired so heavily. They'd held the attack off long enough for some reserves to arrive, but a couple of Japs had made it across the river and tossed a grenade at their spot, which killed his two buddies, and the Japs left Al for dead.

The Navy tried to make a hero out of him. They got people from *Life* magazine and everywhere to interview him, and he just stonewalled them all. It only made him more bitter because he wanted to be shipped home to Philadelphia, but they wanted him in San Diego so he could get the hero treatment. Eventually a movie was made about Al, *Pride of the Marines*, where John Garfield played him.

Al called me Shadow, because that's all I was to him with his partial vision, a shadow. There were some nights I snuck out under the fence and got a couple of bottles of beer. He'd drink a little and I'd drink the rest. During the day I'd get him in a wheelchair and push him up to the wards where the other Guadalcanal wounded were. And, God, these were all young guys, just skinny as rails and with jungle rot and all these other horrid conditions.

Al was still there when I left. After being in the Navy for seven months, on November 6, 1942, I was given a medical discharge. I was heartbroken about it, because I wanted to be involved. Pretty much all guys did then. I tried to talk the Lieutenant Commander, W.W. Demling, out of it, but he said, "No, you'll just be a liability because you'd be stationed somewhere and break out, and it would take two more people to take care of you and that's three people knocked out of the war, and we can't have that." There was no getting around it.

With the medical discharge, I qualified for all the benefits of a veteran. Also on the bright side, I didn't get killed. If I'd become a landing craft operator, as they'd planned, my job would have basically been going back and forth like a duck in a shooting gallery.

I did nearly die in the cockpit of a Mustang fighter during the war, but the incident wasn't exactly Medal of Honor material, as I'll explain shortly.

After my discharge, I moved back home in Compton, and went to work for Douglas Aircraft in Long Beach testing the hydraulic systems on B-17s. They'd just got the line rolling there. I worked the graveyard shift, midnight to seven. I enjoyed that, but I was drinking heavier and heavier all the time, especially working graveyard. I'd go in half-swacked, then about three or four in the morning there was nothing to drink, I'd start to get bleary-eyed and it was all I could do to stay awake. The nights when we were working our asses off, I did fine. But the nights the work went smoothly and you had to look busy, that was hard keeping your eyes open. After six months there, they caught me sleeping for the third time and fired me.

In other respects, it was really interesting being on the home front. All the men were off in the service, and the Douglas assembly line was about half women. With the booze and the women and being 17 years old, it was a lot of fun, I've got to say that much.

There's something I still wonder about today: A lot of these women, if they had a boyfriend who was going to get drafted, they'd get married. Then as soon as he shipped out, they were easy. I mean, they couldn't wait to get knocked up. They wanted to get it done right away so everyone would figure it was their husband who did it. Maybe it was to make sure the marriage stuck, I don't know, but it made a pretty good playing field for a guy like me who was on the prowl, out having a good time. I still wonder how many of these war babies ever knew their real father.

When I got fired from Douglas, I immediately went to work for North American Aircraft in Inglewood for seven months. I started out assembling the rear fuselage section of B-25s. I'd mostly just stand there holding the bucking bar while another guy was riveting. After a couple of months of that, they transferred me to working on the Mustang fighter, basically doing what I'd done at Douglas, filling and testing the hydraulic equipment.

That's where I almost did myself in. Whenever you spilled any of the hydraulic oil on the interior, it created a fire hazard and you had to clean it out using a solvent called permaclor. I was down in one cockpit cleaning the upholstery and I noticed I was starting to get high off the solvent fumes. So I put the rag up to my face and took a big hit, and, Jiminy

Cricket, it was a *helluva* rush!

The next thing I remember, I woke up in a dispensary. Co-workers told me they'd seen me try to climb out of the cockpit, and was half-out and starting to fall when they grabbed me. I was as limp as a rag. When I came around, the doctor told me I was really lucky I wasn't dead because this permaclor was stuff they used in fire extinguishers to displace the oxygen in the air, and I had been suffocating, thoroughly blue, when they hauled me in there. But I was back working the next day.

I didn't get fired from North American. I left, though I don't remember the circumstances. There was a period when I was drinking so heavy that I can't tell you much about it. It was just a mish-mosh.

There are some things I still wonder about today, because I couldn't even remember them the day after they happened. My buddy Don Stewart was in the Navy and had a girlfriend he really had the hots for. He didn't want to ship out and leave her so he went AWOL.

Since he was free on the streets, he decided to get in a fight too, and busted up his knuckles something awful. They became infected, and he wound up at home in bed with a raging temperature, with ugly black lines crawling up both arms. His mother was trying to get him to turn himself in to the Navy so he could get some help, but he wouldn't hear of it.

She called me asking for help. As soon as I got off the phone with her, I called the shore patrol and told them where Don was. They put him in the brig at the Naval hospital in Long Beach. His infection was so bad that he was in there three months recovering.

Here's what I don't remember: Don was under guard in a locked ward, and somehow I got him out of there to visit with his girlfriend in my car for a half hour. I was sloshed, and remember laying a pint of whiskey on one of the Marine guards, but that wouldn't have been enough for him to risk letting Don out. I wish I could remember what line of bull I used, because it must have been good, and you never know when you'll need something like that again.

I was 18 when Dad died in 1944. By then he was living by himself in a little apartment in Long Beach. He and Mom hadn't separated; he'd just go there for his health. He had a bad slide for his last three years, and took a real turn for the worse when I was still in the Navy.

When I'd get a weekend pass, I'd go see him in Long Beach, before I'd start in drinking. I'd lather him up and shave him, because he was really sick, and felt a little better when he looked better. I'd spend three or four hours with him, and then go out on the town.

The thing that really kept him going was following the war. He kept up with it religiously in the papers and on the radio. When Hitler's Sixth Army surrendered at Stalingrad in February of 1943, Dad figured that was the turning point of the war, and he was right. He lost interest after that and began his long slide towards death.

In his last two weeks, it looked as if he could go at any time. That's when he called in a priest, after a lifetime of being anti-church. The last words he ever said to me were, "Take care of your mother."

At the end, he'd be laying in bed just barely able to breathe, and not really coherent. I would be there daily, taking turns sitting with him. On January 8 of '44, I had the afternoon watch. He'd been asleep, nearly in a coma. I was sitting, reading, and noticed he'd quit breathing. I got up real close and couldn't hear anything. My mom, brother and sister were in the kitchen and I jumped up and let out a cry and said, "I think Dad's dead." We called the doctor down the street and he confirmed it.

I had mixed feelings at the time. I knew he wasn't going to be fighting and gasping for air anymore, so there was an immediate feeling of relief. But then I got to thinking about all my experiences with him, and all the things I'd never asked him about himself.

I thought I'd gone through most of that before he died. But that night I went out on the town with Red and the guys, and I could not get drunk, couldn't get with the program at all, no matter how much I drank. I was really shook up. I missed him so much then.

KEEPING THE HOME FIRES BURNING

I had a friend, Charley Raye, who I met at Douglas Aircraft. When he got his draft notice, I bought his fire engine red '37 Ford Club Coupe convertible, and for an extra $10 he sold me the little .22 pistol and box of shells he kept in the glove compartment.

A week or two later, I got drunk with some fellows and we took the coupe for a ride through the business section of North Long Beach. I pulled out that little .22 and started shooting out all the big store windows, like in the cowboy movies, up one side of the street and then down the other. I emptied that gun three times, and the law never arrived. We were so blitzed, we wouldn't have really noticed. The next morning I got to feeling sorry about what I'd done, got rid of that gun and never got another one, until after I had kids and they were grown.

During the war there was a shortage of booze and I drank whatever I could get, including a lot of a crummy tequila made by the Alfred Hart distillery in Los Angeles. I think they just took raw alcohol, put coloring in and called it rye, bourbon or whatever. What they sold the most of was the tequila, because most people then didn't really know what tequila tasted like, so they wouldn't know how awful the Alfred Hart version was. I never drank any paint thinner, but I would imagine it tasted like this stuff.

Occasionally, I'd get a bottle of good bonded whiskey, and then I'd really get whacked out. It was so smooth compared to this swill that you'd just slug it down.

On a typical evening during this time, I'd be lying on the couch and the phone would ring or the door bang, and it would be one of my buddies home on a five-day leave. Whichever buddy it was would have a pocketful of money and would want to go out where the action was, and I was about the only guy around. I'd get on the phone to one of my girlfriends, have her get a friend, and we'd head for a beer joint. Usually it was one on the Eastside called Jess' Place that had dancing to a jukebox and served beer and wine. Then we'd make the rounds, usually heading to Comstock's, which was a cocktail lounge. There was a weird distinction in the law, where you weren't allowed to dance in cocktail lounges but you could in the beer bars.

There were two dance halls in Compton, the Skylight and the Lighthouse, and they both had live big band music, though it wasn't always played by that big of a band. We'd get pretty well oiled up there and then take off for the graveyard or to the end of Wilmington Avenue, where we'd park and neck and see if we could make the grade. Usually we didn't. Then we'd take the girls home and head out to finish off our drinking. The next day we'd do the same thing over again.

Sometimes we'd go to the Pike in Long Beach, an amusement park by the sea where the Majestic dance hall was. It was a swinging place during the war. All the guys who wanted to pick up girls went there, and all the girls who wanted to get picked up were there, which was kind of handy. There was another wild place out by Douglas Aircraft in Long Beach called the Bomb Shelter.

Once in a while we'd go to Central Avenue, which was the real jumping music street in the black part of LA. There was a black guy at the shipyard who I remember telling me, "If you could be black on Central Avenue on a Saturday night, you'd never want to be white again." It was almost that good.

One friend of mine, Gene Christofferson, came home and wanted to go out on the town. We'd gotten as far as sitting on the curb at the Compton PE depot, with a quart of whiskey, trying to figure out which way we were going to go, when a fellow we knew named Frank Moran showed up, on leave from the Navy. So the three of us just sat there and drank that quart of whiskey. Frank must have drunk most of it, because when we got ready to get up and go, he was passed out colder than a cucumber.

Now, Frank Moran was a short, stocky guy with big bushy eyebrows, and wasn't much of a conversationalist even when he was conscious. And passed out, trying to lift him under the arms and tote him with us, Jesus, he was like an anvil with eyebrows.

Gene and I were figuring out what kind of night we were going to have dragging Frank's leaden ass around when we saw a laundry truck sitting there on the street. We opened the back door and it was full of sheets and clothes, so we heaved ol' Frank in there on top, slammed the door and went on our merry way. And you know, to this day I've never seen Frank Moran again.

I was running around with a lot of women during the war, but the only one I was crazy about was Joan, a girl I'd first met when I was up at the Kern River with my dad. We saw each other when we could for about six years. She was a really striking girl, with an athletic swimmer's body, a Roman nose and long, blond hair she wore in braids. Except for being a blonde, she could have passed for an Indian.

With some notable exceptions, romance was a lot slower back then. Joan was about four years younger than I, and we were very slow in getting around to being romantic. We'd just lie around and talk about what we'd do when we were older, sort of like how it had been between my sister Mary and me when I was younger.

Joan lived in Burbank with her family, and with the '37 Ford I'd bought, I was able to get up to see her more. One occasion when I went up there was the first and only time we made love. We went to the movie and her grandmother had to come along as a chaperone. But we sat apart from her in the theater, and we had no more than sat down before Joan wanted to go out to the car. So we did.

We were hardly done before her grandma started tapping

on the window. And, you know, I think she had stood there and watched the whole thing. They hauled Joan off to the doctor the next day and wouldn't let me see her after that.

I was already pretty much persona non grata at her home because of my drinking. But we'd talk on the telephone and meet secretly here and there. On the night she had her senior prom, she phoned to tell me she could see me after it was over at midnight. I drove up there with another couple, and when her date dropped her off, I picked her up. We drove around for a while, and the four of us decided we were all going to go to Vegas to get married.

First we went down to Compton to try to get enough gas ration stamps to make it to Vegas, and I couldn't score them anywhere. By nine the next morning, I'd started to sober up a bit and marriage didn't sound like such a good idea. So Joan had me drop her off a block from her home, and that was the last time I ever saw her.

There was a waiting period to get married in California, where in Vegas they'd marry you on the spot. Fortunately, just getting to Vegas was a bit of a waiting period, otherwise I'd have been married four times over.

There was a guy named Duke Polkinghorn I started running around with not long after I got out of the Navy. I'd hang out at his house a lot, and got to know his mother pretty well, because she and a few neighbor women would be there drinking at nine in the morning. It's really hard to find someone to booze with at that time of day, so I'd sit in with them.

Duke was going steady with a girl named Jean, who looked so much like Ava Gardner that it hurt. One night, I was at a mutual friend's house and somehow or other Jean and I wound up lying on one of the beds, just kissing and having a hell of a good time, when Duke came in. Man, he went and hit me right in the face, not that I was in much shape to notice it. He hauled Jean outside and they started arguing. She told him that she didn't want anything more to do with him, that she liked me.

So I started going out with Jean, and we had a heavy thing for a while. I even bought her a ring. But it seemed we'd only ever get along for a few minutes, and then get in an argument. She could be really good to me sometimes, though.

It was when I was going out with Jean that a guy from La Habra told me about a really fast police car they had in that town. I wondered how fast, so one Friday night a car-full of us drove there and prowled around until we saw the police car. I flashed my spotlight on him and tooted my horn until he chased us. And he did for nine miles, almost all the way to Fullerton, until they caught us and hauled me off to jail.

On Monday, Jean came down with three of her girlfriends and bailed me out, and it was worth the fine I had to pay just to see the look on all these cops' faces when this armada of good-looking broads came in to bail me out.

Before long, Duke had a new gal, Margaret, whose best friend was named Doris. I wasn't all that gung ho about Doris, but because Duke really had the hots for Margaret, I went along with them.

The girls both worked as cashiers at Smith's Market. Duke and I would go in the market, pay for a few groceries at the check-out stand, and Margaret or Doris would reach back on the shelf and slip a quart of whiskey in the sack. When the store closed at eight, we'd go party. One night Doris and I were alone, out drinking, and the next thing we know we're on our way to get hitched in Vegas. We got as far as Barstow and I started to sober up and turned back. If I'd had another quart of whiskey we'd probably have been married.

My best friend then was Red Caruthers, the same fella I'd known since junior high. Red never went in the service because his deformed right arm made him 4-F. His girlfriend, Virginia, had a father in the Navy and her mother had run off with some guy. Virginia lived at home by herself, so that became the party house, where we all hung out, drank our beer and brought our girlfriends.

I was living there for a time, and neither Red nor I had been working. Virginia got really upset that we had flat-out nothing to eat in the house. Women are like that. So Red and I went out and took a job working at a place making packing crates. We started in working, but we'd been drinking all night and were really beat, so we made a cave in the stacked crates and both fell sound asleep in there for the rest of the morning.

We revived in time for the owner to come give us our checks, $8 or $10 or something, and that's the last we bothered with that job. We went to the store, bought a sack of potatoes, milk and other stuff to make potato soup—which may have been the only thing Virginia knew how to make then—and a couple of cases of beer. That made Virginia as happy as a clam.

Around that time, I was going out with a drive-in carhop named Shirley. She was making good money, and the way I looked at it, if you had a girlfriend who was working there was no point in you working. I'd stop at the drive-in early in the evening and she'd give me $10 to go buy some booze. I'd pick her up when she got off at eight, and we'd go to a party or out to the sticks and booze it up.

When Red and Virginia got married in Las Vegas, Shirley and I went along. Somehow, we decided to also get married while we were out there. We arrived in Vegas on the weekend, and it wasn't until Monday morning that you could go to the courthouse and get the license. Shirley was from Boulder City and wanted to visit friends there. So, Saturday night, we had a couple of beers and parked on a hill overlooking Boulder City.

We were talking about this and that, and I was trying to get romantic. She started lecturing me about how when we were married I couldn't drink so much and would have to get a steady job and this, that and the other thing. It worked into an argument that ended up in "Screw you" and "Adios."

The sort of mischief Red and I had been in as kids really

picked up once we were drinking. We stole booty out of cars, and parts off of them. One night we ripped-off the cars in the bowling alley parking lot, several of which belonged to the Compton Police Department bowling league.

Red's brother Doug, who I later worked for in the trailer business, had a gas station then that was sort of a neighborhood hang-out. With the war on you just couldn't get new parts, so we'd sell him stolen Ford carburetors for 50 cents each. To obtain them, we'd bust three half-inch nuts loose with a wrench and clip the gas line with a pair of diagonal pliers.

Doug would dip them in a bucket of solvent that would burn the crud off, so he'd have these shiny carburetors he'd set in the window and sell as rebuilts for $10. It wasn't so much the 50 cents Red and I were after. We just got a kick out of it.

One night we were out, and I needed a generator for myself because my Ford's had gone out. We were coming in from raising hell somewhere and were pretty well sloshed. I had my toolbox in his car because we'd been stealing some spotlights, and I spotted a Ford sedan parked in front of a house down the street from Red's.

He stayed in the car while I went down the block to the sedan. I got the hood up and was taking the generator off when a lady come out of the house and yelled, "Hey, what are you doing?"

"I'm fixing this generator."

"That's my car! Who told you to do that?"

"I don't know, I thought somebody called me and wanted me to fix the generator here."

She started screaming, so I dropped the generator, hauled ass up to the car, and found Ol' Red passed out drunk on the steering wheel. I ran the five blocks home, passing a police car coming the other way.

That was early, maybe 11 or midnight. Come 2:30 in the morning there was a knock on the door and the cops wanted to see me. They cuffed me to take me down to the station.

The hood was up on my car and as we passed it, the cops shined a flashlight on the engine, and the generator was gone. Then, we passed the trash can on the curb, and there was my old generator right on top of the trash. I picked it up in my cuffed hands like it was Yorick's skull, and said, "What the hell is this doing out here? It's a good generator. This shouldn't be here!"

Somehow, that didn't keep them from hauling me down to the station and interrogating me. Then about daylight, I learned later, they brought Red down. They'd run into him passed out in his car, with my tool box in there with him.

The thing was, Red just absolutely could not drink without puking. He would love to have been an alcoholic if he could, but he couldn't. So on the way to the station, he puked in the back of the police car. They made him clean that out with a hose. When they started taking him in the station, he puked again. At that point, they said, "Get the fuck out of here!" and ran him off.

The next day they brought the woman down to identify me, and she couldn't. Of course, I was looking as innocent as I could, and she said, "No, he looked darker." They kept me for 72 hours, interrogating me, and then turned me loose.

I guess I must have had half-a-dozen of those scenes, but I never got charged. I was like Big Louie in *Guys and Dolls*, with "37 arrests and no convictions." Drunk driving was the only thing I was ever convicted of, because I was just dead meat there and pleaded guilty.

Usually the interrogations were like a game. The cops would try to get you to screw up, and you'd try not to. Once, when my pal Don Stewart and I were busted for stealing beer, we made a volleyball out of cotton batting we tore from a mattress, stacked up wooden benches three high and had a pretty good game going there.

The police had to let us go eventually, because, before

Don was a suspect, he'd gone to the guy we stole the beer from and told him if he preferred charges against me that he was going to kick the shit out of him. Don looked sort of like Popeye, with big arms and a small waist, but real stocky, and he could be an ornery little guy. A case in point: we hadn't been out of jail five minutes when he spotted a cabbie who had been putting the make on his sister, and Don beat *him* up.

I don't know how the guy who interrogated us put up with all our bull. He was about 6'4", 180 pounds and had thinning hair: Detective Sergeant Clarence Kissam. Compton only had one detective, and he was it. Whenever they'd book me and my pals, he'd be the one to interrogate us. He'd question us for hours and, though we'd never cop to anything, he did manage to scare the piss out of us every time. Forget the threat of prison: he made it so you'd think twice before doing something wrong just because you didn't want to get interrogated by him again.

Years later, after I'd quit drinking and was doing quite well in the trailer business, I was exhibiting at a trailer show in Los Angeles and he came walking into the display, right up to me, saying, "Maybe you don't remember me: Clarence Kissam."

"Yeah, I remember you." Of course I did. When I saw him coming, I immediately started worrying, "What the hell did I do *now*?"

We went into one of my trailers and he told me, "I knew you'd be here and wanted to talk to you. I just want you to know I'm sure proud of what you're doing. I always knew you were going to do all right. You know, all those times that we busted you? I could have sent you to the slammer any time I wanted. But I always figured you'd turn out all right."

I thought that was pretty neat, because I don't think you have too many law enforcement officers who make those kinds of judgment calls.

Back when I was doing all this petty stuff, I don't think my family really knew much about it. Though I was living at home, I did everything I could to keep it from my mom. And she was in such denial that I could be anything but a nice boy. She wouldn't have believed anything else. She was aware of them hauling me off, but I'd tell her some story about it being a mistake, and she'd believe me. Mothers are like that.

It might seem like I wasn't especially burdened by a conscience at this point in my life, but drink will do that to you. I did have something of a moral ethic, though: I always felt that I didn't want to steal from anybody that had less than I did. If they had more than me, it was alright.

Not too many years ago my wife Donna and I became acquainted with William Randolph Hearst, Jr., and his wife, and they invited us to come visit at Hearst Castle. It's open to the public, but as soon as the last bus goes down the hill, the Hearsts have the run of the place. We went up in a motor home a couple of times and stayed with them for four or five days.

One time, there was a garden hose I'd hooked up so we'd have water in the motor home. I unhooked it as we were getting ready to leave, and it was a pretty good hose. I thought, "Well, shit, I can use that," and threw it in the motor home. Driving home, I'd thought of my policy as a kid, and figured that as long as ol' Hearst had more money than I did, his garden hose was fair game. I guess you don't entirely break old habits.

Of course all the antics I got into as a kid were done with the aid of being boozed up. But once you get sober, you start thinking about consequences, and it's a different ball game altogether. Until then, you do some stupid, regrettable things.

I was always nuts about cars, and I owned a few during the war. For $25, I bought a disfunctional '32 Ford Roadster from Duke that had been sitting in his yard. I made a hot rod of it, taking the fenders off, putting 16" wheels on it and moving the gas tank to make it more like a Model A, which was the hot car to monkey with then.

I drove it in the mountains to Big Bear to meet up with Duke, Red and some guys. Of course, I got famously drunk, and slept in the car that night. In the morning, somebody came by in another '32, revving his motor and wanting to drag. I was still basically asleep, but I fired it up and took off cold from where I was, and went about 500 feet before the engine blew.

Don Stewart had his car up there, and he towed mine a ways while I steered it. I was hungover and got tired of that fast, so I stopped Don and said, "Let's just push this son of a bitch over a cliff and go home." The other guys talked me out of it, and one of them drove it down the mountain, using the clutch as a brake.

I rebuilt the engine, with new rods, rings, inserts and all. When I got it back together I had a piece left over. I thought, "Well, it can't be that important," fired the car up and ran it down the block, where the engine blew up again. That extra part was the gear that drove the oil pump.

I replaced it with a hopped up, ported and relieved '39 Mercury engine that I got for $90 from a guy who had been drafted. It was a real winner, with about 110 horsepower to the Ford's 85.

The Roadster was a fun car to race, but not much good for dating or drinking. Toward those purposes, I bought a '38 Ford convertible sedan. I sold the Roadster for $300 to a guy Red knew in LA. He gave me $100 and was going to give me the other $200 the following week, but then the guy shipped out in the Merchant Marine without paying me.

After a while I decided I'd better get my car back. I knew the guy lived up near the Coliseum, so one afternoon I went up there with three of my buddies. One was a really good looking kid named Paul Schultz who was only 16, but 6'2".

We asked some neighborhood kids if they'd seen a race car anywhere, and one of them said, "Yeah," and pointed to a garage. I pried the doors open enough to look in, and there it was, most of it. The guy had decided he was going to make a Club Coupe out of it and had used a cutting torch to take out the whole back end, generally screwing it up.

We busted the lock off the garage door and just as we were rolling the car into the street, the guy's mother came running out of the house, having already called the police. When the cops came, she screamed, "These guys are stealing my son's car." I let her rave on, and eventually one of the cops turned to me and asked, "What's your story?"

I said, "Hell, he stole *my* car. It's not his car."

"Well, who's got the pink slip for it?"

"I do. It's right in my pocket." And I pulled it out.

The cop checked it out, and said,

"Sorry, lady, it's his car."

Half the neighborhood had gathered around while this was going on. One of them was the girlfriend of the guy who'd had my car. She was real pretty. Ol' Paul got acquainted with her and when we left, he left with her.

A couple of months later, Duke and I were driving down the street in Compton in my '38, and a carload of guys came up alongside us, tooting the horn and trying to pull us over. The guy had come back from the Merchant Marine to find his car gone and his girlfriend taken by a high school kid, and probably was a little upset. He had a couple of big buddies with him too, so I poured the coal on.

This was a Friday night, when they'd have teen dances at the Compton community center. We'd never go in the dance, but it was a great place to hang outside and drink beer with the girls. With these guys chasing us, I barreled into the parking lot. A lot of the local guys were standing around and we ran up, shouting, "Hey, a bunch of guys down from LA want to rumble."

It wasn't like these locals were close friends of mine or anything—they just loved to fight. The LA guys were outnumbered two-to-one and they just got the lungs beat out of them. I stood back and watched them all go at it, and that was the last I ever saw of that guy.

During the war, LA had the Zoot Suit Riots, which was

mainly a bunch of white military guys who didn't want to wait until they were overseas to start fighting, so they took to whaling on the Mexican-Americans, and sometimes on blacks. They had some jacked-up reason for doing that, but the real reason was just that their victims looked different and wore those flashy zoot suits.

I didn't have a beef with anyone. Hell, I had a zoot suit and I loved the thing. But one night I was drinking hard and fell in with a bunch of sailors. The next thing I know, there's a gang of them hanging from my Ford's running boards and I'm at the tail end of a 15-car caravan heading into Watts.

All the blacks were hiding, but there was one guy the sailors spotted running from one place to another, and as I was pulling up, something like 40 sailors jumped him and started beating him. As drunk as I was, I thought, "What the fuck is this?" It was disgusting. There was nothing I could do to stop it, but I was damned if I was going to be a part of it. I put my car in gear, swung a fast U-turn and hauled out of there, not noticing or caring what happened to the sailors hanging on my car.

LA wasn't exactly a hotbed of harmony then, and one night a black guy caused Red and his front teeth to part company.

Several of us used to go to a black-owned place at the corner of Imperial Boulevard and Central Avenue at the edge of Watts, where they'd serve minors. We'd be the only white faces in the place.

Four or five of us were drinking there one night and we got to making some loud, stupid remarks. A big old dude came back to where we were sitting and said, "Get the hell out of here and don't come back." We took one look at him and the gang gathering around, said "Yes sir," and were gone.

Red wasn't with us and didn't know about this altercation. A couple of nights later, when I was busy working overtime, he and Duke went in there to do a little drinking, and this same big black guy came up, furious, "I thought I told you kids not to ever come back here!" I guess we all looked alike to him, so he and some other guys started punching on Red and Duke.

They ran. Red had just got in his car when one of these guys went at him with a blackjack. Later, you could see several dents in the door's steel molding where the blackjack had hit, but one of the blows caught Red right in the mouth and knocked all his front teeth out. Duke got in the car but didn't get his door closed, and a guy was pounding on him until Red got the car in gear and took off.

Red had a plate made for where his teeth had been, and it got to be a real chore when we'd go out on the town. Red, of course, would throw up several times, and keep on drinking. The next morning he'd wake up with his teeth missing, so we'd have to retrace our steps from the night before to find these piles of puke and dig through them looking for Red's plate. We'd always find it. I guess no one else wanted it.

When we were driving, we'd always try to get him to stick his head out the window when he puked, and that worked pretty good. But one night he was at the drive-in standing beside the car. He had to throw up, and, out of reflex, he stuck his head *in* the window and threw up all over the seat. It was for such reasons that we called him Old Pukin' Red.

I didn't have any such limitations on my drinking. Don Stewart still likes to talk about the time I showed up at his place and asked him to take me to pick up my car on Western Avenue. He started arguing that we didn't need to get to my car right then.

"Yes we do. I've got a quart of whiskey in it."

We drove over there, gassed up my car and hopped in it. I started driving, got out the quart and flipped the cap out the window.

Don was incredulous. "What'd you do that for?"

"Hell, we're going to *drink* it, aren't we?"

And we did.

I must have had 50 jobs in this period and right after the war. One company alone, McClatchee, must have fired and rehired me six times.

I started out working nights at a big hot-press making rubber heating conduit connectors for planes. We worked from midnight to 7:30 in the morning, drinking all the time, of course. Another fellow was working on a mixing mill, which was two big, long steel drums. One night he got too close and it ripped his glove off and pulled his hand in. He yanked it out and came in the press room bleeding like crazy. The poor bastard: as drunk as he was, he was still pure white from the shock.

I had a nice '38 Ford convertible by then, which gave me second thoughts. He wasn't going anywhere, so I said, "Just wait a minute, will you?" and got a big piece of cardboard to put on the passenger side. I told him, "Don't bleed all over my car." Then I took him to the emergency room. He'd got so much carbon black in his wounds that eventually all his fingers had to come off that hand.

Another time, I was working as a truck driver for McClatchee. One Saturday they had me take some product into LA, and when I was coming back, there were groups of sailors coming down Alameda Street, hitchhiking back to Long Beach. I started picking them up, and by the time I went by the plant in Compton, I probably had 40 guys on the back of that one-and-a-half-ton truck. I was drinking, and they were drinking and we were all having a hell of a grand time, singing "Chattanooga Choo Choo." I thought we carried a tune pretty well, too, but when I came back to the plant, they fired me.

With so many men off in the war effort, though, they'd keep hiring me back. Once, I was driving for them, and I'd just started out on a delivery when I noticed one of the company cars following me. I made a couple of phony turns, and it was right there behind me. I turned the truck around, drove it to my house, went in and called the office, saying, "Hey, your truck's down here in front of my house. This guy who's following me might as well be driving it. You don't need both of us."

I had all sorts of other jobs. I worked at the Cal Ship shipbuilding company as an electrician's helper. I worked at Fellows and Stewart boat yard making aviation rescue boats. There was a place in Compton that made water heaters. At one of the shortest jobs I ever had, I was put on a rotary drill press. I would put a casting in a fixture, drill a hole in it, tap it, and repeat that three times. The pieces came in a barrel and when I got one drilled I'd throw it in another barrel. It started to get to be fun. I made a race of it.

By two o'clock it was getting to where I might just be able to finish the barrel before my shift ended. I got down to where there were three castings left in the barrel, and maybe 15 minutes to go on the shift, and I was pretty sure I could make it. Then a guy came along and dumped more castings in the barrel, up to the top. I thought, "Oh, great." After working there 7 hours, I clocked out, went home and never went back, because they'd ruined my game.

A familiar enough situation, but posed this time at the Long
Beach Pike with my friend DIck Shuey, 1942.

In my Merchant Marine uniform, 1944. At least my ears kept the hat from sliding off my head.

My Navy discharge certificate. I kept it folded in my wallet, because I'd lied about my age on it, and it helped me get drinks.

THE MERCHANT MARINE

I still wanted to be part of the war, and tried to get into the Army. In fact, I made a big scene at the draft board, drunk. The chief there agreed to give me a shot at it, and sent me on to the physical. But there, they had my medical discharge chart from the Navy, and my skin had broken out a little, so they turned me down.

A lot of guys were sailing in the Merchant Marine, and they didn't care what shape you were in. So in the spring of 1944 I went down and took out seaman's papers. There was no boot camp, no training. As long as they got the $35 union fee from you, they'd ship you out. I didn't have $35 but they needed men, and the official at the union hall said, "There's a ship leaving tomorrow. When you come back on it, pay the $35."

The next thing I knew, I was at sea on a ship called the Coulee Dam. I was a galley man in the steward's department, cleaning pots and pans, peeling potatoes. The pay was $120 a month, and they doubled that when you crossed the 180th parallel into the war zone, plus giving you an extra $5 a day. So it was damn good money, particularly since there was no place to spend it.

One reason I went to sea was to quit drinking. I'd looked at the life I was leading and thought, "Shit, I gotta get some rest. This is just too much work." I figured if I got out on the ocean there'd be nothing to drink and I'd be fine.

And for about the first two weeks I was getting along great. I was eating good and lying out in the sun, and didn't have all that much work to do. You'd think I was on a cruise ship. I was having fun paling around with the rest of the crew.

After two weeks, we were all shooting the breeze one night and one of the guys said, "God, I'd sure like to have a drink." And I said, "You got that right. I would too." When the conversation broke up, I was with the other guy, and he said, "Do you really want a drink?" He opened his locker and pulled out a fifth of bourbon, and I took a big old *glug, glug, glug* and, oh man, it was fine. Then he put the bottle away and locked the locker.

We all slept on deck because it was too hot to sleep in our forecastles. I had my hammock slung under the gun on the fantail. I climbed in my sack and laid there for a minute and suddenly that ol' booze hit bottom and my head started spinning around. Wow, that was good!

So I went down and busted into this guy's locker and got his fifth of booze. I went up in a gun tub, which they hadn't started manning yet, polished off that fifth and passed out.

When I didn't show up to work in the mess hall at seven the next morning, they began searching the ship. They thought I'd fallen overboard. Finally at about nine a.m. they found me passed out up in the gun tub.

I'd busted this guy's locker open and taken his liquor. You don't do that on ships, so I wasn't the popular guy at all. That was really tough on me, getting ostracized. It was such a letdown, because I had been getting along so well with everybody and having fun.

Then I only made it worse. I started drinking everything else: lemon extract, Vitalis, any goddamn thing I could find. I knew my drinking was a problem, but I thought I just needed to cut down a little and get it under control. The idea of not drinking never occurred to me at all, even when the problems it caused were staring me in the face like that.

Fortunately, it wasn't that long a haul. We went from LA to Guam. The Navy had sunk some old ships there to make a breakwater. Our ship started drifting and ran aground on the breakwater, crumpling the forepeak, where the fresh water supply was. So we never even got in the harbor. Some Navy tugs pulled us off the breakwater; a tanker came up and we disgorged our cargo of bunker oil and went back to LA, 60 days after we left.

I was back on the town with a good payoff in my pocket, but within 24 hours I was flat-ass broke.

When I went back to the union hall, I still owed them the $35 plus two month's dues. But they needed hands, so they put me on another tanker, the Sacketts Harbor. We shipped out on April 13 of '44.

I was on that boat until September of '45, after the war ended. We spent most of that time going back and forth through the Panama Canal, loading up on oil at Curacao, then dumping it off at whatever the newest island we'd secured in the Pacific was.

I was still working in the galley, but I wasn't working much. There was a steam line running through there, and I got them to tap it and attach a steam hose to it. When I'd hit the dishes with that live steam, it would clean them in an instant. I usually had my shift done in 40 minutes.

I'd hang out in the galley, though, and learned a lot from the cooks. Sometimes I'd stay up all night with the baker as he'd make the next day's bread and pies. In the Merchant Marine, they were all real pros, out of the big restaurants or hotels.

The seaman's union had a lot of clout, so we weren't just getting shit on a shingle. It was a union rule that at every lunch and dinner there had to be a choice of three entrees. A lot of the time we didn't have the third entree, but we'd get around that by having a tray of beef tongue in the refrigerator. For the whole goddamn trip we'd have that one tray of tongue we'd put out, and nobody ever ordered it.

As long as the ship was underway and you had the routine going on, everything was pretty peaceful. But we'd be at anchor for long times because we were a floating oil storehouse. Then the crew would get testy and nasty, a whole different feeling.

One night I got in a hassle with the chief cook. He said something and I said something and he clobbered me, got me down and was beating my head on the steel deck. I got loose and grabbed a fire ax off the wall. I chased him all around that ship, and I meant it. If I'd caught him I'd a hit him with that fucking ax, because I was really pissed. Mine wasn't the only fight like that, and it always happened when we were at anchor.

Aboard ship, I made booze in crocks, using cherries, sugar, water and a little bit of yeast, coming up with a brew that was maybe 15 % alcohol. One morning, I was pretty hungover and the chief steward wanted me to get up and start washing the dishes. I told him to leave me the hell alone. But he kept on, and I jumped out of bed—I was sleeping on deck then—grabbed him around the neck and started beating his head on the rail and tried to throw him overboard until someone came along and broke it up. Jesus, we really didn't need the Japs.

The Sacketts Harbor had a 5" gun aft and a 3" gun forward and four banks of 20 millimeter anti-aircraft guns. Along with the 60-man crew, there were 20 Navy guys. They were short three Navy people to man the guns, so they asked for volunteers from the civilian crew. The Merchant Marine ships all had a union steward, and ours let us know we weren't supposed to do that, because we were civilians and if we bore arms and fell into the hands of the enemy, they could shoot us.

Of course, I volunteered. They put me as second loader on the 3" gun, a no-brainer, but you'd wear a helmet and felt like you were in the action. We had all sorts of gun practice, at floats and balloons they'd let off the ship. We'd blaze away and never hit a single thing.

There were only two times I saw the enemy. One was near Truk, when a Japanese plane spotted us. We were terrified we'd have a destroyer on our ass, but nothing ever came of it. The other time we were with the entire fleet, in a staging area for the next invasion. It was near dark and we were tied up to a Navy ship, discharging our cargo into it. The Navy boats had movie screens and projectors on them, which we never had. Our crew was over on the Navy ship waiting for the movie when the alarm went off for general quarters.

Being the second loader on the 3" gun, I busted out running to get back to my ship and my battle station. But because we were loading fuel into their ship, it had been sinking lower while ours was rising up. Our deck was way up there and I had to scramble around to find a ladder. Climbing up, I lost my hold twice and fell back to the deck, I was so excited trying to get to that gun.

By the time I got there everybody in that harbor had started shooting, but no one knew what they were shooting at. Our gun didn't have a target, but we were blazing away too. Several people in the harbor were killed from falling anti-aircraft shells. Meanwhile, two Japanese planes came in real low. One crashed and burned on the deck of a carrier. The other one tried, missed and crashed on the island. We could see the plane blow up, and thick oily smoke rising from it.

As much as you hear about the science of war, a lot of it is still like kids with rubber band guns. If the Japanese had concentrated on having their subs take out our oil tankers, we couldn't have carried on a war. But they didn't feel that tankers were a worthy, honorable target. Ships like mine were only carrying the lifeblood of the whole damn fleet, but we didn't have the status to the Japs that a destroyer did. That was a lucky break for us, because tankers like ours were easy pickings, and we'd have blown up without much coaxing at all. If the Japanese had gone after us, and had they hit the Panama Canal instead of Pearl Harbor, it might have been a very different war.

When our ship would come into Panama, we'd inventory what we had onboard and replenish that with new stores. So on the way in, we'd deep six everything, chuck it overboard, so we could have all new supplies.

We'd also pick up our mail in Panama City. I wrote a few letters home, but not many. My mom always wrote to me, though. She'd cut out the *Dick Tracy* and *Lil' Abner* comic strips for me from the Sunday funnies, and boy, those would go round the ship.

For a boozer, Panama City was heaven. That town was wide open.

Things you couldn't get anywhere else during the war—French perfume, Swiss watches, nylons—were available in Panama, in the jewelry stores and souvenir shops. At the end of the main drag there was one big hotel, the Intercontinental, that was about eight stories tall and dominated the town. All we cared about, though, were the four big saloon nightclubs. They had all kinds of liquor, and they all had rooms upstairs where the whores operated.

One night, one of our mess guys, who was only about 15, went upstairs with one of the hookers. He got his shirttail stuck in his zipper; the hooker started making fun of him; he got angry and charged at her; she came running down the stairs screaming; and some of the staff started beating on him, so the guys from the ship started beating on them. Next thing you know, it was frantic, like a wild west movie. We started throwing chairs and absolutely trashed the place.

The Panamanian police and military were one and the same. They all dressed to the nines and could be tough characters. When they came in, I lit up the stairs, with another guy from the ship right behind me. They caught up with him at the top of the stairs, and he clobbered a cop with a pitcher that was sitting on a table. He fell back on the other cops, and we both went through the window and got back to the ship.

They jailed six of our crew, though, and wouldn't let them go until we paid something like $1500 in damages. The skipper got us each to kick in $30 to get our guys out. Most of us had already blown through our pay, so it was an advance against our future wages.

I spent a lot of time in Panama, and on Curacao, which at the time was a Dutch island. It was a neat little place, but stiff. The Dutch Queen was there in exile, because the Netherlands had been taken over by the Germans, and the island was like something from the old days of imperialism.

The big deal on Curacao was the Shell Oil Company refinery. They had maybe 2,000 blacks working in the refineries, and the rest of the inhabitants were Dutch, living in a walled compound. It was patrolled by huge uniformed black guards— the shortest of them was at least 6'4"—and the merchant seamen weren't allowed in. They were protecting their daughters.

For 16 months, it was just back and forth between there and the war zone.

When the war ended, VJ Day, we were about a day out of Panama and a day into Curacao, and, boy, did we have a huge celebration on the ship. We had all these porthole blackouts—which had blocked our cabin lights from enemy planes but also blocked any fresh air from coming in—and the first thing we did was chuck them all over the side. Then we shot off all our flares. Everybody had been hoarding a bottle for the occasion. The second mate and one of the engineers were the only ones sober onboard that night.

In Curacao we needed to get some work done on the ship, and then, they said, we had to take another load of oil to Japan. I got up a full head of booze and thought, "Shit, no way. The war's over. I'm going to get off this thing and get home some way."

On past stays on Curacao I'd befriended some black guys who had big schooners that traded between the islands— fruit, rum and things. They had no quarters, so you'd sleep on deck on a coil of rope or whatever. There was no head, either. But they always had plenty of fruit and rum.

I made arrangements with one of these guys to take me to Port Au Prince in Haiti, maybe a four day trip. I figured if I could get that close to the States, somehow I'd get the rest of the way home.

I'd been staying with the black guys for about a week

while my ship was in dry dock. I wasn't showing up to work in the galley, so they were looking for me. It got to where the schooner was going to sail soon, so I snuck aboard the Sacketts Harbor around two in the morning to get my seaman's passport and a few things. I was just leaving the ship when *whoom*, they put the arm on me and locked me in my forecastle.

The next morning they took me to the skipper, who tried to impress on me the importance of our getting fuel to Japan so our ships could get home. I told him as far as I was concerned the war was over and I just wanted to get home. He said "Well, you can't do that," and had me locked up again.

The official report read: "This man was absent from his duties, August 16, without valid reason. Seaman's reply: nothing to say."

I was sitting there under lock and key wondering where the hell I was going to get something to drink when I heard a scratching outside. They were still working on the hull in the shipyard, so I stuck my head out the porthole and gave a shipyard worker $6 to get me a quart of whiskey from the Dutch seaman's club. He'd make $3 on the deal, a day's pay for him. That got to be a daily thing, and every day the skipper called me up to talk to me in his office, and I'd be whacked out. He never did figure that out.

When we sailed, the skipper let me out of my forecastle and I was back to duty working in the galley. He'd still call me into his office every day. I told him, "When this thing hits Panama, I'm going over the side. I'm not going out to sea." Once a ship gets under way, they're not going to stop to get you.

Finally he said he'd sign me off in Panama. But he told me, "You'll probably be there for two years. There are tons of displaced guys stuck trying to get home, waiting for a vacancy on a ship." I just didn't care.

There was a buddy of mine on the ship, a pretty good drinker but nothing like I was, who had the same notion of getting off, though his reason was piles. So the captain signed the both of us off, on September 3, 1945. On the canal zone side that belonged to the US, they had a barracks where you'd get a bunk and meals, and you could go into Panama City every day.

My buddy, Ronnie, was a weird-looking guy, with really kinky, curly hair and a pocked face, like he'd had bad acne as a kid. But he could make other people look good. He'd been a set painter and sketch artist at the Hollywood studios. He did a sketch of me, and it was really good. That gave me the idea that we could make a few bucks from the soldiers and sailors throwing their money around in the bars. I'd show Ronnie's sketch of me around, and tell them for $10 they could have one to send home. With me lining up the work, Ronnie was probably doing ten or fifteen portraits a night for nearly a month. He kept all the money for himself. As I mentioned, he wasn't as blitzed as I was.

One night, as we were coming in late from the saloons, the desk man at the barracks desk told us that if we were looking for a boat to the States, one was passing through in 20 minutes. We threw all our stuff together, got a cab, jumped in a launch and caught sight of this Liberty ship coming through. It didn't even slow up for us; we boarded it on a Jacob's ladder.

They didn't have any idea who we were, so Ronnie told them he was a chief steward, and I told them I was a chief cook. Those jobs were filled, but they put us up with the ship's chief steward. He was a superlative drinker and had a couple of cases of booze he'd brought up from Peru.

We were partying on that ship day and night, literally. For the ten days we were at sea I never slept. It was the damnedest thing. I just stayed whacked out of my head. I found out later that this booze from Peru, called Pisco, was laced with cocaine. That's what kept me awake.

The boat landed up-river at Philadelphia. We were kept in quarantine, as a ship always was when it came in from a foreign country. There were so many ships arriving that the inspectors were all backlogged. So we were stuck for days with Philadelphia sitting right there. Goddamn but we wanted to get off, being gone as long as we'd been.

One day a launch pulled up with mail for the ship while we were standing along the rail. Ronnie had maybe three grand pocketed from his drawings. After the launch guy dumped the mail off, Ronnie got his gear and told me, "Come on. Let's get the hell out of here," and we jumped in the mail launch. The guy yelled, "Hey, you can't do this!" Ronnie flipped him $100 and he hauled ass out of there with us. I never did get discharged from that ship.

The mail carrier took us to a ladder on a rusty old steel pier. Right at the pier head was a saloon, and, boy, was I glad to be on United States soil again. Wow! All I remember about the saloon was a big bowl full of crab legs and a nut cracker.

Did I see the Liberty Bell? No, all I saw of Philadelphia was more saloons. Ronnie and I planned on going up to New York, but somehow we got separated. I was stumbling down a street in Philadelphia, wearing my ship khakis, when an old guy on a stoop said, "Hey, soldier, you want a little action?"

And I said, "Yeah. Man, why not?" You have to remember I'd been at sea a long time. He took me up to the second floor in his brownstone, and he had a nice looking gal there, except she looked like she was on drugs. The old guy said, "Have at it," and I did.

I spent the night there and the next morning he fixed breakfast. I said I had to get to the train station, and he said, "Why don't you stay here? I'll take you to New York in a couple of days." But I split. I'm not sure what his thing was. I guess he liked to watch. And the woman was kind of a zombie, though she was a nice looking one.

I got to the train station, and as luck would have it, bumped into Ronnie there. We made it to New York, but every place we went was just overrun with soldiers and sailors celebrating. We caught a cab and asked the driver if there was a place where there wasn't as much competition. He took us to a dance hall away from the downtown. There, we wound up with a couple of Army nurses. One was a mousy little gal and the other was a tall brunette Ronnie ended up with.

We danced with them and then they took us home. We stayed with them a week, and, Christ, the mousy one I was with was boozing as bad as I was. Nearly all I remember from that time is that every afternoon I'd wander out of the apartment to a bench on the lawn in front of a library. I'd sit in the fresh air just to get myself together a little bit, and then it was back to the apartment.

Ronnie had lost his sea bag on the train from Philadelphia. After a week it showed up at Penn Station and we went down to collect it. I guess I wasn't navigating very well, because they set me on a stool in a bar adjoining the station while Ronnie and the girls went to get his bag. I hadn't sat there very long before I thought, "I want to go home. I'm tired of all this stuff."

I called my mother collect and told her I needed some money to get home. She wired it to a Western Union office a couple of blocks down the street. I went off in that direction, and didn't see Ronnie and the girls again. (I did see Ronnie years later, and he'd married that gal he was with.) Wiring money took a while back then, so I crashed for two nights, September 15 and 16, at a flophouse, the Seaman's Church Institute building, for 85 cents a night.

Once I got the money from the Western Union office, I bought two quarts of whiskey and a bus ticket to Los Angeles. I woke up in Indianapolis, got off the bus to buy two more quarts of whiskey, got on the bus, and woke up in Tulsa, Oklahoma, just long enough to look out the window. Then I passed out again and the next thing I remember was Tucson. I was all out of whisky and money, so I had a glass of beer.

All this time I'd somehow held on to a Bulova wristwatch with my name engraved on the back that my mother had given to me when I graduated from the tenth grade. I hocked it for $5 on Main St. in L.A., got a haircut and bought a clean shirt, and rode the PE down to Compton. I got off a couple of blocks from my house, and since the last drink I'd had was that beer in Tucson, I was practically cold sober for the first time in months. I ran all the way to my home. I'll tell you, that's quite a feeling, seeing home after so long. I hadn't been there for 14 months, and then only for about 20 minutes between ships.

Me, Hank, Thelma and Oskie Christoffersen
in the alley on Clinton Street.

With my '32 Ford 3-window coupe.

I wanted a little pussy,
I got a little pussy.

Finding new ways
to get high, 1943. I'm on the
shoulders of the 16-year-old
Paul Schults.

THE PARTY YEAR

After the war I tried to go to school and do one or two constructive things, but '46 really was a party year. I still have a lot of canceled checks from that time, and most of them were cashed in saloons. With the war over, consumer goods were coming on the market and everybody had high hopes. It was a good year.

On the New Year's Eve leading into 1946 there was a big party in Santa Monica. I went with a little ol' gal who had a fiancée off in the Navy. We were both blitzed, she got a little bit romantic and I got a bit more romantic. At the stroke of midnight while everyone was hollering "Happy New Year," we were on the back seat of the car. We weren't thinking too much about the new year.

I probably wouldn't even have remembered that night with her, but I soon found I had to. Her boyfriend mustered out of the Navy a month later and they got married. Before too long they got in a big fight, she told him about us, and he came looking for me. I must have dodged this big, mean old son of a bitch for four years.

After I'd arrived home from the Merchant Marine in late 1945, I started hanging around the gate of the Ford assembly plant in Long Beach, trying to get hired. They paid well, and in cash. Every morning, a Ford guy would stand there picking a few hires—just going, "You, you and you"—from the 30 or 40 guys there. After a couple of days, I noticed that he'd ignore the gentlemen and pick the ones who pushed and shoved the most. That was Ford policy, to hire the aggressive types. Once I saw it worked like that, I made sure I got hired.

They put me on the chassis assembly line, bolting splash pans and other parts on '46 Fords. They were the same design as the '41 Fords, since everything had stopped cold during the war.

The chassis were coming by at a good clip, but I found that if I worked up the line a little bit, I could get ahead enough to run to the men's room and smoke a cigarette. When I'd come back, I'd be behind a bit. I'd catch up, get ahead, and go smoke another cigarette.

When they saw a worker doing that, though, they'd add more work on him. So they kept adding and I kept getting ahead and smoking. One day I was just going like crazy—it was like that *Lucy* episode where the assembly line keeps speeding up on her—and the next thing I knew I woke up in the infirmary.

I'd passed out. When I got my senses back, the doctor told me, "You're going to live. You're all right."

I told him I was just trying to do too much too fast. He said, "That's exactly what you were doing."

"Well, I'll try to slow down a little bit."

"No, I've seen guys like you and you just don't work on assembly lines, so you're out the door," he said, and I was fired, just like that. They wanted you to keep up, not to be aggressive to the point where you keel over. That was on January 5 of '46. I'd lasted there about a month.

My next job was at the Supercold company, which was shifting its production back to making refrigeration units, having made bomb bay doors for Liberator bombers during the war. I was a material handler.

I met a gal there who I asked out, and she said yeah. That same week I was invited to bowl with the plant's bowling league on Saturday night. I bowled with them and started drinking, and totally blacked out.

At work Monday morning my timecard wasn't in the rack, just a note to see the boss. I went in and he said, "I guess I don't have to tell you what this is about. You'd better clear out of here."

I said, 'No, what did happen?"

"You know. Go on now."

To this day I still don't know what I did, but it must have been one big-ass bowling alley faux paux. After that, the gal didn't want to have anything to do with me, either.

A friend of mine, Dick Shuey, was still in the Navy, stationed on a ship in San Diego. One Saturday, an acquaintance went with me when I drove Dick down there from Compton. We started to drag race with some guys we knew in another car. I was able to out-drag this guy and get way ahead. Then I'd pull over, kill the engine and lights and we'd sit there drinking. When the other car caught up we'd do it again.

A while after Dick passed out, a cop stopped us and asked what we were doing. He asked if we had any whiskey on board and I said, "Yeah" and handed him my half-full quart. Just then Dick woke up and shouted, "What the hell are you doing?" and tried to snatch the whiskey back from the cop. I was hanging onto the door because I couldn't stand up. The cop looked at the whisky, handed it back to Dick and let us go. I've never understood that.

Near the Coronado Island ferry things started getting a little hazy for me, though I do remember taking off on the ferry ramp a tad early, being airborne for about two feet and knocking the ferry gate in a million pieces. After we dropped Dick off, we wound up later in Tijuana in a saloon, and near daylight we decided to drive to Mexico City, totally shit-faced. We headed generally south until the road ended, and I went over a drop-off, landing in a baseball field. It was a total miracle I didn't kill any of the kids playing there.

Several of the adults there lifted the car up, shoved it on the road and told us to get the hell out of there. The car didn't sound the same, because I'd lost the tailpipe and muffler. A little later, I sold the spare tire for money to buy another bottle. On Wednesday, the guy with me managed to cash a couple of checks, and we kept at it.

I got home on Friday, having left the weekend before. I'd done all this atrocious stuff and could have killed 40 kids, and I didn't think anything about it at all. Hell, it was just another day.

I started looking through the want ads in the *LA Times* and saw one that read, "Veterans, earn big money, and travel the US." It sounded like a lot of fun, so I went down and talked to the sales manager, who was set up at the Biltmore Hotel. He misrepresented the hell out of the job, unless being dumped on a street in El Monte is your idea of traveling the US.

At 9 a.m. the next morning ten of us were dropped off in a residential neighborhood in El Monte with salesmen who were going to show us the ropes.

The salesman I was paired with started banging on doors with this pitch about a veteran's rehabilitation program to help vets recover and get through school. It was all bullshit, but he made a heavy emotional appeal to the housewives. Then he'd explain how we'd get points for magazine subscriptions. I went to five or six homes with the guy, and he closed every sale. The fucker had big tears in his eyes.

Then he asked me to do it, but I got tongue-tied. I just flat-out couldn't do it. During lunch, I told the boss that I wasn't up to it, but he said I couldn't get a ride back to my car until 5, so I might as well try again with another guy.

This next salesman only had one arm. He'd lost it in an auto accident as a kid, not in the war. But he was sporting a khaki shirt with a couple of ribbons on it, and the arm all pinned up. This guy was good. He closed every sale too.

After several sales, I told him, "Hey, I'm going to go down to the gas station at the corner to use the bathroom. I'll be back in a minute." I went down to the intersection, stuck out my thumb, and caught a ride back to Los Angeles.

Even if I'd been starving, I couldn't do that sort of scam. It was such a line of bullshit that I couldn't believe it myself. I did have some morals.

A friend who'd got out of the service told me he was

going to attend LA City College, and that sounded like a pretty good thing to me, because you could get the GI bill to help. Despite being in the Navy such a short time, I was getting $20 a week mustering-out pay for a year. Everyone called that the 52/20 club.

So I moved up to LA and in with a family I'd known from Compton, the Cristoffersons. They had a big two-story house at 1749 Clinton Street in the Echo Park district of Los Angeles. I was with several guys sleeping in a room over the garage, while the family and girls lived upstairs in the house. There must have been 15 of us living there, from two years old to 60. The lady that owned the place collected $10 a week room and board. Since most of us were getting $20 from the government, that was fine. Before long, I worked it so I moved into the living room, with a bed that pulled out from under the stairs.

For a while I dated one of the Cristofferson daughters, Loretta, a divorcee a couple of years older than I was. We were going pretty good for a while, but Loretta had a little girl and probably wanted someone stable who would provide for her. We drifted apart, and I'm pretty sure it had to do with my drinking. I was pretty busy with other gals anyway.

At LA City College I wound up having to take dumbbell English and other make-up classes. My high school had issued me a diploma when I joined the Navy, but that didn't give me the credits the college wanted to see.

Meanwhile, on the college job bulletin board, one listing was for an office boy with a car. It paid 65 cents an hour plus mileage, so I answered it. It was for the Association of Motion Picture Producers, at the corner of Western and Hollywood Boulevard, in the publicity office on the third floor. I got the job, and it was keen.

The office was run by a fellow named Arch Reeve, a really super guy. He had a hunchback and had to have all of his clothes custom made. It was his policy to put out a news release every day, whether there was any news or not. The release was made up of industry items: figures and grosses, labor hassles. I'd mimeograph them, deliver them to all the newspapers and entertainment rags in town, and keep a scrapbook of what made it into print.

Another of my duties was to stop off at the liquor store to pick up soda water and scotch for Mr. Reeve. I'd also chauffeur him on Thurdays, when he'd have cocktails and lunch at Lucy's with all the studio publicity heads. Sometimes he'd introduce me to these industry big shots like I was going to amount to something myself, which embarrassed me.

There are certain people you have an understanding with right away. Mr. Reeve and I were on the same wavelength. He was 60 and I was a punk kid, but I was the only one in the office he really talked to.

He liked me and even offered to help get me hired at MGM as a junior publicist. I thought about it, and decided their schedule didn't fit my schedule at all. I would have to quit school—which I wasn't doing much at anyway—but it really would have screwed up my social life. I told Mr. Reeve I'd better stay where I was.

Meanwhile, I was living at that Echo Park nut house with all those guys. I'd get up and get to school, still high from the night before, make it to eleven o'clock, then have a couple of drinks on the way to the office. I'd be in good shape until I'd finish up about 8 p.m. and go out on the town again. Like I said, 1946 was party time.

From the Christofferson house, we'd catch the street car all the way down Sunset Boulevard to the Aragon Ballroom at the Santa Monica Pier on most weekends. We'd drink and dance until 4 in the morning. Lawrence Welk was the Aragon's perpetual headliner. Welk usually played the slow dances and the older people would be out on the floor. That's when we'd drink or walk out along the beach. We'd dance to the bands that would come on when Welk came off. They weren't name bands at all, but they were good.

Our neighborhood in Echo Park was nicknamed the Aimee District, because it was near Aimee Semple McPherson's church. She had been sort of the Bob Schuller of her time. She'd started as a tent revivalist, and put on such a show you could have sold it as vaudeville. Eventually, she had thousands of followers and was all over the radio. Her headquarters was the 5,000-seat round, domed building near us, Angelus Temple. And, God Almighty, she had a rabid following. A lot of the people had bought houses in our neighborhood just to be near her.

They must have had a lot of faith. Her son Rolf was running the church then, because Aimee had died of a drug overdose in 1944. Some years before that, she'd disappeared off the face of the earth for a month. She turned up in Arizona a month later claiming she'd been kidnapped. Soon it was found out that she'd actually been shacking-up with a lover in the Hollywood Hills.

When we'd go to the park to play around and drink beer, people from Aimee's temple would come around and invite us to attend the services. The first time they did that we were just about out of beer, so we thought, "Oh, what the heck, why not?"

We attended the service, and when they passed the plate down, Jesus, it was full of money. So we reached in there and grabbed handfuls of it and stuck it in our pockets. As soon as we got out of there, we ran down and got some more beer. That got to be a regular means of income for us for a while.

A fellow named Bill Marsh would hang out at the Christofferson's. His dad had been a studio electrician for years. The union had a thing where the only new members they'd take in were sons of members that had been in the service. Bill qualified, and got his electrician's card.

He was living in a little apartment near Santa Monica and Western and suggested I move in with him. I'd bombed out of college by then, things were on the outs with Loretta, and

Bill's place was closer to my job, so I moved in.

He was making big money at Paramount. I was making my pittance from the producer's association, but I was such a bullshit artist then. I'd show people my payroll stubs from the Motion Picture Association, after I'd altered the numbers to make it look like $2247 instead of $247.

Through my job, I was always getting tickets to radio shows and other events in Hollywood. People would stand in line hoping to get into those. Bill and I would have four tickets and we'd walk down the line until we saw a couple of pretties. We'd grab them, see the show and take them out afterwards.

When I was a little bitty kid, maybe five years old, a couple of older girls, maybe 12 or 13, had lured me into an old abandoned house in my neighborhood. They said if I'd show them my private parts, they'd give me some candy. I thought that was a good deal, so they looked me over real well and gave me the candies. I bit into one and holy Toledo, it really *burned*! I'd never seen red hot chiles before, and that's what they'd foisted off on me. There was probably a moral to this experience, but it was lost on me.

I was always getting in trouble over girls. When I was in the 7th grade, during gym class they'd had the girls and boys on separate sides of the gym. But I'd always drift over to the girls and start sweet-talking them, until the gym teacher whacked me in the rear end with his whistle strap. Even earlier, in the 4th grade there was a girl on my street named Ann with whom I was really smitten. I'd try striking up a conversation on the way home from school, but she wasn't taking to that at all. One day she just lost her patience and really clobbered me over the head with her lunch box. I went down like a shot, and afterwards figured I'd better forget about having anything more to do with her. Too bad. By the time she got to be 16, she was the *ugliest* thing you ever saw in your life, with a beard.

When I moved in with Bill in Hollywood, I wasn't exactly handsome. I was pretty average, even less than average because I was skinny. But because of Frank Sinatra, that was kind of *in*. I was about the same build. I was also a fair dancer. Loretta and I once won first prize—a crate of oranges—at a swing dance. I really never had much of a struggle getting girlfriends. I was able to strike up a relationship with any of them I zeroed in on without too much trouble.

Bill and I were out chasing every night. There were nine zillion gals living around Hollywood then trying to get into the movies. The fact that Bill worked at Paramount and I worked for the producers' association impressed the hell out of those gals, so we had good livin'.

Bill was with me the night I got busted for my third drunk driving offense, on our way out to the Aragon. I was speeding and whipping in and out of traffic, and here came the flashing lights. They threw me in the West LA jail.

In September of 1946 the court took my driver's license away and put me on probation. I had to leave my job because I had to quit driving. Which I did, for about a month. Then I went right back to it, driving without a license.

Bill and I had also been stealing stuff for no good reason. One morning after a real wild fracas we wound up in the parking lot of the LA Country Club, and went through a number of cars, stealing golf clubs, blankets, whatever.

The next morning, I woke up and looked out the window and there at the curb was my little '32 Ford coupe parked with the rumble seat open and all this crap we'd stolen just piled up in it for anyone to see. After that Bill and I figured we'd better go our separate ways or we'd wind up in the pokey.

So at the tail end of 1946 I packed up my things and moved back in with my mother in Compton.

I was always a dapper drunk. Since I didn't
fit the stumblebum image, most people
didn't even know I was sloshed.

TRAILER CASH

When I moved back home with my mom in Compton, I thought about going back to school, but didn't. About the only thing I learned in college was to not go to college. In one of my classes I read an essay by the successful publisher William Allen White titled "I Never Went to College." White felt he'd advanced himself a lot more by being out in the working world.

So I followed my brother Speed into the trailer business. Speed had been working for US Rubber for nearly 20 years, since he was 16. He had a good position there, with seniority and security, but he chucked all of that to work for a trailer company in LA. He was making really good money there, and that kind of appealed to me.

I'd always liked playing in my father's cobbled-up Model T rig in our yard as a kid. And when my dad and I had been staying at Kern River a guy came in towing a brand new 16-foot trailer that had been made somewhere in the East. I got to take a look at it, and that barge was the way to go. Most trailers made in the '30s were elegant, like yachts, because it was the wealthy who bought them. This one was really tricked out. Since my dad and I had been living in a little tent by the river, using orange crates nailed to a tree for shelves, it looked like a mansion to me.

Trailers hadn't been a big business before the war, but there were housing shortages when everyone came home from overseas and started families. The idea of living in a trailer started to look good to people, particularly when sleeping in a ditch was the alternative. So, after the war, trailer parks came into being, and they were springing up everywhere.

With that new breed of buyer, the post-war trailers usually weren't anything fancy. They'd have a propane stove, an icebox, a few cupboards, a full-sized bed and a fold-down one. There wasn't a bathroom, because they were difficult to rig up.

Before Speed had been working at the one trailer shop very long, a guy named Lee Black started the Blackhawk trailer company right in Compton. Speed and a whole gang who had been working this place in LA came to work there.

Speed suggested I look into the business. He didn't recommend me to the boss—he says I was just too unreliable then—but he didn't say anything bad about me either. Lee Black hired me and I went to work there in January of 1947.

At Blackhawk the employees were paid piecework and the rates were really high. But right as I came on there was a slow-down in the business, and after two weeks the boss put everybody on an hourly wage. Nearly everyone quit, including Speed.

Suddenly, I was the old hand there. The company started hiring new people, and I was put in charge of a crew attaching the metal siding to the outside of the trailers. Unlike the aluminum the industry used later, this was heavy-duty war surplus, so hard that we found we had to drill it before we could drive a nail through it.

Blackhawk was a free-wheeling enterprise, with more room for initiative than the other places I'd worked. This wasn't by design, but because the plant foreman was an old drunk, a building construction guy who knew nothing about building trailers. If any of us had a problem with anything, all he'd ever tell us was, "Well, you figure it out."

I was always good at practical things, and I really liked that there was no set procedure for doing the job, so any method I came up with was all right.

I also found I worked well with people. We were an efficient little crew. In no time at all, the station behind me couldn't get the units to us fast enough, so the boss put me in charge of them too. Within six months, I was in charge of the whole shop.

Of course, I was still drinking heavily. Every noon I'd cross over to the bowling alley, top my lunch off with a couple of hookers of bourbon and go back to work. At night, I'd be out guzzling until two in the morning, and be on the job at seven, still high, to get the plant going. And it was all clicking for me.

I was 22 years old, getting $2 an hour and a $5 bonus for every trailer that went out the door. We were building about 15 trailers a week, so I was making about $155 a week, big money then. I went right out and bought a new maroon Ford Sportsman woodie convertible.

I didn't have that car for too long, but I did have it long enough to catch my future wife's eye.

Considering that we've been together for 52 years, it's always amazing to me that my meeting Donna Mae Setterstrom was so coincidental. I had that woodie sitting in my front yard, and, as I was getting in it one day to go downtown, a fellow I barely knew from around the corner came up. With scarcely a how-ya-doin' he asked, "Are you going downtown? How about a ride?"

"Yeah, c'mon, jump in."

So we took off and were talking about this and that. I don't remember why, but instead of heading downtown, we made a left and went up Compton Blvd. And there, sitting on a bench waiting for a bus, was Donna and another girl

I said, "Wow, look at that!" and he said, "Yeah, and I know 'em." So we pulled over and started jiving with them, trying to get them to come with us in the car. They wouldn't, but we made arrangements to meet them at the Starlight Café across the street that evening. And that's when Donna and I started to go together. I had that brand new car and she had stars in her eyes over that.

If I hadn't come out of the house right as this guy was coming around the corner, and if I hadn't turned left instead of right, and Donna hadn't been sitting on the bench just then, she and I wouldn't have been. I think there must be a certain amount of fate or guidance in life.

Most of the gals I chased around with were pretty fast. But Donna was a straight-laced girl from the right side of the tracks, and I liked that. Meanwhile, she thought I was the greatest. I was a young man and she was 17, and that might have been part of my appeal. The new Ford convertible probably didn't hurt either. Whatever it was, I could do no wrong with her. That really touched me. She didn't criticize me, even for my drinking.

Of course, she didn't see the worst of it. She had no idea I was an alcoholic. All she knew about alcoholics was the popular image of the ill-kempt stumble bum. I dressed well. I'd always go out looking pretty good, even if coming back was a different story. But I was different around Donna. The only time I'd see her was when I was trying to put myself together. I'd get myself reasonably sober and take her out to a movie or something semi-respectable.

While I was working at Blackhawk, Doug Caruthers— Red's brother who'd run the service station—had a business delivering trailers from the factories to dealers. One day he was picking up an order at Blackhawk and told me, "Hey, John, I want to get a place building trailers. I've got some money saved up. You want to come and work for me?" to which I said, "Hell, yes."

The boss at Blackhawk had become high-minded and hired some consultants. They expanded the operation way beyond anything that made sense. The expansion wasn't getting much more production than we'd had before and the overhead was probably twice as much. I was becoming pretty disenchanted with that.

Then the consultants put in an efficiency expert over me who would walk around looking important. He wasn't doing anything because he didn't know what to do, but he had some good credentials from somewhere. The son of a bitch was only in the way, and I resented it.

One day there was a trailer hooked up to a delivery truck,

ready to go, and this expert came up and insisted, "There's something not right with this trailer. A door inside needs adjusting. You can't ship it until you get that fixed."

So I just jumped in there myself and fixed it. I got out and told him it was ready to go. He said, "Are you sure?"

"Yeah, I just fixed it."

"Well, I'd better check it."

He climbed in the trailer with his clipboard, and as soon as he did, I slammed the door and signaled the driver to take it away.

That got the expert out of my hair for a couple of hours, but he was hopping mad when he made it back. It can be pretty hairy stuck in a trailer when the driver doesn't know you're back there, and he got bounced around a bit. But when he dragged me into Lee Black's office, all I said was, "Hell, I didn't know he was in there," and my boss believed me.

It wasn't too long after that when Doug came in one afternoon, said he'd found a trailer factory to buy and asked, "You still want to come to work?"

I was excited because, working for him, I'd be able to design the trailers, which was something I really wanted to do. In my opinion, what we'd been building at Blackhawk was a lot of nonsense, with more material, money and labor than was needed. I could see lots of better ways to do it.

After work one day, I went with Doug to look at an old trailer plant in an alley in Compton. There were four half-built trailers from when the owner had gone belly up, a table saw and a few tools. It was just a bunch of crap, and Doug told me the guy wanted to sell it to him for $10,000.

"Jesus, Doug, you could do a lot better than this dump for that kind of money."

"It isn't exactly $10,000. I'm trading him a $10,000 race car for it," he said, and that was OK because his car probably wasn't worth crap either.

Doug made the deal and I went to work for him in early 1948 at a salary of $125 a week plus $5 a finished trailer. Doug had sold his house and taken on a partner who had $1,800, so he had some working capital to get started. We called the company Viking.

When I left Blackhawk, I went into my boss' office and told him, "Hey, I'm out of here. I'm going to work for another guy. If you don't kick these efficiency experts the fuck out of here and do something drastic, you ain't going to be in business much longer."

He hardly even looked up, and said, "I'll be all right, smartass." Six months to the day later, he was in chapter 11 and gone.

The Viking factory had about 30 feet of street frontage, but it went back 250 feet from there, in a couple of open-sided sheds running the length of the alley. The sheds weren't even fenced in, so anything we didn't want stolen we had to lock in the office at night.

The initial crew there was Doug, Red, their father, the guy who had put in the $1800, me and two kids who would come in after school to sand and mask the trailers for painting.

Soon, we hired a couple of more guys and were getting five trailers a week out of that chickenshit alley. I'd designed an 18-foot trailer that was pretty neat and sold to the dealer for around $1200, which was $300 or $400 less than most similar models.

It wasn't like I was designing the Eiffel Tower. Trailers were simple. You'd buy a chassis from a supplier and on that you'd build the floor with two-by-twos nailed together, with cardboard on one side and plywood glued on the other. You'd bolt it onto the chassis, and put Linoleum on it. You'd build the sidewalls on a jig table, and nail those to the floor. You'd buy the cabinets ready-made, install them, then put the top on, wire it, put in the light fixtures, varnish the inside, paint the exterior and put a stripe on the outside, which was aluminum siding you'd mold and paint. You'd do that on an assembly line, with maybe a half-dozen trailers in progress.

Ever since I was a kid, I'd loved designing and building model airplanes. (I still do. With all the development in Southern California, we fliers kept running out of places to go. Finally, a decade ago, I bought a tract of land in Lost Hills, north of Bakersfield, and donated it to the model airplane club.) With the planes, I'd learned to build something with as little material as possible without sacrificing quality or structural strength. A lot of that experience went into my trailers.

I left out a lot of things on the model I designed. The industry was putting crummy paper insulation in the floors, and I skipped that. The trailers weren't very far off the ground, but everyone was putting steps on them that cost $10. I left those off, too. Some of the things the industry did were holdovers from the days of luxury trailers, and the dealers and the public really didn't care about them. I left them out and the result was a nifty little trailer, priced cheaper than the competition.

Doug had known all the dealers from delivering trailers, so he set up dealerships overnight and the trailer sold like crazy. We were off and running, zingo!

I was making good money, enjoying it and drinking like a fish. For what I was getting done, I worked cheap, so Doug didn't mind if I was a little sloshed.

Doug's wife, Johnnie, was another matter, though. I'd got on her bad side during the war, when she'd run Doug's gas station while he was off working as a machinist. Every single time I'd gone in there, she'd want to see my ration stamps before she'd pump me any gas. It would always be this back and forth:

"Let's see your stamps."

"I got 'em. Put the gas in."

"Let me see them."

"Put the gas in, dammit."

She'd finally put the gas in, and I'd give her the money

and haul away: no stamps. I'd see her in the rear view mirror, absolutely livid. But I'd come in next time and give her the same argument, and she'd go for it again, like Charlie Brown with Lucy's football.

Johnnie's one of my oldest friends now, but when she was running the office for Doug at Viking, she hated me with a passion. I'd have the shop in order before I went home at night, so it could get going at seven the next morning without me. I wouldn't be needed there until nine or ten. Johnnie, meanwhile, would have been there since seven, just getting more furious with every minute. But Doug knew I was getting the job done, so I could get away with that.

Some people didn't even notice that I drank. One New Year's Day back then, I was supposed to take my two nieces and their mother—Jerry's family—up to the Rose Parade. On New Year's Eve I was at a party at the Christofferson's, and sometime during the night I passed out with some broad in a bedroom. About five in the morning the telephone started ringing. I somehow heard it and found the receiver. It was my mother reminding me about my nieces.

I straightened myself up, took a couple of belts out of a bottle and headed out to get them, so I was in pretty good shape. I had an uncle who lived in Pasadena at the time and I dropped the girls off near his place. Then I found a saloon in Altadena that opened at 6 a.m. and watched the Rose Parade on their TV (this was the first time it was televised).

I was pretty well hammered by the time the last float rolled by. I went to pick up my charges, but the traffic coming out of Pasadena was so heavy I couldn't make any headway whatever. It occurred to me that the Pacific Electric track went to within half a block of where my uncle lived. I drove my Sportsman up onto that live electric track and took it all the way to my uncle's house. And those kids told me years later they had no idea I was drinking.

Donna's parents, Elizabeth
and Emil Setterstrom.

Donna Mae Setterstrom,
the future Mrs. Crean.

Donna was a Meglin Kiddie,
as was our future friend
Donald O'Connor. It was
such an honor that few
noted the division of labor:
The Kiddies danced; the
Meglins got paid.

Donna, seated, in her
high-cultured youth,
obviously before she met me.

Donna and my wedding picture,
Las Vegas, 1948.

HITCHED

I was making good money at Viking, but was spending most of it on drinking. I knocked out the transmission and rear end on the Sportsman while drag racing. I had it in the garage and got behind on the car payments because, again, all my money was going into booze. I signed the car over to one of Blackhawk's road salesmen. He paid the garage bill, took over the payments and was supposed to give me $300, which he kept putting off.

Even though I'd gone from driving a sleek mahogany and ash woodie convertible to puttering around in a '41 Oldsmobile, Donna was still hanging in with me. Her father had me pegged as bad news, but everything I did was OK by her. I'd come by every two or three weeks, when I sobered up, and take her out.

After we'd been going together about six months, I was out alone at a Compton saloon one night. There wasn't much happening, so the bartender and I were talking. He started telling me how great married life was—about the companionship and not being lonely—and said that I ought to get married.

In the party year of 1946, you couldn't go into a saloon anywhere that wasn't three deep with people. But by 1948 there was hardly anybody in the bars. Things had settled down. Most of the guys I had been chasing around with were married.

I was wandering around out there like a lost dog. I had a few girlfriends still on the string, but none I'd even think about marrying. That's where Donna came in. When I thought about it, she was the only one I'd really want to marry. So this bartender sang a pretty good song to me.

The more I thought about it, the more marriage seemed like it might be a good idea. I went to a pay phone in the bar, called Donna up and asked her if she wanted to get married.

And she said, "Oh, yeah." She was thrilled, not the least bit judgmental that I was drunk, proposing over the phone from a saloon.

We let Donna's mother in on it, but we knew her father would have no part of it at all. We snuck off, eloped, to Las Vegas. First, though, I got a couple of large buddies and paid a visit on the guy who was stiffing me on paying for the Sportsman. We yanked him out on his porch, hauled him down to the supermarket to cash his paycheck, and got my $300. With that I bought a set of rings and some clothes and financed the trip.

I'd stood up with my friend Oskie Christoffersen when he got married. He and his wife, Eloise, went with us to Vegas, as did a girlfriend of Donna's. We took my sister's car, a nice big Buick. I just told her I was borrowing it for the evening, not that I was taking it to the next state.

In Vegas, we looked up friends of Donna's who lived there—cocktail waitresses whose husbands were blackjack dealers—and got them to come along. We got a license at the courthouse and then found a Lutheran church right outside of town.

It was fairly early in the morning and there was a guy outside in his overalls hammering on the side of the building. I asked him if the preacher was around, and he just said, "Yeah," and went in the house.

He came out with a collar on, took us into the church and Donna and I got married. While we were taking the pictures afterwards, the preacher was out there again in his overalls, banging away.

This may all sound like it was a little off-the-cuff, particularly given the previous times I'd started off toward the Vegas altar, but I was dead serious. When the preacher was saying "forever," man, it was *forever*. I was hearing that. And I was tickled to death. I really wanted to get married to Donna. That was May 8, 1948, and I'm still tickled.

We didn't honeymoon at all, but headed right back to Compton. Donna's mother had rented us a little vacant one-room house across the street from where they lived. It had a Murphy bed in the main room, and an add-on lean-to kitchen built on the back, with a similar bathroom. The rent was $15 a month. Donna's mother set everything up for us, furnished it and put food in the cupboard.

She and my mom got together and wanted to have a big reception for us. They cooked up a party for a Sunday afternoon, July 11, and sent out a pile of invitations.

But I had a little Mustang motorcycle—a dealer in Compton had been selling them for hardly anything down—and the day before the reception, I'd gone out riding with a buddy who also had a cycle. We went to the cycle shop, and from there to Comstock's saloon. We got to drinking, and I never thought about going home at all.

Instead, around 8 p.m., I was barreling through town on my cycle. It being Saturday night when the stores were open, there were policemen at both crosswalks. I came charging through with the engine wide open.

I don't really remember too much of this, I was so out of it. But the cop who ran me down told me all about it later. He'd busted me several times before and was a pretty decent guy. He told me I somehow managed to swerve around a corner, rode a block, stopped, fell over and couldn't lift the motorcycle back up. This wasn't quite the evasive maneuver the moment had called for, and the cops poured me into a squad car and tossed me in the clink.

That was my fourth drunk driving arrest. I was already on probation and hadn't been reporting to the probation officer, so I was dead certain I was going to get a year in the slammer. I also figured, given the way Donna's dad had no use for me already, that was the end of the marriage.

And I thought that, even as far as Donna was concerned, that was the end of the marriage, because I'd been a real asshole already in the short time we'd been married: Maybe I'd come home from work or maybe I wouldn't.

I wasn't very responsible, the handiest example being that when I'd taken off on my motorcycle, I'd told Donna I'd be back in an hour, and didn't come back at all.

As long as you have plenty to drink, you don't have any conscience. But cut off from the booze in jail, I felt terrible about what I'd done.

Needless to say, they had to postpone the reception.

On Sunday, Donna came to see me in the jail. I told her to get my boss, Doug, to bail me out before I had to go to court Monday morning. The only thing I could see to do was to jump bail and get the hell out of town. There was a trailer company in Tulsa, Oklahoma, where I was pretty sure I could get work. Donna saw Doug, but he said no way was he going to bail me out.

So Monday morning I went to court and pled guilty, because I wasn't anything but guilty. I was astounded when the judge only levied a fine of $50 (that I could pay off at $5 a week) and turned me loose.

I couldn't figure out what had happened there. I learned later that Donna's mother was a good friend of this judge, and she'd smoothed it all over with him.

It wasn't long after that when I got rid of the motorcycle. I went with Red to a Baldwin Hills motorcycle hill climb and burned out the clutch. I don't know how many payments I had due on it, but I figured, screw it, just leave it there. But as I was walking down the hill some guy asked me about it, and offered me $100 for my equity in the thing. He gave me the cash right there. Red and I went to a saloon on Sepulveda Boulevard and we shut the place down, spending most of that $100.

For the most part, though, I simmered down after my reception-day arrest. Donna and I set up housekeeping, and life really got easy. I could stay at home in the evenings and drink, and not get in trouble. With Donna there at home, I wasn't out chasing around in the bars after women, which had been a lot of work. So I fell right into married life. It was a great way to go. Donna and I really got cozy with each other, and every night was like a honeymoon in our little shack.

Some people need some adjusting to married life, because they're used to privacy. Growing up at home, then in the Navy and Merchant Marine, and with various roommates, I'd never lived alone, and still haven't ever. If I needed privacy, I had a garage, shop or car I could go to, and that was enough.

Donna and I would occasionally go out and have a bit of a social life. Because of my arrests, I wasn't driving. There was an old guy who would pick me up and take me to work. On weekends I'd hang around at Donna's folk's house, trying to get in good with the old man, working in the yard or whatever. He'd go down to the store and get two cans of beer, one for each of us. What the hell anyone wants with one can of beer I'll never know.

Meanwhile, he kept telling Donna he'd pay for a divorce anytime, but she wouldn't hear of that. She says now that she never had a moment's doubt that she'd married the right guy, that she knew I was too smart to keep on like I had been. Her mother was on my side, too, and I never could understand that. She had every confidence in the world that I'd turn out all right.

Not many weeks after the wedding, Donna's dad was banging on our door one morning, saying his wife was dead. She'd been very sick for a while with some manner of heart ailment. I took care of the funeral arrangements, because the old man was pretty shook. Through no doing of mine, it was about the biggest funeral Compton had ever seen, just because Donna's mom was such a loving person and was involved in helping a lot of people. Her death sobered me up, for a couple of weeks.

We didn't live in that little house across from Donna's dad for very long. Viking was making a ton of money and we outgrew our alley location. We had a dealer in Anaheim, on Manchester, which, before the freeway was built, used to be on the main route from LA to San Diego. The dealer had a motel with a big front yard; that's where he sold his trailers. He told us about a building nearby, at Manchester and Ball Road, that was for sale.

Doug was sick with some persistent ailment then, so I was running the plant while his wife Johnnie was running the office. Doug's partner was still in the picture, too. The three of us drove out to Anaheim, in Orange County, to look at the building. I went ape over it. The layout was perfect, 20 feet wide and 300 feet long, surrounded by 10 acres of paved ground. It was an old orange packing shed, and the property came with a nice four-bedroom farmhouse.

We met with the lawyer of the old gal who owned the place and cooked up a deal where Doug could buy it for $50,000 on terms, leasing it with a five year option. We had production like crazy when we moved out there.

The old lady wasn't moving out of the farmhouse for a while, though, so we built a trailer for Doug and his family. They moved into the Orange Grove Trailer Park near the new plant. Donna and I got a trailer there too. We got a little television, which was just catching on then. As I'd mentioned, most trailers didn't have rest rooms then, so there were community facilities in the park.

Viking's sales manager, Bob Fowler, moved into the same park, and I don't know how Doug put up with us. We were both drinkers and were always arguing about the trailers. I'd be wanting to make them as cheap as we could, and old Bob was wanting to fancy them up. We were at cross purposes all the time, and Doug had to referee.

Before too long, Donna's dad loaned us the money to buy a lot on Orangethorpe in Fullerton and finance building our own house. We moved into it when it was only partly finished.

Orange County was still mostly orange groves then, and was mighty quiet. Garden Grove was just a one-block village. Anaheim was only a little bigger, maybe two blocks long. There was scarcely any night life to speak of. There was a little saloon right in the middle of the orange groves about halfway between where I lived and worked, on Euclid, called the Hideout. People came there from all over, because there wasn't much else.

Donna got pregnant three months after we were married, and we had our first son, Johnnie, in May of 1949. While Donna was in the hospital going through labor, I was there every minute, and it was a long labor. There was none of that being in the operating room with your wife then. The expectant fathers were consigned to a waiting room. There were maybe five other guys in there with me. But eventually they were all gone, and I was still sitting there.

In the middle of the night the doctor told me that if Donna hadn't had the baby by eight a.m. they were going to take it out by C-section. That scared me, because I didn't understand what they were talking about.

Finally, around six in the morning, the contractions accelerated, and Johnnie followed along presently. Doctors didn't have any of the tests that they do now, and there was such an anticipation: not knowing if it was going to be a boy or a girl, worrying if it would have two heads or three arms. When it all came out well, that was a great feeling.

When we brought Donna and the baby home from the hospital, I was so protective. Her dad was behind the wheel, and I was telling him how to drive: "Dammit, don't brake so fast!" The whole world changes when you've got a baby on board.

Even before Johnnie was born we had been getting baby-headed. We'd called on an ad that offered refurbished vacuum cleaners for $9.95. The salesman came over and brought in a vacuum cleaner that must have been missing all the blades from its fan, because it had about as much suction as your grandmother.

Then he said, "Here's a little better one than that for $19.95, and showed us one that was nearly as bad. Finally he came in with a better model that worked. For his closing pitch, he covered the hose with his white handkerchief and put it against our overstuffed furniture, and it showed some dirt on it. He looked right at Donna and said, "And you're going to let your new baby live in this *filth*?"

Zingo, we signed for it. The *down payment* was $9.95, and the rest was $80. The guy was a total snake, but, thinking of our baby, we fell for it.

Newlywed. Am I the luckiest man on earth, or what?

DAM DRUNK

Doug Caruthers was a stand-up guy, and probably the best boss I ever had, but that didn't keep me from quitting in a huff several times. And quitting didn't keep me from going back to work for him again.

Doug was a real banty rooster, a hot tempered little guy. When things wouldn't go his way he'd scream and holler. That's one reason I'd quit, because when he'd start hollering at me I'd tell him to go fuck himself. I wouldn't bend to it, which just made him madder.

On one occasion, I was glad he was hot-tempered. There was a guy working in Viking's metal department who was really screwing up. I went out there to fire him, and he squared off on me. If he'd put as much into his work as he did into pummeling me, I wouldn't have needed to fire him. I was ducking out of his reach as best I could, but he was wearing me down.

Doug heard the ruckus, ran down there, grabbed a 2"-by-2"-by-8' rafter beam and came after the guy, swinging that. You could hear the beam whooshing through the air until he'd backed the guy out into the parking lot.

That was Doug. He always had a dog, and his damn dogs would take on his personality: They were ornery bastards who'd as soon bite you as anything.

Doug and I would invariably start arguing about the product—whether a trailer should have a single sink or a double sink, things like that—and I'd dig my heels in. When it came down to him having his way, I'd walk out.

One of those times—near when Johnnie was born—I quit to work for Terry Coach, a company in Southgate owned by a guy named Roy Clayton.

Donna and I had been living in the half-completed house in Fullerton, but Donna's dad wanted to get it finished, so he got us to move back in with him in Compton. His house was a lot closer to Terry Coach, so there was no reason to be in Orange County anymore.

Roy Clayton was a big, broad-shouldered guy, with a head that was small for his body. He had a gruff way about him, though he was well-meaning. He could see that I was boozing a lot, and one night he said, "John, I'd like you to stay a little after work tonight."

I thought, "Oh hell, I'm going to get canned." But he sat me down in his office and told me about himself, how he'd been a boozer and had been sober for three years as a result of going to Alcoholics Anonymous. He told me how well that had worked for him, and, goddamn, I was really enthused.

We sat there talking until about nine p.m., and when he got done, I said, "That's a hell of a story. If I ever find that I'm drinking too much, I'll probably do the same thing." So I went my way and didn't think anything about it.

Not long before this, I'd been on a boat Doug had in Newport Harbor. We were all drinking, and I was sloshed. As we were leaving, at the car I remembered I'd left something on the boat, probably a bottle. I went back to fetch it. As I was stepping off the boat, I slipped and fell in the bay. I was hanging on this float, but was so drunk I couldn't climb up on it. Meanwhile, they'd taken off in the car and it was a while before they noticed I wasn't with them. They came back and pulled me out. I was shaking and shivering, freezing. But, no, I didn't have any drinking problem.

While I was working at Terry, Doug had gone into the business of retailing his trailers. Meanwhile, his production rate at Viking had gone down to almost nothing. He was having a tough time getting those few trailers skinned—putting the aluminum on the outside—so I started moonlighting over there. Donna would come along and help me and we'd skin the trailers as piecework, for so much a trailer.

One night I was there and Doug came out on the plant

floor and started griping about how the retail business was the pits, telling me, "I'm just building enough to fill the retail orders, onesies and twosies. What can I do to get out of that?"

I was always product-oriented, and spent a lot of time on dealers' lots seeing what customers wanted. I told him, "Get out of this onesie-twosie stuff and go into production building a 24-foot trailer. They're popular right now and I bet you'll do great with them." That night we made a deal for me to go back with Viking, and he gave me a $1000 bonus.

I designed the 24-footer and got it into production. As I'd thought, they sold well and we had a good profit margin in them. We were building three a day and shipping them right out.

Then one of Doug's dealers up near the Grand Coulee Dam in Washington State came up with a deal in which he wanted us to bid through him on a government contract to build trailers for the dam crew. They needed fifty 33-foot trailers built in six weeks. Building that different size would have meant converting our whole production line.

Doug asked me if I thought we could handle the government job. I told him it would be tough, just balls to the wall, to get it done.

He took the job anyway, and at a really reduced price. I couldn't see how he was going to make any money, but he had stars in his eyes because it was a government contract.

We lost a lot of time getting the production line switched over and up to speed. To finish the trailers in the time allotted, in the last week we had to crank out six units a day, 30 units in a week. We got them out, but they were pretty shabby. The workmanship was not good at all and we shipped them out with a lot that needed to be fixed.

I had been running two shifts, and was working 18-hour days. I was drinking heavily too, and was a mess. I'd passed the point of diminishing returns, where I was doing more harm than good.

The trailers arrived in Washington with roof leaks, plumbing leaks, electrical shorts, poor varnish jobs, you name it. The government people wouldn't pay Doug until they were up to snuff. Doug sent his brother Red and me up there to get the trailers fixed up enough to where they'd OK them and release the money.

We flew up to Seattle and took a little puddle-jumper through the canyons to Kennewick, where the trailer dealer was who had got Doug involved. The dealer also had a car dealership, and he picked us up in a nice new Oldsmobile. He drove us to his lot, and Red and I had to drive 150 miles to the dam from there. He tried to put us in some beat-up car, and I said, "Hell, what's the matter with this Oldsmobile here?"

He said, "This is an expensive car."

"Well, shit, we're not going to drive that old clunker."

We went back and forth on that until he let Red and me take his Oldsmobile, which we totally destroyed.

At the Coulee Dam, we got acquainted with the government inspector right away, and he was as bad a boozer as we were. We'd meet out on the job in the morning, fix a few things on the trailers and he'd sign them off. Then we'd go into a government canteen to sit out the rest of the day drinking beer. We'd buy all the beer, so this routine suited the inspector fine.

It was just cold and nasty up there. We were staying in a crummy little hotel in Coulee City, with a convenient bar on the ground floor and two floors of rooms. Red and I were sleeping in one double bed in a room on the third floor. The roof slanted way down, so there was just barely room to move. They'd have the steam heat on, and by midnight you'd be so hot you couldn't stand it, so you'd lay on top of the blankets. Then they'd turn the heat off and by four in the morning it was freezing cold.

We kept up this routine for six weeks, working in the mornings and drinking and partying the rest of the time.

In Washington, they didn't serve any booze on Sunday, and one weekend Red and I weren't ready for our Saturday night to end. It was only 100 miles or so to cross the border to Coeur D'Alene, Idaho, so we decided to go there. We set off in the dealer's Oldsmobile, and as soon as we got out of town we hit a pea-soup fog.

We came to a T in the road, where one way went to Seattle and the other to Idaho. We went neither. We left the pavement, I slammed on the brakes and we skidded right over the edge of a cliff. There was a cable guard rail there, and we were hanging on it. The car was almost vertical and the front end was all smashed up on the rail.

We got out of the thing, carefully. Before long, a couple came along in a pickup truck. The guy had a big old log chain he hooked to the Oldsmobile and pulled it back onto its feet. I jumped in and it started, so away we went to Coeur D'Alene.

We pulled up in front of a saloon about daylight. I got a look at how much damage we'd done to the Oldsmobile, and it was more than we could cover up short of burying the thing. As well as we could figure, the missing license plate was back at the scene, along with all that ripped-out guard rail, and I thought, "Boy, we'll probably hear about that."

We spent the day drinking and then headed back to the dam. We stopped at the accident scene but couldn't find the license plate.

We kept calling Doug for money, because we were spending it like drunken sailors. He finally said, "You guys just come home." Red flew home but Doug wanted me to first go to Seattle, where the government was opening bidding for another 100 trailers.

I was supposed to drive the Olds back to the dealer who had loaned it to us, and then take the bus in to Seattle. But I took one look at that car and thought, "I don't think so." I just abandoned it in Coulee City and hopped on the bus there. I think Doug finally had to pay the guy for the car.

I called my uncle in Seattle—one of my mom's brothers—because I'd never seen him. I made plans to visit him and to find out about the trailer bids. But by the time I got to Seattle, I was so homesick, and drunk, that I went straight to the airport and flew to Los Angeles.

Flying home, I knew that I'd really screwed things up, that my drinking had made a mess of the trip. And while I was thinking this, I drank a pint of whiskey on the plane.

Donna's dad picked me up at the airport. He'd never liked me anyway. I was the enemy, and I was drunk. He gave me the news that his daughter, my wife, was in the hospital with a miscarriage. She'd already had a rough week because her little dog had been run over in front of our house on Orangethorpe and nobody had even picked up the body.

We went home, and Donna's dad went on to bed. I got in my car and drove to the hospital to see Donna. It was midnight, and they, of course, wouldn't let me in. I made a big scene pushing my way in, saw her, and left before the police got there.

Then I got pissed off at Doug for not letting me know Donna had been having these problems. I went over to Doug's and tried to get him out of the house so I could beat him as senseless as I was. He wouldn't come out, thank goodness, and I finally ran out of steam.

I woke up the next morning and thought, "Oh shit, this is fucking awful." I got in my car to go in to work to apologize to Doug for messing up in Washington and the whole thing. Then I thought, "There's no point in doing that if I'm just going to keep on screwing up."

I thought about what Roy Clayton had told me about Alcoholics Anonymous. I turned the car around, went to Roy's place in Southgate and told him, "Man, I'm ready." I spent the whole day with him, and he was telling me all the good things about getting sober.

That night he, his wife, Donna and I went to an AA

meeting in LA. Some old guy talked for what seemed like six hours and I wasn't a bit impressed. I had no interest. But on the way home, Roy kept talking and got me all excited again. Just as a result of that talk, I stayed sober for five months.

From age 16 to 25, the longest I'd ever stayed sober was 29 days on a bet, which I lost because the bet had been for 30 days.

I didn't think there was any deep-seated psychological reason for it: I drank because I liked it, and figured the trouble I got in was just the price you pay. You know what it's doing to you, but you always figure the next time is going to be better. But I'd reached a point where I knew it wasn't fun any more.

In that five sober months everything went right. I couldn't believe it. It occurred to me that the reason why I was always so hammered was also the reason I was so poor. In those five sober months I bought a new house, bought a new '49 Plymouth convertible, and got my own business started.

Everything was just coming up roses. So on one hot summer afternoon, I stepped into a saloon, got a bottle of beer and drank it. I got another bottle of beer and drank it, and then went about my business. I went home that night, went to bed and went to sleep, thinking, "I didn't get drunk. I don't have a problem anymore. There's no reason I can't have a couple of beers now and then."

The very next day I called on Kit Trailers in Long Beach. It was near quitting time, and the purchasing agent—who later turned out to be a real thief—said, "How about going down to the saloon for a drink?"

I said, "I don't drink anymore."

"Oh, what the hell, come on down. One won't hurt."

So I went with him, got drunk and didn't draw a sober breath for six weeks. That was the most miserable fucking time in my life. Before that, whenever I drank, I could function, could usually go to work and get things done. But in that six weeks I was just a wreck. I'd be fading in and out, meaning to get things done but putting them off until I could function, which wasn't on the calendar.

I became suicidal. I was going to crash my car, was going to drown myself in the ocean. I was so pissed off with myself for getting blitzed after I knew better. I felt like I just wasn't worth a shit and was bad news for everyone around me.

One night I was sitting in a saloon in Compton and I got to thinking about ol' Roy being sober for three years and the way it had been for me in the few months I was sober. I was usually so rummy that I didn't know what was going on. If I hadn't come to my senses for a few moments right then, I could have stayed that way forever.

Even in the haze I was in, I suddenly knew as clearly as I've known anything that it's better to be sober than drunk. I decided right then, "I'm going to go find out what it is those AA people are doing, and whatever it is, I'm going to do it!" I set my half-full glass down on the bar—this was August 16, 1950—and that's the last drink I ever had.

The next day I became acquainted with the AA people in Compton, and became very active in it. From that point on, my life totally changed for the better.

I took AA dead serious. Knowing how screwed up I'd been from drinking, I was really anxious to do everything that was necessary. It was hard. It was frightening.

The main tenant of the AA program is that we come to believe that there is a power greater than ourselves who we assume is our creator.

The AA book suggests that, upon awakening each day, we ask that our actions and thoughts be directed by Him. Upon retiring each evening, we review our day by asking if we've been helpful and kind, and we give thanks for the day's blessings.

The program also adopted the old Serenity prayer: "God grant me the serenity to accept the things I cannot change, the courage to change the things I can, and the wisdom to know the difference."

It was amazing to me how much easier life got as a result of these simple concepts and the resultant actions.

One of the things you have to do on the program is make amends, to apologize to all the people you wronged when you were drinking, and clean up the messes you created. I had a few of those.

I was still in violation of probation for my drunk driving in West LA five years earlier. That was good for a year in jail, and every time I'd seen someone who even looked like he might be a probation officer, I'd duck around a corner.

I went uptown and turned myself in to the probation officer. He dug out the file, and said, "This is a long time."

I told him, "I'm on this thing called AA, and have to go around squaring up old problems. So here I am."

He asked if I could pay the $30 remaining on my fine. I did and he gave me a receipt, and said, "Forget it." I practically flew down those courthouse steps because I'd felt for sure I was going to jail for a year.

It got easier squaring things as I went along. A lot of the amends were just financial, where I'd borrowed money and not paid it back. And a lot of it was just making apologies to people who really weren't much interested.

There was one situation, though, that went back even longer than the probation matter. Since 1946, I'd been dodging the guy who'd married that woman I'd slept with on New Year's Eve. I knew him, and he could be a mean son of a bitch.

I knocked on his door and told him, "Hey, Pal, I ain't going to be dodging you no more. If you want to take a poke at me, just do it right now."

"What the hell are you talking about?"

"The last time I saw you, you said you were going to kill me."

"Aw, shit, I was just kidding."

He didn't even remember it, and for years when I'd seen him coming down the street, I'd been scared to death.

Though Donna had been married to me through two years of my drinking, she didn't really feel I'd wronged her much. I'd done a lot of things that she didn't take that seriously. She was weird that way. I'd take off on a Friday night and she wouldn't see me until Tuesday, and she didn't get all that upset. She said she knew I was too smart to keep on drinking. I think that's one of the reasons why we've stayed married all along, because she had so much faith in me and was so willing to accept things.

Once I really stopped drinking, those were fun days for us.

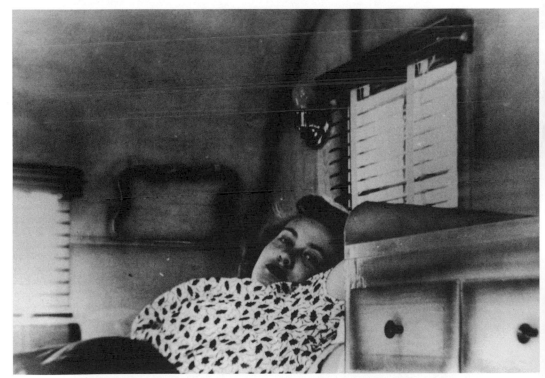

Everything good in one place: Donna pregnant with Andy, with, overhead, the Venetian blind design that started it all, in the first Fleetwood model trailer, 1951.

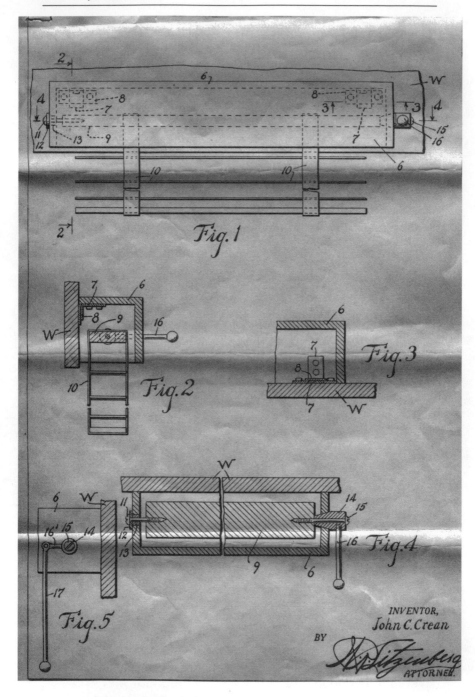

The patent drawing for the Venetian blind design
that put me in business for myself.

DRIVING BLINDS

During my initial jag of sobriety, I didn't even try going back to Doug. Instead, I got a job working for a guy, Ralph Byrnes, in Long Beach, selling Venetian blinds and light fixtures to the trailer industry. This was in late 1949, coming up on Christmas. I remember that because, when I first went to meet him at his home, Ralph was playing the hell out of a 78 RPM record of Gene Autry's "Rudolph the Red-Nosed Reindeer." He thought it was just great, and then thought it was great all over again, and again.

I was on commission with Ralph, and the going was pretty thin. His light fixture sales were OK, but his blinds sold for 10 percent more than trailer companies were paying for the competitors' blinds, and they were identical. The only account Ralph had for them was with Kit Trailer, and that's because he was paying kickbacks to Kit's purchasing agent.

I got Ralph to go with me to his Venetian blind manufacturer in Long Beach, and I asked the head man there, "If you can't make this thing any cheaper, can't you make it any different? There's no way we can sell it the way it is."

He said, "Nah, I've been in this business all my life and this is as cheap as anyone can make them, and there's no diffcrent way to do it."

"How am I supposed to sell the same blinds everyone else has for 10 percent less? I'm not that damn charming."

We got in a bit of a tiff, and finally I said, "If you can't make them any better or cheaper, by God, I bet I can."

"If you can, why don't you?"

I said, "I think I will," and walked out of there. That same evening I severed relations with Ralph because it really wasn't bringing in any money for me. I figured I'd probably go back to work for Doug or Roy because I needed to start making some money. Donna was pregnant with our second boy, Andy, and we were still living with her dad.

I had the sample blind I'd been toting around, and took it apart. There was an expensive little mechanism that the cords went through to open and close the blinds. I figured, "Why not just put a lever on it?" In a trailer the blinds aren't up that high, so you don't need the dangling cords like you do in a house. I got some parts and pieces out of the junk in Donna's dad's garage and I made up a set of blinds that had a little lever, and it worked like a million dollars.

I got in the car and found suppliers for the slats and the wood and everything else I'd need. Then I did my arithmetic on the costs and found that, given what blinds were selling for, there was a lot of margin.

The one hitch was that I needed something for the lever. I didn't have the money to tool up for a new part, so I went scrounging through the manufacturing plants in South LA.

One plastics place I checked was making trick salt shakers, the kind where, when you pushed a button on top, salt would drop out the bottom. The top of the shaker was shaped just about right for my purposes. So I drilled a hole through one, and, abetted by some model airplane glue, I had a blind with a lever. I put a screw in to adjust the friction, and the finished thing looked and worked fine. I named my design the Control-Eze and took out a patent on it.

With that unit, I went into business for myself, under the name Coach Specialties Manufacturing Company. Despite my nearly ruining him with the Washington fiasco and making a drunken scene on his lawn, Doug became my first customer. He liked the fact my blind was different. I had the sample set up on a board where you could flick it back and forth like a camera shutter. Features like that gave the sales guys something to talk about.

Doug was building ten trailers a week, and made an initial order for ten sets of blinds at $25 a set. He gave me the

$250 in advance. That was my starting capital, and the only capital I ever took in, until years later when we went public on Wall Street.

Doug wound up being a good customer, and until the day he died we were good friends. He eventually sold his company to some of the guys who worked there. His 10 acre property adjoined Disneyland and he later sold that to Disney for a good chunk of change. He pretty much retired then and spent the rest of his life racing midget racers, winning the national championship several times.

A piece of advice I'd suggest to anyone is to learn your business on someone else's dime. If you want to make widgets, go to work for a widget company. Do well and work cheap, and you'll get promoted. As long as you learn how to make all the widgets, how to sell them, where to buy the material and everything else, then you can go off and take a crack at it yourself.

Because I'd made the rounds in the blind business, I knew how many windows each manufacturer's model had, and how many Venetian blinds would be needed for the entire industry. I figured if I could get half of that business, I'd be making just a bundle of money. I priced my blinds out so that I'd make 50 cents a blind, no matter if it was a big one or a little one, because that was easy to figure.

While I was getting started, I wasn't making any money at all, and Donna's dad was paying all the bills. It goes without saying that he still hadn't warmed up to me.

I was eligible to collect unemployment insurance, and he'd been on my case to go down to the unemployment office to get it. Just to salve him, I did, and while I was standing in line, Don Stewart—my old buddy I hadn't seen since I chased around with him before and during the war—turned up in line right behind me.

We exchanged the whatcha-doin's and I told him I was starting this little business. He'd been selling vacuum cleaners and hadn't been doing very well. He asked if I could use any help, and I said, "Yes, but I don't have any money to pay anybody." He asked if I could pay as much as he was going to collect on unemployment, which was $20 a week, and I felt I could probably do that.

He said, "Boy, I'd like to go to work for you then."

Don and I just left the line, and we never did get our unemployment.

Up to that point, I'd been making the blinds in my father-in-law's garage and borrowing a neighbor's air compressor to paint them. There was no way that setup could handle much volume.

The same day I ran into Don at the unemployment office, he found an old garage for rent, where the owner had an auto repair business next door. He rented the garage to us for next to nothing, and agreed to let us put a hole through the wall and hook a hose up to his air compressor. That evening we moved all our junk there from Donna's dad's garage.

We saved money in so many ways that it was easy to compete. Initially, Donna strung the blinds, which was slow, tedious work. When we got a little bit ahead financially, I hired a woman who was experienced at that. She'd string those things up almost faster than you could watch. What we paid in piecework for that, at nine cents per blind, was most of the labor cost. The rest—the painting and the sawing—I did myself. While I was making the blinds, Don called on customers, made sales and delivered the product.

There was one main company in the blind business, and they were used to being the only deal in town. Their chief salesman was a big, fat pompous bastard with a Cadillac, named Al Sangston. He was the kind of guy it was fun to do in. Our blind was better and cheaper in every way, and we started knocking off his customers right and left. Every time Don came in with one of this guy's old accounts we'd just laugh like crazy.

Our delivering a better product for 25 percent less wasn't

our only advantage. The competition was packing their blinds in bundles by their size. The manufacturer would have to store bundles of each size blind, tear one open to get a 72" blind; tear into another package for the next smaller size, and so on.

From my production background, I knew it was an advantage to the manufacturer if I packaged mine by the set, so that's what I did. Each bundle would contain the blinds needed to finish one trailer.

The blinds mounted on the wall with a bracket, and, typically, the worker would have to measure where that bracket went for each window. I'd provide manufacturers with a jig that would fit in the corner of the window. You'd tap that with a hammer, and that would mark where the blind bracket mounted. That got rid of the measuring, and the installation went three times as fast. Al Sangston didn't know squat about things like that.

Within five months I had way over 50% of the business and had $10,000 in the bank. In 1950 that was a pot of money. Houses in the area then were topping out at $11,500, and that was for a three-or-four bedroom, two-bath house.

It was also at five months that I had my six week drinking binge. Don took care of me during that time, because I was a total mess. He covered for me with our accounts, drove me around so I wouldn't crash and did everything but spoon-feed me.

I tried not to let Donna know how far gone I was. She was busy with the kids. I'd been drinking the first two years we were married, so she probably didn't think too much about it.

The business almost surely would have folded during my binge if Don hadn't held it together for me then. Once, when he was ferrying me around, I got to insisting that he stop at a bar and let me get a drink. I was becoming belligerent. Don simply stopped the car, got out on the pavement and said, "I tell you what, if you can whip me, you can go across the street to that bar. If you can't, you get back in the car and I'm driving you home."

I saw he really meant it, and that backed me down. That's the kind of guy Don was, and is.

Once I stopped screwing up and got on AA after my six-week binge, the blind business took off like a rocket. Having seen how little I was capable of accomplishing, I became really ambitious to see just how much I could accomplish, and I was thinking clearly enough to follow through on that.

The business was running so well that in the spring of 1950 I decided to start building trailers. I had really liked designing them for Doug, but I knew I'd like it much better when I didn't have a boss who would argue about the designs. The first trailer I built in May of that year was a 13-footer. It was a pretty clever little design, and inexpensive.

Roy Clayton, my old boss who had told me about AA, was one of my Venetian blind customers, and he heard through the grapevine that I was building a trailer. He gave me a call and said, "I sure as hell don't want to be buying any blinds from a competitor."

I just said, "Well, whatever."

He said he wanted to look at the trailer and came over. He liked the design and told me, "I can't build nearly enough trailers for my dealers. How many of these do you think you can build?"

I guessed 10 or 15 a week. He was surprised by that, but he went on, "How about us forming a corporation? I'll furnish all the material. You just build them and I'll sell them to my dealers."

I thought that was great, so in the early summer of 1950, we formed Dixie Enterprises, Incorporated. Roy and his partner were 51 percent owners and I was 49 percent.

Our building was only 1600 square feet, but we were able to set up a little assembly line there after we moved the blind-making business across the street to another building Don rented. I was up to building 15 trailers a week in no time at all. Both the trailer and blinds businesses were going great guns.

One day the phone rang and it was Roy, saying, "Hey, gotta stop building trailers. The season's over. Shut down 'til next spring."

I said, "Hell, I just got started." I was really disappointed, but that's the way Roy did things. It was standard for the industry then to build little vacation trailers from spring through summer, and then in the wintertime they'd switch over to making big house trailers. Roy had never built a big trailer and didn't know anything about them. He was just in the habit of shutting down and hibernating until spring. That made no sense to me at all.

I called him back and said, "Roy, I bet I could sell quite a few more trailers. Would it be all right if I designed another trailer, put the name Dixie on it and tried to sell it?"

He said, "You won't sell any, but if you think you can, go ahead."

I cobbled up another small trailer, a 15-footer. I changed the interior, and put a different paint stripe on the side. I was always price-conscious, and, in the shop I had, the overhead was virtually nothing. I was able to price the Dixie trailer at $595 to the dealer.

After I got the first one built, I hitched it behind my car, a '49 Plymouth, and went on the road. Over a weekend driving around Southern California—and not even going to Roy's usual dealers—I took 40 orders, enough for a month's production. Most of the manufacturers had already switched to the bigger trailers, and there was an actual shortage of vacation trailers. The next week I took a trip up the coast to the Bay Area, inland to Sacramento and down through the Central Valley, and I sold another 40 of them.

We built these little Dixies for a couple of months. Then, as it was getting to be the winter season, I decided I needed to build a big trailer. The building I was in was just too small for that. The trailer company where I'd originally gone to work in

Compton, Blackhawk, had gone broke and the plant was sitting empty. It was a good-sized but ramshackle old place that had originally been a Hudson or Nash dealership. I was able to lease it cheaply.

I set about designing a 35-foot trailer, which was about as big as anybody built then. I made mine with a bathroom, which not many people were doing because the plumbing was complicated.

You were on your own creating your product then, with no government standards or red tape. The industry pretty well policed itself. The dealers were very careful about what they bought, so everything had to work and be well-constructed.

The new 35-foot Dixie went like crazy, and soon I was making 10 a week. They wholesaled for about $3500 apiece.

We were doing a brisk business, but there was still an awfully small gap between success and failure. There was one week in which, to cover the paychecks we'd issued on Friday, Don and I had to hit the road and sell a trailer over the weekend.

We took off Friday afternoon, pulling a 35-foot trailer with a '49 Plymouth. This was before freeways, and it would take three hours to go 100 miles. Going over hills, we'd be in low gear at 5 or 10 miles an hour.

We called on dealers all the way up the Central Valley but no one was biting. It was getting into Saturday night when we hit Sacramento, where I had high hopes for one dealer because he'd been selling a lot of my trailers. As we drove up to the lot, though, I saw that he had three or four 35' Dixies just like mine sitting there. I thought, "He's overloaded. No sense in stopping."

Instead, we went over to the Bay Area and down to San Jose, where I was pretty sure a dealer would take it. There, the guy hemmed and hawed around and decided against it. It was rainy and cold and that was the end of the line.

Just in case he'd sold something over the weekend, I called the dealer in Sacramento, and he said, "Goddamn it, John, why didn't you stop the other night? I saw you driving right on by. Jesus Christ, I need a trailer real bad." It turned out the ones on his lot were already sold. So we drove two hours back up there, sold it and got back to the shop just about daylight Monday morning.

It wasn't too long after that when Don was having fits with his wife, and one day he said, "Piss on it. I'm tired of this," and bailed out of there. He packed up and left the next day to get a job in the lumber camps in Northern California. He was gone for two years. When he came back, he and his wife got right back together.

Don never came back to work for me. He took a job working for a chassis manufacturer, and worked nightclubs playing piano and singing. He eventually bought his own trailer company and did pretty well. After nearly 60 years of knowing him, he's still one of my best friends

Everything at my little trailer operation was working out just beautifully, until Roy started getting bored over at his place. There wasn't anything doing at his plant, and he was having marital problems, so he started hanging out over at my plant and telling people what to do. Along with pretty much stepping on my toes, Roy was a gruff old guy, and the way he was ordering people around rubbed them the wrong way.

It really annoyed me, to the point where one day I told Roy, "Look, there's no point in the both of us being here. If you want to run the place, you run it and I'll just get out of here. You take an inventory and figure what the place is worth and send me my 49 percent."

He was shocked and said, "What's the matter?"

I said, "Hell, I don't need you around, and you can probably do real well without me."

Later, his partner, an accountant, came over to the house and tried to talk me into staying. He was afraid Roy wouldn't run things as well as I had. Meanwhile, Donna's dad, my mother, and everybody else, it seemed, was really on my case for wanting to leave, insisting, "It's the biggest opportunity you'll ever have in your life."

But the 49 percent deal didn't fit my personality at all. I wanted to be the boss. I didn't want to have to argue with anybody. Dixie was making money. It was really a swinging thing. But it wasn't fun for me any more. So, in June of 1951, after 13 months with Dixie, I just picked up my pencil and a couple of things and walked out. That was the end of that era.

Donna, a Fleetwood and our trusty Plymouth, camping in 1951.

Donna watching me watching her,
on the Colorado River, 1951.

Hitting the road in style, with a prototype 10-ft. fleetwood.

Donna with both hands full;
Johnnie and Andy, 1951.

FLEETWOOD

I'd had the blind shop going the whole time I was making the trailers with Roy. It had moved several times, and by the time I split with Roy, it was located behind another trailer company in Paramount. Of the five guys I had working there, a couple had some experience making trailers with me at Dixie. I designed an 18-footer with twin beds and got them started building the prototype. Then Donna and I went off to Las Vegas for a week, just enjoying ourselves.

After that week I came back and really went to work. I was starting off in good shape because I had good relationships and credit with all the material suppliers from making the Dixies. I also had solid relationships with a lot of dealers.

I thought the 18-footer was a pretty good trailer, but when I took the prototype around the LA area I only got orders for six units. I decided to go up the coast again.

I had told Roy I was going to make trailers when I split with him. When he asked what I was going to call them, I didn't want him to think I hadn't given it any thought, so off the top of my head I said, "I'm going to call them Fleetwood."

I hadn't really settled on a name when I left on my trip, though, so I took a piece of polished aluminum about the size of a license plate with me, figuring I'd take it to a sign painter once I'd decided.

In the trailer industry, a lot of people were borrowing from Detroit. There were Ramblers, Roadmasters, Saratogas and others, all taken from car names. The more I thought about it, Fleetwood, being a Cadillac name, was a good one. I couldn't think of anything better. In Santa Barbara I found a sign painter, and the script lettering he used to spell Fleetwood on that aluminum sign became the logo the company used for years and years.

(Of course, once we'd had a bit of success, we started getting threatening letters from General Motors' legal department telling us to cease and desist from using the Fleetwood name. We basically just ignored them, and they never got serious about doing anything about it. Then, years later, they came out with a motor home called the Glenbrook. They hadn't bothered to check to see that we had a registered trademark on that name, so we made an agreement with GM then that they could use Glenbrook if we could keep using Fleetwood.)

I didn't actually get any farther north than Santa Barbara with that first Fleetwood trailer. I called on a dealer there who had handled the Dixies. My new trailer got an immediate response from him, inasmuch as the first thing he said was, "What do you expect me to do with a piece of shit like this?"

I was pretty taken aback by that, and asked, "What do you mean?"

He proceeded to just pick it apart, saying, "Nobody buys twin beds, and the galley is too big and the whole thing is a stupid size nobody wants..."

I asked him, "Well, what *would* sell then?"

He showed me a used little 12-foot Mainline trailer that had been built right after the war. It had a full bed in the back, a little dinette in the front where two people could eat, a galley and wardrobe. It didn't look like much to me, but he said he sold every one he could get his hands on.

It was getting late, so when I left him, I just checked into a motel. That night I got to thinking about a trailer like the one he'd shown me, sketched one up, and in my head tallied a bill of materials. I decided the guy was absolutely right, that it would really be a winner.

I cut the trip short, headed straight back to the shop and canceled materials for the 18-footer. We finished building the six for which I had orders. Then I got to work producing the 12-footer. I was moving so fast then that I'd split from Roy in

June, had made and dumped the 18-footer and designed the 12-footer before July was over.

My new model was what we called a single-wall trailer. You'd use half-inch plywood and no studs, just the aluminum on it and no insulation. It really was a slick little rig.

I had a fellow working for me, Carl Jenson, who had been a salesman most of his life. He had been working on a political campaign for one of the LA supervisors, and the guy lost. Carl had ulcers from all that, and a doctor had told him to do some exercise to get over them. He asked me for a job with manual labor and I had him in the shop building sidewalls.

Just as I was getting the 12-footer into production, Carl came to me and said he was feeling pretty good again and was going to quit and go into real estate. But he asked about taking a trailer to go deer hunting in San Luis Obispo County first.

I'd thought about using Carl for a sales guy, because he had a background in it and I didn't have a good salesman after Don Stewart left. I asked Carl, "Hey, before you go out hunting, how about taking the trailer on a tour around the LA area one weekend and seeing what you can do?"

He hitched the trailer behind his Buick, and came back with a stack of orders. We'd offered a package where the trailers wholesaled for $445 apiece, but the dealer had to order a truckload of them, which was four trailers. Nobody had ever made a travel trailer you could buy for $445. Usually they wholesaled for between $600 and $700. Carl had sold sets of four trailers to something like 15 dealers, so we were really off and running.

My cost was probably $395, and the $50 I made was a pretty good margin. At four trailers a day, that was $200 dollars profit, which was a bundle in 1951. Dealers sold them for about $595, and they sold fast, so that was a big swat for them.

The little Fleetwoods were a bargain, but they weren't perfect. One time, Carl and I went fishing in the Sierras with one. The first night, we pulled off the road, bundled up, and went to sleep. Some time in the night, the butane regulator froze and the furnace went out. The next morning when I moved to get out of bed, I couldn't, and neither could Carl. Our blankets had frozen solid to the walls, because there was no insulation. We pulled and tugged, and eventually only got free when the blankets tore. They were still stuck to the walls.

I built 500 or 600 of the 12-footers, and I still see them around. In fact, right across from Village Crean today, there's someone living in one of those little Fleetwoods. He should be glad it never freezes here.

We built those trailers until about Christmas time of '51. Then it was the same song, second verse: I had to get into a bigger trailer, though I wasn't really forced into it, because deer hunters were still buying the little trailer.

The trailer business has always gone through fluctuations, and when business slowed for several companies in the early '50s, they assumed that trailers were only a dying post-war fad, and they bailed.

One of those companies, Normel, had the large building in front of us, and when they folded, the landlord invited me out to lunch. He asked me about renting the big building and I told him I couldn't afford it.

He said, "I tell you what, why don't you take it for six months, and if at the end of six months you're not able to pay the rent, just move out and pay me nothing?" I gave it a shot and moved in. I designed another 35-foot trailer and went into production on that, while keeping the little trailers going too.

Our new 35-footer wholesaled for $3,295 and was the first trailer on the market to have three doors. Usually, trailer doors would open on the living room or the bedroom. My new door led into the kitchen, and it was very popular, because the kitchen gets the most traffic. We soon had production up to ten a week.

I wasn't big on options. I bought two colors of paint, and if you didn't want a Fleetwood with a green stripe or a

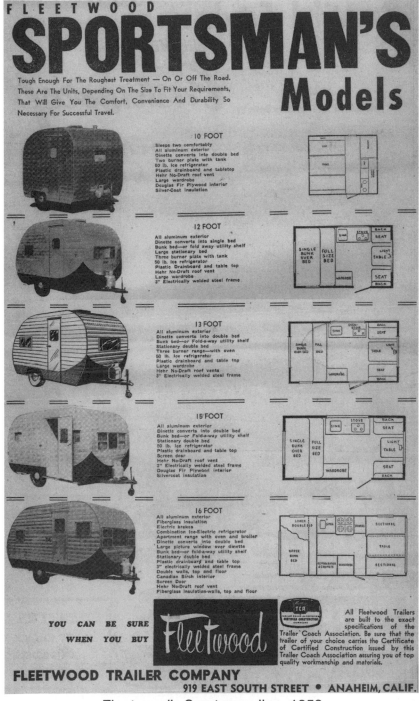

Fleetwood's Sportsman line, 1953

yellow stripe, you were out of luck.

I did try making a variation on the 35-footer, though, a cottage trailer with wood siding and a shingle roof. I thought it was a good idea and it was fairly inexpensive, but it just didn't arouse any interest. I wound up making only eight of them. The wood siding and pitch roof made a better house than a regular trailer, but it looked like a little shack.

The other problem was that the damn thing leaked. I took one around to dealers in Oregon and Washington, and it rained constantly. While I'd be showing the trailer to a dealer, water would form on the moldings where the leaks were, and eventually collect into big drops that would plop down. I'd keep one eye on the moldings, and would point out the refrigerator or some other feature to distract the dealer while I'd use my handkerchief to dab the drops off the ceiling.

The standard 35-footer had immediate acceptance from the dealers and did very well. It was a hassle building both the big and the little trailers in the same facility, so I formed a partnership with Carl and a fellow named Harry McCulley to set up a separate company to build those in Gardena, called C&M Manufacturing Company. I think I retained 50 percent and they had 50 percent between them.

A market arose for some 31-footers, so I rented another building and formed a partnership with Speed and another guy, Johnny Payne, to start making those. That plant was in Norwalk, and it was a pretty good setup, except that it was next door to a meat packing house, and it had flies like crazy. We'd gone along there for maybe a year when Harry and Carl started yet another trailer place in Gardena, so I had four locations going.

Donna worked in the office in Paramount, taking care of the books and the purchasing. Business was going so well that she needed some help. We ran an ad and a fellow named Dale Skinner applied. He looked like a Nebraska farm boy— affable, tall, big and corn-fed—which is what he was.

He'd recently arrived in California from Lincoln, and

had already answered another company's ad for a warehouse superintendent job, and took it. Then he found that their idea of a warehouse super meant pushing a hand truck around and moving crates. So when he saw our ad in the local paper for an accountant, he was interested. He was really a hick, but, man, he was good. We hired him in July of 1952, Donna broke him in, and he just took off from there.

I hired another fellow to be our purchasing manager, a job he'd had with a big firm from Chicago. He'd hardly been with Fleetwood any time at all before I couldn't believe how out of balance our inventory was. Every department was short on things we needed to get trailers done and out the door. I fired the guy on the spot. Then I went in the office where Dale was working with Donna and told him he was our new purchasing manager.

Dale immediately got flustered and asked, "What the hell does a purchasing manager do?"

"Well, I guess he purchases."

Dale was scared to death, and kind of stammered when he said he'd give it a try. Then he sat right down with our lists of materials, got relationships going with the suppliers and did a beautiful job. That was Dale, right up through when he became company president, always sure he wasn't up for the job, and then blazing right through it. I never, ever would have made it without him. He was very disciplined and I respected his opinion enough that he could rein me in when I'd come up with a wild-ass idea.

Dale had been with us for well over a year when I noticed that he hadn't taken a single day off. I asked him, "Aren't you ever going to take a vacation?"

He responded that with his third kid having just been born, he didn't have the money to go anywhere. I handed him a credit card and the keys to my new Lincoln and told him to come back when he got some rest.

I drove his old Ford around in the meantime, and that

wasn't fun at all. When Dale got back to town, I asked him to go to lunch with me one day, and we stopped by a Lincoln dealership on the way back. I pointed out a two-tone green Mercury and asked, "What do you think of that, Dale?"

"That's a beaut," he said, to which I replied, "Well, you'd better like it. It's yours."

In March of 1953, I moved my plant to an even larger building at 919 East South Street in Anaheim. Meanwhile, I must have moved the venetian blind shop ten times in two years, from one little location to another.

Some trailer dealers would pay on delivery, but a lot of them expected you to extend them credit. There was one dealer, one of the oldest and most respected in LA., to whom everyone extended terms. Carl got to be friendly with him, and we got to where we'd deliver trailers to the dealer through the week. Then every Friday Carl would go there and get a check for the previous week's supply of trailers.

One Thursday night the dealer called Carl and told him, "Hey, tomorrow come down and pick up the trailers you delivered last week. I'm not going to need them."

Carl asked, "What's the matter?"

"Never you mind. You just get down with the truck and get those trailers out of here tomorrow."

So Carl did the next day. Friday night the dealer killed himself. He'd been playing the horses and had girlfriends stashed in two or three different apartments around town, and had been broke for quite some time. He'd been flooring the same trailer contract—where a finance company fronts the money for the trailer and then the dealer owes the finance company— to two or three different finance companies, who each then thought they held the deed on it. So he'd wound up owing several different companies for the same trailer.

Needless to say, he was behind the eight ball for a huge amount. It was only because Carl had been a good friend of his and he knew we were just getting started that he had us pick up the trailers before he checked out.

Though the dealer hadn't paid us for the trailers, the finance companies had paid the dealer for them, and it was their position that they owned them. We didn't want to get caught in the middle on that, so we shipped the trailers out-of-state to other dealers right away. When the main finance company called us, wanting to know where the trailers were, Carl told them, "I don't know, they're not around here."

As a result of that, the finance company put us on their shit list. That wound up being a good thing. Though that company financed most of the trailer business in the area, they weren't all that good. We went to a small company in Los Angeles, Pacific Finance, to floor our trailers and buy the retail contracts. Pacific Finance did OK by us, and financing trailers blossomed into a pretty good thing for them. After seeing their success, a few other companies got into the business then.

Soon after I quit drinking, Donna and I had been able to buy a house in Compton, and we were still living there. While we both worked at Fleetwood, we had a baby sitter watching the two boys. One day, I stopped at home to pick up something, and couldn't help noticing that the sitter was sitting there drunk while the kids were just tearing the place up, unattended. That's when I decided that Donna should become a full-time housewife, so I fired her.

I'd been a Democrat all my life. One day, though, I was driving up to LA with one of my sales managers, Walt Paulson, and politics came up. When I told him I was a Democrat, Walt said, "You're a *what*?" He was really surprised, saying, "Jeez, that's kind of dumb. Haven't you ever noticed that all the rich people are Republicans and the poor people are Democrats?"

I was a Democrat because, in the neighborhood where I grew up, everyone was. And, sure enough, it was a piss-poor neighborhood. I thought, "Well, shit, I'd rather live in the nice part of town." So the next day I went and registered Republican. It was strictly a pragmatic decision.

Dancing at home, 1954.

The exterior.

Paradise, 1950's style.
The living room of our home in Garden Grove.

Andy with his buddy—
and future Olympic swimming medalist—Gary Hall.

Circumnavigating our pool in Garden Grove. If we print this
small enough, you might not notice that I'm flipping the
camera off.

It wasn't actually too long after that, in early 1953, when we moved to a nicer neighborhood. One morning, one of my employees told me a company was building some good homes in Garden Grove that were available for a low down payment. They'd put a tract in where the houses sold from $18,000 to $22,000. There was just no market for them because everybody was buying their homes on the GI Bill, which would only finance a house that was $11,500 or less.

That lunch hour, I ran over to look at them. I really liked one, and the salesman asked, "You want to buy it?"

I told him it was a little pricey for me. He asked, "Can you come up with $1000 down?" I said I didn't have anything like that. Next he asked if I could make payments of $80 a month if they let me move in. I found out later that $80 was the interest the builder was paying on the construction loan. As long as I promised to come up with the $1000 down payment within a year, I could move in. I signed all the papers and bought the house right then, for $80 down! I went home to get Donna, and, boy, was she excited.

I got almost as good a deal from a swimming pool builder, and we were set in our own little paradise. We got to know the neighbors right away. The builder had been selling houses to customers like us: people who looked like they'd eventually be able to pay for them. My next door neighbor was a jeweler in Wilmington, with two kids Johnnie and Andy's age. Two doors down was a doctor at the Veteran's hospital in Long Beach.

Another neighbor kid, Gary Hall, learned to swim in our pool, and later won two silver medals and a bronze swimming in the '68, '72 and '76 Olympics (that was his son, Gary Jr., in the '96 Olympics). Johnnie made the local newspapers in July of 1958. A neighbor kid, a three year old wearing a cowboy outfit with the holster and the whole bit, fell into our pool, and Johnnie, who was nine then, jumped in and saved him. He won a Cub Scout of the Month award for that.

We had a really neat six years in Garden Grove, having parties with the neighbors and enjoying life.

The year after we moved there, I bought my mom a house a couple of blocks away from us. I think she was proud of me by then, as much as she was capable, but I never got much praise out of Mom. I don't think it bothered me that much, because by that time I was getting plenty of support from Donna and others. Mom was always more interested in trying to straighten out my brother Kenny from his drinking.

Once the trailers had really taken off, I'd sold the blind shop to Kenny on an earn-out, and he went great guns with it. It was the worst thing I ever could have done for him. For about a year he made money hand over fist, and it was the first time in his life he ever had any surplus cash. He got to boozing again and playing the horses. Meanwhile, he was married and had three kids to take care of.

In no time at all, he wasn't making deliveries and was losing customers. He and his wife, Peggy, separated when he went on a big drunk. She got a restraining order, and he was supposed to send her so much money a week. He didn't do it, so she had him thrown in jail.

By that time there was nothing left of the business, because it was so far in debt and behind on the rent. Customers hadn't received deliveries. Screwing up like that had created new business for that pompous fat guy, Al Sangston, who Don and I had chopped down years before.

Peggy had been trying to run the shop, and she called me up, at her wit's end. She had decided she wanted to close the thing out, and the landlord wouldn't let her take anything out of the building until she paid the rent.

When I gave Kenny the business he had leased all the machinery from me for a dollar a year, so it was still mine. I took a truck and a couple of guys down there and started loading the machinery in the truck. The landlord must have had a neighbor watching for that, because we hadn't been there fifteen minutes when he came flying in, furious.

We just kept on loading the equipment as he was stomping up and down. Then we rode off.

All that was left was a little bit of inventory, some nuts and screws, just crap. I called Al Sangston and said, "Hey, we're closing up the blind shop. If you want to come down here and buy the rest of the stuff, I'll let it go pretty cheap."

He jumped in his Cadillac and ran down there, looked around and asked, "What do you have to sell?"

"You're looking at it right here."

"I don't see anything that's worth anything."

"There's a lot of good stuff here."

"What do you want for it?"

"$10,000."

"$10,000 for this shit? You've got to be kidding!"

I told him, "Well, it's worth $10,000, and I've either got to get rid of it or go back into the blind business."

He thought for about half a second on what that would mean to his sales and said, "In that case, we can probably use it." He gave me a check for $10,000, which I gave to Peggy. That was the end of the venetian blind business for us. And it wasn't long after that when they stopped using them in trailers. Everyone went to drapes.

SALE OF BEAUTIFUL JAGUAR—This is one of the beautiful new Jaguar cars, made at Coventry, England. It's being turned over to Johnny Crean, head of the Dixieland Enterprises of Compton. The $4000 car with a 160 horsepower motor has a top speed of 132 miles per hour. Tony Koos, local dealer for Jaguar (Jeep, too) hands Johnny the keys.
—Photo by Harry Laugharn, jr.

Jaguars were so little-seen in the early '50s that my buying one made the local newspaper.

Wanna race? Behind the wheel of the Jag.

Achieving lift-off in my Porsche Roadster.

From *Auto Sport Review* magazine, 1953

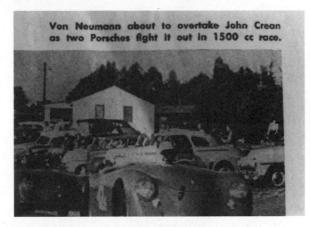

Von Neumann about to overtake John Crean as two Porsches fight it out in 1500 cc race.

John Crean's Porsche leads Jack Milne's Singer into the first corner of the Desert Trophy race.

From *Motor Sports World* magazine, 1953.

RACING TO THE BRINK

During the war, Don Stewart, Red and a bunch of us used to drag race on the streets. With rationing, we could only get a limited amount of gasoline, but we couldn't think of a better way to use it up. We'd hang out at the drive-in, and guys would come around from other areas to challenge us. The police had to know it was going on, since there would be a regular parade of our cars heading out to Wilmington Avenue. They rarely bothered us, though.

I had my little '32 Roadster with a Mercury engine in it, and it was fast enough to beat everyone around Compton. I finally had to slow up because of my tires. You couldn't get new ones, or even retreads, due to the war, and mine were worn down about as thin as a rubber.

As I got older, I still really loved a hot car. When I was starting in the blind business, Donna and I went to an auto show in Los Angeles and we just flipped over a Jaguar XK120 on display there. We both went, "Wow, what a car!" I was still deeply in debt as a result of my drinking, but I told Donna, "As soon as we get out of the hole, I want to get one of those things."

I had worked out a budget to get out of debt in 18 months. But, because I wanted that car so much, I started moonlighting and doing everything extra I could, and was out of debt in six months. As soon as I could afford to, in March of 1950, I ran down and got one of those Jaguars.

Sports car racing was just starting in California then. The XK120 was touted as being the world's fastest production sports car—with a top speed of 132 MPH, and I decided to take it to compete in a race in Pebble Beach. A few days before the race, I let one of my plywood suppliers take the Jaguar for a spin and he somehow managed to destroy the transmission. I barely got it back from the shop in time to make it to Pebble Beach.

Back then, the first three races you could enter would be novice races. Because my car was this sharp Jaguar, they placed me in the front row, next to a Cadillac Allard—a light English car with a big Cadillac engine—which at that time was one of the winning cars.

Being an old drag racer, I came off the line right as the flag came down. Man, I left that Cadillac way behind me. I was the first driver into the initial turn, and stayed half a lap ahead of everybody for that entire lap.

But when the Jaguar shop had fixed the transmission, they hadn't fastened down the floor mat. So, as I was going about 120 on the short straight, heading into some winding curves through a wooded area —whoomp!—the mat flew right up in my face! You could have thrown a tiger in the cab and I wouldn't have been more scared. I couldn't see a damn thing. I got off the gas and mashed the mat down with one arm, while the whole field passed me.

I managed to get going again and still finished sixth out of some 50 cars. Aside from nearly dying, it was such a rush that I was hooked.

Bill Stroppe and I fixed up an MG Special, and I raced that for a couple of years. There were only five or six races a year, weekend things, because it was a new sport. Of the small set of people involved in racing then, several went on to lead the sport. Phil Hill, who was also driving a little MG then, became world's champ.

Racing was more popular on the East Coast, and there was some big money involved in it. Jim Kimberly, a Kleenex heir, was racing Ferraris and other big-ticket cars, while Briggs Cunningham was building up Chrysler Specials. I once took my MG to Elkhart Lake, Wisconsin, for a race.

My business had been doing so well that I wasn't really paying much attention to it. I hired some people who had good reputations in the industry, and I presumed they were whiz kids who'd be able to run things better than I could. I placed them in charge of sales, production and development, while I was out screwing around with the race cars. Donna and I really were having a marvelous time with that.

I began competing in a little racing Porsche that was custom-built at the factory with an aluminum body about as thick as an eggshell. It could really go. I bought it from Johnny Von Neumann, who owned Competition Motors, the only Porsche distributor on the coast then.

To get the Porsches, Johnny also had to agree to carry Volkswagens, which had just been introduced in the States. In 1953 any sort of foreign car was a novelty on the road then, but the Bug was just too much of a joke for most people. Johnny couldn't sell any of the six he'd had to order. I started feeling sorry for him and bought one, and so had the first VW on the streets on the West Coast then. It was a fun car, and people were always curious to ask about it. Donna and I bought the new Beetles in '98 too, and it was the same thing over again. We never get the sort of attention in our Lamborghini or Mercedes that we do in the Beetles

I'd been doing fairly well racing the Porsche. I was never winning, but usually came in second, behind Johnny Von Neumann. He was probably a better driver than I was, but his shop prepared both our cars for the races, and there was also no question that they were prepping his car better than they were mine.

We ran as an informal team, and he consistently came in first, with me right behind him in the second slot. That wasn't bad, but I also thought it would be great to beat him. I tried hard, with the result being that I blew up my engine three times. The Porsches were far better than anything else out there, but you could only push them so far. I'd over-rev mine to get a little more speed before I shifted gears, and *blammo*.

Johnny never got upset by my blowing the engine, since he'd win the race *and* get the job of fixing my engine for $1500 to $2000 each time. It was damn foolishness on my part: his car was just faster.

While I was racing my brains out, Fleetwood was slowly going to hell, thanks to these "experts" I'd hired. I woke up one day in 1954 to find we had a yard full of trailers, with virtually no sales, and accounts payable up the kazoo. The company was teetering on the brink of ruin. We were nearly a quarter of a million dollars in the hole.

Approximate to the time I realized this, I had a race in Chino. That race was the third time I'd managed to edge by Johnny, only to have my engine blow. I climbed out of the car, walked back to the pits, and made the decision right there that I'd had it with racing. I had to get back to work.

I told Johnny to just haul the car in, fix it and sell it. (The Porsche company later bought this car back. They'd only made nine of this particular model—it didn't really have a name, but the car was later dubbed the Porsche America—and wanted mine for the Porsche museum in Stuttgart, where you can still see it today.)

I'd also made a deposit on a new Porsche 550 Spyder and had been waiting nearly a year for that to arrive. I told Johnny to sell that to somebody else.

Some time after the Chino race, I had a phone call from Johnny telling me that the ship with the Spyder was going to dock in the states soon, and was I sure I didn't want it? Then I got a telegram from the factory in Germany congratulating me on the car and telling me how special it was.

And it was special. The Spyder was the first Porsche with an overhead cam. The model I'd been racing was a push-rod job. When you strained it too much, a valve would break, and the pieces would destroy everything in the engine. But you could rev the 550 to almost any speed without breaking a valve. It was a tremendous machine. It went on to rule the sport for about five years.

Johnny did everything in the world to get me to buy it, because he knew I was experienced in Porsches. When the car arrived at his shop, he called me again, "Jesus, John, this is a hell of a car. You sure you don't want it?" I held firm. Then he called me again to tell me he had a buyer there for it, giving me a last chance to keep it.

I told him, "Look, I don't want it. Sell it!" And he sold it to James Dean, who managed to kill himself in it a couple of days later while driving up to Pebble Beach. I think Dean was destined to do something reckless, but it's too bad he had to do it in such a great car.

This is what trailer salesmen looked like, circa 1951.

A 40-foot, two-bedroom 1956 Fleetwood, one of the low-cost, no-frills models that saved the company.
Well, almost no frills—we got dealers to deliver the models with flowers in the front planters.

RECOVERY

Racing had become an obsession with me, and I knocked it off the same way I knocked off booze. I didn't call any of my racing friends. If they called me, I wouldn't talk to them. 1 didn't go near a racetrack for three years. That was easy enough at the beginning, because I was wrapped up in trying to steer Fleetwood away from destruction.

I had four plants going then: my Anaheim plant, two with Carl Jenson and Henry McCulley and the one with Speed and John Payne. There were well over 200 employees. When the plants were going at their peak, they were making over 50 trailers a week.

While I hadn't been paying attention, the price had been creeping up too high on the trailers coming out of the Anaheim plant, and the quality had been dropping on the ones from the other plants. When there was a sudden downturn in the trailer business, we were in no position to weather it. It didn't look like I'd be able to hold anything together, much less four operations.

So in one night I got rid of the three other plants. I called Carl and Harry and told them, "You take over the liability, and you can have my 50 percent. Those two operations are yours now." Then I went and woke Speed up around midnight and told him the same. We sat and talked a while, and I told him I thought I might be able to hold onto the one plant in Anaheim.

Speed, Carl and Harry had a rough time for a while, but they were able to pull their operations out of the fire. Harry was a good production man, and Carl was a great salesman. They did well until Carl got to gambling and was tapping the till, and it broke them. Speed and Johnny Payne's operation became the Flamingo trailer company. They eventually took on new investment partners, though, and it cut their stake in the ownership. I think Speed wound up with 10 percent.

Once I began to sort things out at my Anaheim plant, I started thinking I'd been too optimistic when I'd told Speed I might save things. It was a real mess. I had trailers that weren't selling because they were overpriced and not giving the customer value. I had disgruntled employees because they weren't being treated right. I had tons of bills and creditors who were really starting to hound us.

I stayed in the office late one night trying to plan the best way to liquidate the place and go get a job somewhere. Instead, my mind kept going back to trying to figure out where I'd gone wrong. Here Fleetwood had been blazing away, and now I was mired up to my neck.

I finally figured what it came down to: I'd become an asshole.

When a guy starts in business, he's doing everything he's supposed to do. He's totally concerned about the customer, about the product being the best it can, and being the best value. He makes sure he's treating his employees right.

It's only when people get successful, have money in the bank and everything is wonderful that all that changes. They start taking their customers for granted and treating their employees wrong, and it all goes out the window. That creates room for another business to come in and do everything right, because the big, established guys are out of touch. It's human nature. They become assholes.

That's what happens to most businesses and that's what happened to me. I'd been off having fun with my race cars, and leaving Fleetwood to be run by these "experts" who really didn't give a hang because it wasn't their business.

I sat in my office most of the night, jotting down a list of how I was doing things then and how I'd done them when I'd started, and it was all different. From that, I put together a company policy that simply went back to doing everything the way I had when I started. And that's been the policy Fleetwood has followed, almost, down to this day.

There was a good chance, though, that I'd never get the opportunity to implement the policy. My creditors had a meeting and decided they were going to appoint a receiver to oversee my business, to take charge of the cash I received and dole it out to the suppliers.

The creditors sent a committee of three to my office to tell me they were going to hobble me with this keeper. I told them, "That's fine and dandy if you want to do that, but the day that keeper walks in, I walk out, and you aren't going to get a fucking nickel."

They said, "What's wrong with a receiver?"

"If you guys get the hell out of here and leave me alone, I can probably lift this thing out of the hole, and you'll get every dime that I owe you. But if you put that keeper in here, it'll totally upset the apple cart. I won't be able to sell any trailers, and it won't work. So take your best shot." Then I threw them out.

They had a subsequent creditors' meeting, at which a pair of suppliers to whom I was deeply in debt came to my rescue. One was a window supplier named Elmer Hehr and the other was a metal supplier named Roland Sahm. I didn't hear about this until later, because the meetings were private, but they basically said, "Hey, you'd better leave him alone, because he will walk out. We know him."

Thanks to them, I got some breathing room. Taking stock of my situation, I had three damn good men--Dale, my production manager Cliff Breitweg and my sales manager Walt Paulson--fifteen production employees, and $250,000 of debt. With that hand of cards, I wound up bringing Fleetwood out of the hole and paying off all the creditors within six months, before 1954 was over.

It was a lot of work, but one of the nice things about that is if you're busy, you don't have time to worry. I wasn't losing much sleep anyway. I had a reputation in the industry as being one of the best production managers and designers there was, and could have found a job anywhere the next day. Doing that actually would have been getting rid of a pain in the ass. But I'd dug the hole I was in, and I liked the challenge of getting out of it.

I decided to go back to making just one model, for one price, and selling it for cash. I designed a simple 35-foot trailer based around a popular floor plan. I priced it at what our cost would have been at that time.

My purchasing manager, Dale Skinner, who was already my right hand man then, looked at the price and it scared him to death. He insisted, "We'll never make any money that way!"

I told Dale that wouldn't be the case once we got our supply costs down. When you got in trouble like we were, suppliers raised prices on you. And, running as inefficiently as we'd been, building 15 models and paying all these supposed experts (whom I'd just canned), there would be plenty of room for profit.

That turned out to be the plant-saving routine. The first thing I did was go through the shop and clear out all the inventory that was laying around, ranges, refrigerators and all this junk left over from all the different trailer models we'd built. With that gone, I built storage for one week's supply of the materials we needed to make our one new trailer model. It changed the plant to where it was really a super-efficient operation. There was so much more room to work, and the trailer was so easy to build, that we were able to make a much higher quality trailer.

It wound up being a very low-priced unit, selling to dealers at $2695. Most other 35-foot trailers, including our previous one, went for about $3500. Something else we gave people that no one noticed was two extra feet. The maximum the law would allow on the highways those days was a 35-foot trailer, so we called ours a 35, but it was really 37 feet. We built those oversized trailers for ten years and never got called on it. What was really funny was that so much of the competition

We were poor in '54, but Fleetwood clicked in '56.

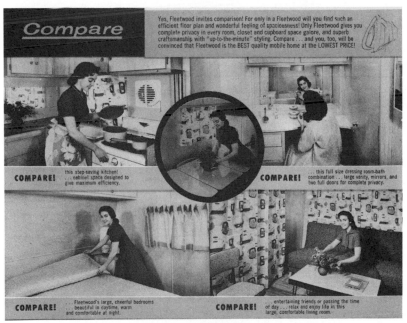

(Inside of brochure)

tried to copy the trailer and get all our features into 35 feet, and you simply couldn't do it.

About a year later, Dale and I happened to be in Long Beach near Kit Trailers. I knew the owners, so I suggested we drop in. One of the owners, Dan Pocapalia, was there, and he didn't look entirely comfortable to see us.

"Well, I suppose you came here to see it," he said.

"See what?"

"You know what you want to see."

"What are you talking about?"

He took us to their back lot, and they'd bought one of our trailers, had taken it all apart and had built one exactly like it. I told him, "That's kind of interesting. When are you going into production on it?"

And he said, "I'm not. I can't build that trailer and make any money. It's impossible." No one else had the sort of efficient operation we did.

Walt Paulson, our sales manager, went out on the road with our prototype. We devised a unique program: that this was an exceptionally low-priced trailer, and that the dealer had to agree to buy 12 of them over a year's time. That was probably the first time an approach like that had been tried.

A lot of dealers weren't greeting us with open arms at that point. To clear out all the unsold trailers I'd had sitting on our parking lot, I'd taken out ads in the *LA Times* and the *Herald Examiner* and sold the trailers directly to the public, which dealers always hate, for obvious reasons. But the new 35-footer was such a good design and such a value that they couldn't turn it down.

Walt signed up 40 dealers between Seattle and LA and on out to Denver and Albuquerque. Our production rate was ten units a week, so with forty dealers, we were always out of trailers, and so were the dealers. Our production was below demand, and that's what brought us out of our slump.

That was one of the tenants of my new policy: **controlled production**. The way my former experts had run things, they'd increase production when they had a couple of good sales weeks, then when things would slow down they'd lower production.

Before they came in, I'd kept a controlled production that was lower than demand at the highest time of the year. We didn't exploit as much market as we could, but we never had to slow down or speed up. We were able to keep the same employees all the way through, and that was really an important thing. When you have a manufacturing operation that's not steady, you don't get good quality and it's very seldom profitable.

Another advantage of limiting production to be less than the demand was that dealers didn't have to do any drastic discounting to sell one of our trailers. Because there was more demand than product, and because they were a good value to begin with, dealers could make a decent margin on our units, which made us popular with them. Years later, one dealer in El Monte told me that whenever he hired a new salesman, he'd take him into a Fleetwood trailer, open a kitchen drawer and say, "There might as well be a $500 bill in here, because that's how much more we make on a Fleetwood than we do on anything else."

Dale kept track of the payables. Some of our debts were up to 120 days, and he paid off those first as fast as he could, then the 90 days, and then the 60 days. He handled all the creditors who called constantly wanting money. He didn't bother me with that, so I was able to function at 100 percent. So often when people get in debt, they're so whipped trying to stave off creditors that they can't do their job.

When we got current, man, we had a party.

Despite Dale's fears about our pricing the unit too low, we had a net profit of roughly $300 per trailer. At ten a week, that was $3000 a week, making a quarterly profit of $39,000. I'd started an incentive program that paid quarterly, and even while backing down our debt in that first quarter, 30 percent of our net was paid out to my three managers and myself. They got 6³⁄₄ percent, about $2,600 each, and I got 10%, $3,900. We could each have bought a new car for that kind of money then.

I'd had **profit-sharing** even before that, but it had been a doled-out thing instead of company policy, which it became in the mid-1950s. All of our managers since the mid-1950s have been on a low salary, and the bulk of their pay comes from a portion of the net, which is given to them in bonuses. It's written-in, so they have a feeling of proprietorship. That's worked very well over the years, for them and for the company. There are also profit-sharing plans for the production workers and other employees.

As a result of having hired the experts who almost ruined us, another of the policies I adopted was to almost **always promote from within the company**. When I needed a sales manager, if there was some guy working on the line who looked like he could clean himself up and do the job, then he became a sales manager. I scarcely hired anybody from outside at all. It gave the guys in the plant some incentive, knowing they could go from the assembly line to management if they had the gumption. I knew how much that had meant to me when I'd worked for other people. I've had a lot of good people come to Fleetwood to start as assembly workers, because they knew the opportunity was there.

A policy that wasn't as popular initially was that no one at Fleetwood was allowed to sell factory-direct to customers anymore. My salesmen had thought selling direct was keen, because we'd make an extra profit then. But when we did that, word invariably would get back to the dealers—as it had when we'd cleared out our overstock—and they'd be furious. So I laid down the rule that we'd **sell strictly to dealers**. Since then we never even had a resale license, so there was no way we could sell a trailer direct.

Another big change in policy was that we stopped

advertising. I determined that we would **spend no money on anything that didn't go directly into the product**. That policy eliminated all trailer shows, all advertising and public relations, and we quit the trade associations we belonged to. We still had product brochures, but we put a minimum of expense into them.

We really stuck tight to that. Unless something went directly into the product, we spent no money on it. It's a damn good policy if you want to give people value, because that stuff doesn't add a thing to the product.

That remained the company policy, but it came to be liberally interpreted. If some well placed ads or promotions lead to far greater volume, that can benefit the product. But I think that Fleetwood eventually went overboard in the other direction, hosting dealer meetings, sponsoring events and other things that don't directly support the product. That has driven the company overhead pretty doggone high.

I have an absolute hatred of being in debt. That has been in my blood since way back. In my drinking years, my standard operating procedure was to stretch myself out in debt as far as I could, so that when I'd get a paycheck none of it was mine. I'd pay the bills and wind up with fifteen cents.

In business, I'd taken out a bank loan at one point, and the bank became fidgety and called in the loan. I suddenly had checks bouncing all over the place. That situation bothered me so much that I decided I would never, ever in my life borrow another nickel from anybody. And I didn't.

It became a bedrock policy at Fleetwood that we would strictly **grow through earnings and never borrow money**. Through the years I was strongly criticized for that by people on Wall Street and others. In the high-flying times when everyone was borrowing and leveraging, I kept Fleetwood out of it. I was under a lot of pressure from within the company as well, but I just flat-out wouldn't let them do it. Then when the bottom fell out of everything, and everyone was going belly-up because they couldn't pay back their loans, I was a hero.

But they don't remember that during the rosy times.

If any company should have become fat and complacent in ensuing decades, it was Fleetwood. It became the biggest company in the world in each of our four fields—motorhomes, travel trailers, folding trailers and manufactured housing. But because I wrote down those virtues that a young company has and made them company policy, it kept our feet on the ground.

Everybody who came to work at Fleetwood read our policy, and they found out pretty fast that it wasn't just words: that was the way we did it. In all the years I was there, my biggest job was protecting that policy, because there was always somebody who wanted to shoot off from it in one way or another. Since I've retired, the company policy has gone right out the window. That's perilous, because that policy *is* Fleetwood.

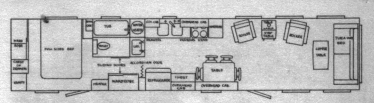

Study this floor plan, notice how every available inch
has been used. The 14 foot living room which opens into the
spacious dining area gives a never before had feeling of space.
The walk around bed, the large bathroom, the great amount of
work surface in the kitchen, the placement of the space heater
are but a few of the conveniences to be found in this plan.

FLEETWOOD HAS IT!

Heat where the cold begins! . . . under windows along
walls . . . Fleetwood perimeter heating . . . surrounds you
with warmth.

When you buy the trailer of your dreams, make sure you
get a heating system you will be willing to live with.

Fleetwood's fully automatic GAS (either natural or manufactured) forced air heat is adequate even in sub-zero weather!
. . . and it's clean . . . no black smoke or messy oil drums
to handle.

Fleetwood's heating system with the 40,000 btu Duo-Therm,
the all metal, fully insulated ducts, the adjustable floor regis-
ters, is the finest ever offered in a mobile-home.

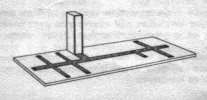

Our brochures weren't fancy, but we did our best in them to
show people how our trailers were better.

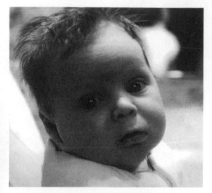

Susie, taking a good look
at 1961.

How did I Keep our trailer
costs down? I made my kids
build them all. Johnnie visits
the Waco plant in 1959.

The kids BS—
Before Susie. That's Andy, Emily and Johnnie.

BOOM

Fleetwood made its recovery in 1955, and our success was a steady ascent from there. We put a new plant in Waco, Texas in 1956, then in Nampa, Idaho in 1957, Douglas, Georgia in 1958, Crestline, Ohio in 1959, Carbondale, Pennsylvania in 1960 and so on. We put in a plant a year for ten years, and they all did wonderfully.

Six months after we'd gone to bat with the new 35-foot trailer, a fellow came to work for me named Bill Stearns, who had been assistant to the president at a company called Nashua. They had several plants around the country, and I was interested to learn how they did that, since I sure hadn't had any luck before with absentee management.

Stearns had written to me about coming to work for Fleetwood, and I'd responded that we couldn't afford anybody at the time, but that I'd like to talk to him if he was ever on the West Coast.

On Christmas Eve, 1954, I stopped in at our plant to pick up a couple of the kids' presents I had stashed there. A guy was sitting in a rented Cadillac at the gate. He looked like he should have been a history teacher, with big glasses and combed-back hair, but it was Bill Stearns. He wasn't with Nashua anymore, and had come out to California hoping to get hired. I talked with him for a while, but mainly told him to stop in after the holiday.

When he presented himself, I told him again that I didn't think I could hire him. He said he was willing to come to work even on the assembly line, so I said, "Fine, you've got a job," and had him building cabinets. He probably figured he wouldn't be on the assembly line long, and he was right, because he could be a tremendous help to our growth in a number of ways.

He was the one who got us involved in conducting

market research, which he said they'd always done at Nashua to find what models and sizes sold. We didn't know a thing about that.

Though Fleetwood only had the one model, we were still expected to make yearly changes to it, just like in the auto industry. With one of the systems we learned from Stearns, we soon had the model changes down to a science. Our sales manager had a log book with a form. Every time he'd get a complaint or a suggestion from a dealer, he'd log it. We'd look those over every 30 days, and if any complaints or suggestions repeated very often, that told us what to do. It was pretty damn easy. If several dealers said they needed a kitchen with a 10-cubic-foot refrigerator, we knew there was a demand pushing that.

Stearns also suggested we do market research by going through the State of California trailer registrations. After doing a job like that, you can see why someone had to invent the computer. We got bundles and bundles of registration cards, because the Department of Motor Vehicles wouldn't just give you the cards for trailer registrations, but for cars and just about everything else with wheels. The serial numbers the industry used at the time were coded in such a way that they'd tell you what size a trailer was and how many bedrooms it had. So once we sorted out all the trailer cards from the pile and tallied their serial numbers, we had solid figures on what people were buying.

We found that two-bedroom trailers outsold single bedrooms by about two-to-one, while we had only been building a one-bedroom trailer. I jumped right on that information. By April of 1955, I had a new two-bedroom model rolling off the production line, another 37-foot 35-footer. (Later, when the maximum length allowed on highways was raised to 40 feet, we came out with a 40-footer, which, since I always liked to push at regulations, was actually 42 feet.)

Our one-bedroom model still had some unneeded

features left over from when our prices had gotten out of hand. For the two-bedroom, I really got down and dirty, leaving out anything that wasn't essential, and I passed the savings on in the price. It was a new, unique floor plan, and dealers picked up on it so enthusiastically that we soon dropped the one-bedroom model.

At this point Fleetwood was only making house trailers. I'd gotten out of the travel trailer business when Fleetwood was teetering and I'd given those factories to my partners. By the end of the 1950s, most companies had settled on making either house trailers or travel trailers, with only a few manufacturers making both. (Nowadays travel trailers fall under the recreational vehicle heading, while the politically correct term for house trailer now is "manufactured housing.")

On the housing side, after 1955 we pretty much had a lock on the low-cost unit. Most of the other manufacturers felt they had to have all kinds of fancy extras, and it was really just an ego trip because the customers didn't give a shit. They wanted to get in out of the rain, turn on a light and have the stove work—that's all they cared about, and that's what we gave them.

Prior to our comeback with the lower-priced trailer, our warranty expense had been too high. Dealers would complain about our units arriving with things they had to fix, and a lot of that was just them ripping us off. They'd charge us for problems they said they had to repair, and we weren't there to know if they did or not.

We came up with a new warranty, where if a trailer had an electrical short or a leak in the roof or plumbing, we'd fix it. Aside than that, there was no guarantee at all. Instead, dealers were expected to inspect a trailer when they received it, and if there was anything wrong they weren't supposed to accept it.

Our expense in servicing that warranty went down to practically nothing. Sometimes there'd be some nit-picking thing where a dealer wouldn't accept a trailer, but our product was in such demand that the driver would simply take it down the road to the next dealer who was dying to have it.

We generally put a very high quality product out there, one that gave real value. For example, at a time when most companies were still wiring their electrical systems with lamp cord, we were employing the type of wiring you'd find in houses. There weren't any government standards causing us to do that, just the competitive marketplace and a pride in our product.

I was a stickler for quality control, and that sometimes meant being tougher than I liked. We had a number of displaced Latvians working for us in Anaheim. Russia had taken over their country, and the local Lutheran church had sponsored them into the US. The ones I hired were good workers, tickled to death to have a job.

A consistent problem we'd been having was with plumbing leaks. We found it was all human error, where a worker would screw a fitting on temporarily, figuring he'd tighten it later, and then forget about it. So I laid down the law, that anybody who put a fitting on and didn't tighten it was going to get fired, just like that.

One day I was showing our assembly line to a dealer. Just as I was telling him about that policy, I reached down to demonstrate it by twisting a fitting on a water heater, and damn if it wasn't loose. The guy who'd screwed it in was one of these Latvians, and I fired him right then and there. He broke out in tears. I felt absolutely rotten, but that's the way it was. And we had damn few plumbing leaks.

We had very few problems with our trailers because our controlled production meant we had a steady workforce who kept the quality up. There was so much more demand for our trailers than we could fill, though, that I started getting anxious to open other plants.

I wasn't interested at all in building an empire, but it was very important to me for my employees to have an expanding organization in which they could grow. Having worked for other people, I found you only really gave it your all when there was some opportunity for you to get ahead. If I wanted to keep the good people I had, I really needed for them to be able to advance, which meant a bigger operation.

Again, Bill Stearns' organizational experience from his time with Nashua had a lot to do with our successful expansion. I just recently read a book Henry Ford wrote in 1924, and I thought I was seeing ghosts, because Ford's policies and procedures for running a company were almost identical to mine. I'd almost bet that the guys at Nashua had read this book, because a lot of the ideas I got from Bill Stearns are in there: the standardization of product, the tight materials management, putting value in the product, cloning plants.

We suspected Texas would be an excellent place for us, and the market research techniques we learned from Stearns confirmed that. Then we wrote letters to all the chambers of commerce in central Texas, shopping for the best deal, because they were all anxious to get some industry in there. Most of them had nothing going except cotton and agriculture.

Waco responded the most positively. I drove there and negotiated the deal to put a plant in. The city would give us the property and build the plant on it, then lease it to us for one percent a month of what it had cost them to build. Their cost was $65,000, so our rent was to be $650 a month.

The plant design was a clone of our Anaheim assembly line, and so was the personnel. The people we were grooming to be the management for Waco spent nearly a year working alongside their counterparts in Anaheim. When they got to Waco, they knew their stuff. It was the same on the factory floor. We took the lead men for each station in the California plant, seven or eight of them, and had them go to Waco to train the lead men there. The workforce we found in Texas was terrific. They really wanted the jobs.

While the plant was under construction, we set up offices in the Roosevelt Hotel, which was one of only two hotels in town. There were no motels. Since we didn't do any advertising, our sales manager would sit in the Roosevelt and introduce the product to dealers over the phone. Our prices were very low, and we could quote our sales numbers from California in our pitch.

It turned out that a lot of dealers already knew about us, and were anxious to take on our trailers. There was no manufacturing down that way in Texas and they'd been getting their trailers from up north, so we were a pretty easy sale. Dealers were afraid someone else in their area would get us first. Long before we opened in Waco, our sales manager set up enough dealers to take the product when it came off the line.

Opening that plant required some close timing. We'd made good money through the year in Anaheim and had just enough to secure all the machinery—which I bought second-hand, driving between Waco, Houston and San Antonio to find it all. If we had it set up and running in time, got the trailers built and delivered and took the money in, everything would work out fine, with no capital shortage. But doing that was really close.

We'd copied all the jigs and fixtures in Anaheim and stacked those up on a big old trailer. I made the trip down to Waco with the truck. We were on-schedule until we got to the New Mexico border on a Friday. The load was 40 feet long, and the maximum they'd let us take through the border without a permit was 35 feet. The permit had to come from Santa Fe and took three or four days to obtain. We didn't have three days to lose, so we found a welder in a little town by the border and had him cut off the back end of the jigs. We threw them on top, welded them into place and went on through.

One reason why Waco had been so anxious to get our factory was that they'd been having a drought for the past couple of years. With nearly their entire economy tied up in agriculture, that was disastrous for them.

Just as we were getting the plant running, a big rainstorm

came in. Suddenly, it was like everyone in town had turned into Gene Kelly. People were out in the streets, dancing in the downpour, stomping in the gutters. You've never seen happier wet people in your life.

Meanwhile, we were running on such a tight schedule that we had the plant open before we'd even laid the parking lot. The big rain came before we'd put the asphalt down. The ground was so wet that when the roller went over it, there was water squirting up everywhere out of the ground.

The driver said, "Hey, this won't work. You have to do this when the ground's dry."

I told him, "We don't have time for that. Just put it *down.*"

Some of our best people went down to Waco, like the plant manager Cliff Breitweg, who I first met when I worked at Supercold right after the war, and the production manager, Clint Dorsey.

Fleetwood's cabinet shop in Anaheim had been run by a woman named Flora, whose husband, Clyde, also worked for us. They were some of the ones who went down to get the Texans up to speed. Flora was tremendous. I could sketch a design on a piece of plywood—we didn't use drawing boards—and Flora would whip out a perfect cabinet. I'd never let her actually run the saws, though. That's because at Blackhawk, Lee Black had his wife helping out in the shop, and she got her right hand horribly disfigured in a table saw. That's bad enough for a man, but for a woman it's horrible.

When I had the Anaheim lead crew in Waco training the Texans, we all lived in one apartment complex. We had a lot of fun, always joking around. Our first night there we were all together in one of the rooms, and suddenly Flora jumped in the air and stomped down on the floor, right on a scorpion. It scared the hell out of me, but she didn't give it a thought.

Along with the people we sent to Waco, there was some good local talent. Bill Ducas started with us in Waco and rose in the company until he became a division production manager. He first came in looking for work one day when I was in the shop sweeping down, pushing a broom, and he asked me, "Where's the boss? I want to see about getting a job."

I told him to go to the Roosevelt Hotel between six and eight p.m., which was when we did our hiring. At five o'clock, I'd go there, shower, put on a suit and tie and sit down behind a desk. Ducas walked in to see about the job and mentioned that the janitor at the plant had sent me over—didn't recognize me at all. He never would have made a good detective, but he was great at what he did.

We initially hired 40 people from the Waco area. When they first came to work for us, they were riding bicycles or driving beat up old trucks. Within a year, there were 35 brand new cars in the parking lot. Because most of the local employees lived on farms, which were producing again thanks to the rains, the money they were making with us was like a real jackpot for them. We tried to help out by scheduling their vacations around the harvest time so they could get their crops in.

The timing of building the Idaho plant a year later wasn't as critical as Waco, because we had the income from the two plants to work with. We had another problem up there, though. In the '50s, the mountain states were dominated by three men who each controlled strings of retail lots. The dealerships they didn't own had to do their bidding anyway, because these guys had the financing tied up. There was a bit of collusion between them, dividing the territory up, which was illegal but they were getting away with it.

They dictated what trailer lines the dealerships would carry, and that was determined by which manufacturer would give them the biggest discount, which as they meant it was a nice way of saying kickbacks. But even if you were paying tribute to these guys, if they could squeeze a bigger amount from someone else, they'd drop you like a hot potato. You'd have merchandise coming off the line, and they'd call and say they didn't need you anymore.

When we went into Idaho, the dealers insisted they had to have the discount. Our price was as low as it could be, and it was one-price-fits-all, so I told them no way. It looked like this was going to be a major hurdle. But we went to Pacific Finance, the company we'd convinced to handle trailers when the California finance companies were hassling us. We got Pacific to put offices in Idaho and finance our trailers for the dealers there. It turned out to be a whale of a deal for them, and for us too. Eventually, Pacific was doing business throughout the mountain states.

One of the three big dealers, Harry Goldberg, was actually a super guy, and a great American success story. His dad had passed away when he was just a kid, and Harry was supporting his mother, selling papers on the streets of Denver, and loaning money. He went from there to having a pawnshop, and from there a finance company, which wound up being Aetna Finance.

For all the influence Bill Stearns had on Fleetwood's operations, he wasn't with the company for all that long. He was a real mixed blessing, because he had tremendous knowledge and skill, but he also was the kind of guy who would just make people hate him immediately. He had such a nasty personality that whenever he'd meet with anybody, I had to follow behind Bill and reassure them that everything was all right, and not to pay too much attention to his ranting.

Everything had to be his way. Our trailers had a rounded shape, and we used a plywood laminate to make the round bows in the sidewalls. Bill's former company had used regular lumber, sawed it thin and then soaked it in a 20-foot galvanized tank so it would bend. Plywood, meanwhile, would bend without our having to soak it.

Bill insisted that we had to make the bows with lumber. So every one of the plants had to buy one of these hog troughs for soaking the wood. Unbeknownst to Bill, we went right ahead using the plywood. But any time Bill was going to make a visit to a plant, I'd get on the phone and tell them, "Well, you'd better get out your hog trough." They'd be there soaking the bows until the moment he left.

In July of 1957, after Bill had been with Fleetwood for two and a half years, he called me one day and said, "I've been doing some organizational work with Gibson, Dunn & Crutcher and Arthur Anderson" —our lawyers and accountants—"and I've got some documents all ready to go. Why don't you and Donna come in and look them over, because they need your signature."

We went to the office, where Bill was waiting with representatives from our lawyers and accountants. He handed me the papers he'd prepared. Reading them, I saw that he'd contrived things to split Fleetwood into separate sales and manufacturing companies. He was to be the chairman of the sales company, and I was supposed to run the manufacturing company, which was obliged to sell exclusively to him. Once he had control of all the dealers and had accumulated enough capital, he could just say "adios" to me.

I was absolutely flabbergasted when I looked at what he'd drafted. Bill had been getting paid very well, with great bonuses. I'd made him vice president, and here he was taking me for some kind of idiot.

I gathered the papers up, threw them in the trash, and said, "This meeting's all over." I told Donna she might as well go on home. The lawyers and accountants were surprised because Bill had let them think these changes were being made with my knowledge.

Ol' Bill's face went red and he started to have one of his temper tantrums, which he'd never done with me before. While he was blustering in my face, telling me how wrong I was and how crucial he was, I said, "Bill, you just pack your stuff up and get the hell out of here. We don't need you anymore."

Then he started to calm down, and said, "It'll take me

about a week to get things cleaned up."

"No, you've got exactly one hour to get your ass out of here. You'd better figure out how." There were three big guys in the office who were 100 percent loyal to me, so he knew we had the horsepower to physically chuck him out.

While Bill was with Fleetwood, he was so effective that I hardly had to do anything. But he made the mistake of thinking he was irreplaceable. I'd done very well before he joined Fleetwood, and, while he was with us, it hadn't been easy smoothing over his rages.

When he left, he took our blueprints, our lists of material sources and other company information with him. He started his own trailer company in a vacant trailer factory in Fullerton. He coaxed ten of our dealers to invest $10,000 or $15,000 apiece to finance it, and started manufacturing a trailer that was identical to ours.

But, with his angry nature, Bill couldn't get anybody good to work for him, and he couldn't get up production. His business was a mess. I don't think Bill got ten trailers built, and those were pure shit.

Bill got mad better than anyone I ever met. I mean if anything didn't go exactly his way, his face would turn crimson and veins would rise like a gopher trail on his forehead. After he'd been in business about 60 days, he was having one of his trademark fits, and he dropped flat dead.

Before he had pulled his little power play with me, he'd sent Dale Skinner, my purchasing manager and right hand man, out of the way, down to Texas. As soon as I ran Bill off, I phoned Dale and said, "You'd better get yourself home, because you're the new vice president."

Just like every other time Dale got a promotion, he nearly rolled into a ball because he didn't think he was worthy of it, but he was always dynamite, the best man for the job that I could hope for. Although I was officially the president until 1970, when Dale was given the title, he actually did most of the work a company president usually did.

While Dale used to worry if he was good enough for Fleetwood, Bill Weide initially suspected that Fleetwood wasn't good enough for him.

With four plants going in 1958—Anaheim, Waco, Georgia and Idaho—we needed someone to more or less be a controller and take care of the finances. Bill had been working for a company that imported cookware and was recommended to us by our accountants.

Dale gave him a call, and Bill came down from LA to see about the job. When he drove by the office, he just kept on driving, because it was such a pathetic-looking shack. Bill was going to head back to LA without even stopping, but he later told me he figured, "What the hell, I've come this far." He went in and talked to Dale, was impressed with everything but the office, and signed on.

He was the first person to come to work for us who had any sort of credential. He was a CPA. He was also a college grad, which was pretty rare for us at the time as well.

Bill is also Jewish, and there were damn few Jews in the trailer business then. Actually, with the exception of the movie business, all of Southern California had a kind of country club attitude then. Bill had graduated second in his class at USC, but many less qualified gentiles had landed better jobs at law or accounting firms.

When Dale was interviewing him, Bill stopped him and told him that he was a practicing Jew, and that if that was a problem they'd best not go any further. Dale said, "I'm a Methodist, but don't practice much. John Crean's a Lutheran. If you think you can get along with us, you'll be okay."

His being the rye amid all that white bread never caused him any problems. Bill is a great people person, and everybody in the company was crazy about him.

I didn't even meet him until he'd been with us three months. He was holed away in the office, and I was everywhere but there. One day I went charging in there in my greasy overalls looking for Dale, and Bill started hollering at me, because most people weren't supposed to be in the office, and he didn't know who the hell I was.

Bill never did learn much about how to build a trailer, but he became Dale's right hand man for a number of years, and, later, president of Fleetwood.

People have told me that you can train people or change them, but I never bought that at all. If a guy couldn't do the job, I just fired him and got someone who could. When I was hiring, I never looked at a person's education. People who weren't afraid to work, who were willing to start at low wages, with the idea that there was opportunity ahead: they were the people we hired. And most of the time they turned out to be great people.

We had some stiff requirements, so a lot of people didn't qualify. In those early days, we'd never hire anybody for management who wasn't married. We wouldn't even talk to them. We figured married people were more stable.

I've never been big on unions. Usually they're just driving a divisive wedge between the employees and the owners, and you never feel like a team. If you're treating each other fairly, unions aren't necessary.

The first year we were building our two-bedroom trailers, 1956, we had a big strike. We'd simply replace the workers who went out, but we had pickets for six months.

After Bill Weide came aboard, we had him handle our union negotiations. He had no prior expertise at that, and I have to admit that Dale and I put him in charge simply because we could, as both of us hated dealing with the unions.

In 1959 the Sheet Metal Workers of America tried to orchestrate a work stoppage at the Nampa, Idaho plant. Bill had some of the lawyers from Gibson, Dunn & Crutcher give him a one-day crash course on labor law and then he went up to Nampa (We couldn't afford to send a lawyer with him). The union's head representative was future Supreme Court Justice

Arthur Goldberg, who must have thought Bill had a weak bladder, because Bill kept excusing himself from the meeting. He was actually going out and calling our lawyers back in LA to get some handle on what Goldberg had been talking about.

The labor strife rarely became violent, but it was nasty in Carbondale, Pennsylvania when the union struck there in the 1960s. That plant was always a pain in the ass, with constant labor problems, and the strikers turned violent. The families of the plant management were getting threatened. It got so bad they had to move out of their homes and live in motels and places out of town.

I went to Carbondale during the strike. In the morning, the pickets were all standing outside the plant, keeping warm with fires blazing in steel barrels. As we drove past the picket line, they pelted the car with rocks. It was a rented car, so we could give a shit.

The strike finally resolved. When you've got guys throwing rocks at you and making threats, that's against the law. It should have been halted. But the labor attorney we'd hired to work for us wasn't doing anything. I went to see him and said, "Man, let's get an injunction. This can't go on."

And he said, "I can't get the reputation of being a union buster." So I fired *him* on the spot, and had to go to Scranton to get somebody to do the job.

You have to negotiate with the unions, but it would always come to the striking point for them when we would refuse to collect dues for them from our employees. When they couldn't get that they'd just walk away, because they never could get employees to ante up the dues on their own. It was a sweet deal for the union if we'd collect it for them. I didn't think it should be my business to be pulling union dues out of my workers' checks, and I wouldn't budge from that. When the unions knew they couldn't get that, they'd cave. We're still non-union.

Not too many years after we started the profit-sharing

for management, we instituted one for the production employees. We'd know how much labor we could afford on each unit to make it competitive in the marketplace. We'd assign that cost to the product, and if the employees could build it for less than that amount, the difference would go into a pool to be distributed at the end of the week to employees, in proportion to their hourly wage.

The program was a slow starter. But once the plants and employees got the hang of it, a few of the plants were even getting units built in half the time they had been. The employees started taking home twice the wages. That was good business: it stopped turnover, it stopped unions, and kept us competitive.

PUBLISHED OCCASIONALLY BY FLEETWOOD TRAILER CO., INC.

VOL. 1, NO. 3   ANAHEIM, CALIFORNIA   APRIL 29, 1955

RADIO CELEBRITY MAKES HOME IN FLEETWOOD

Charley Raye, one of America's most unique radio personalities makes his home in a 35 foot Fleetwood. Charley, who originated his show two years ago on a Honolulu station in the Hawaiian Islands, recently brought his show to Station KGER in Long Beach, Calif.

Charley's is a one-man show. He performs the part of writer, pianist, recording technician, sound engineer, singer, news commentator, reporter and announcer. Pictured is Charley at work with all of his equipment installed on and around his piano.

His show originates from a restaurant on "Restaurant Row" in Long Beach, where he also entertains the diners while on the air.

One of the interesting parts of his show is interviewing different celebrities on his "beeper" telephone, a phone with a device installed which emits a signal every 10 seconds to let the per-

Continued on Page 2

Al Pio Celebrates First Year in Trailer Business

Al and Irvyle Pio, who own and operate Al Pio Trailer Sales, at 14041 S. Harbor Blvd., Santa Ana, completed their first year in the trailer business this month.

Al and Irvyle Pio

Al operated a used car business in Westminster, California for eight years prior to entering the trailer field. When asked why he switched from cars to trailers, Al replied, "When I used to buy a used car, I was usually buying someone else's headaches and passing them on to someone else and then taking all the blame." When asked if he didn't have any "headaches" with trailers, he replied. "Yes, but I used to be a carpenter and I can fix them."

Irvyle does all the paper work for the operation and acts as saleslady when Al is out servicing or delivering a trailer. Al employs a part-time service man but does a big share of the work himself.

Al sold 188 trailers in this first year, including used, vacation and all. He

Continued on Page 2

I wrote the Fleetwood Newsletter, which featured my friend Charley Raye in this 1955 issue.

CHARACTERS COUNT

Some people think that persons in the trailer trade are akin to aluminum siding salesmen and patent medicine hawkers, but I've only known a couple of out-and-out crooks. There was no shortage of characters, though, and some of them didn't mind working an angle that was a little bent.

One of my favorite characters was Charley Raye, the guy from whom I had bought my Ford coupe and .22 pistol during the war. He wasn't in the trailer business, but that didn't stop him from selling a bunch of them anyway.

I didn't see Charley until years after the war, because he'd wound up in Hawaii doing an all-night radio show. He came back and opened a saloon in Long Beach that did a great business, largely because he was the entertainment there. He had a late-night radio show on a Long Beach station, and it didn't hurt that he could tout his nightspot on the air. Once Charley got a business going great guns, he'd sell it. What the new owners didn't know was that once Charley would move his piano out and open a new place, the audience would go with him.

He'd keep selling trailers out from under himself too. Back when Fleetwood still had a resale license, Charley would come to the Anaheim plant and I'd sell him a trailer wholesale. He knew a banker who would finance it. Charley would live in it, meanwhile putting an ad in the paper to sell it to someone who'd take over the payments. He'd borrowed more than the damn trailer was worth, would pocket the profit, and buy another trailer right away.

Charley didn't look like much, but he was all personality. He could really hustle. He'd go roaming around Long Beach in the middle of the day in a new Eldorado convertible. Any time he saw attractive girls, he'd pull over and give them a card for his saloon, telling them they could have free drinks. Of course, when you've got the girls in a place, you've got the guys, and he had things rolling.

He really had a way with women. He'd be playing the piano and meet an attractive gal, and his opening line would be, "Did you ever sleep in a house trailer"

"No."

"You want to?"

He was surprised how many said "Yeah." One night, Charley had taken a gal to his trailer and had her in the sack there. About two in the morning when he was all done with her, he told her to get out so he could get some sleep. She said no, she wasn't going to go. He started getting rough with her, and she pulled out a .38, leveled it on him and told him she was staying. He kept arguing, and she opened up with the thing. She shot five holes in his roof and floor.

So he let her stay the night, and the next morning I got a call, "Hey, John, can you come fix my trailer?" We hauled it in the plant and put some new panels on it.

When the Disneyland Hotel had just opened and didn't have much business, Charley at one point had five broads stashed there in different rooms, and none of them knew about the other ones. He carried on pretty much the same routine until 1959, when he died when he crashed an airplane he'd just bought into Mile Square Park in Fountain Valley.

I've had a couple of people in my operation who turned out to be a little shady, but not too many. Usually when someone's act seems too good to be true, it *is* too good to be true, and I avoid them.

I had a sales manager in Idaho who was a heavy drinker. I didn't know it because the plant manager there would always cover for him when he went on a spree. I also didn't know until much later that they had a partnership with a dealer up there. Because we limited our production, Fleetwoods were hard to get, and these two fellows were shipping a lot of units to this one dealership and taking a piece of the action.

It wasn't criminal, but it wasn't fair, and I would have fired them if I'd known about it. Before I did find out, the plant manager had retired and I'd already had to fire the sales manager for his drinking. He was a real mess, which is what happens when you've got someone covering for your drinking like that. If he'd been fired ten years sooner, maybe it would have turned him around. Instead, his drinking killed him.

There are some con artists I've met who just thoroughly enjoy stealing. They were personable and had all sorts of skills, but ripping people off was just so much fun, that's what they wanted to do.

Remember the guy I had to shake down for the $300 he owed me on my Sportsman so I could marry Donna? That was D.J. Wymer. I first met him when I was working at Blackhawk. He was Blackhawk's sales manager on the road, a nice looking guy with a super personality.

His scam was that he'd tow a demonstration trailer behind his car on the road and sell it. He'd endorse the check to whoever it was made out to and go to the bank, cash it and take the money. The manufacturer who sent him out with the trailer wasn't getting paid, but D.J. would come back with a story about how the dealer didn't have the money but would send a check soon, and that the dealer intended to buy a bunch of trailers. Usually the dealer actually would.

Meanwhile, D.J. would do the same thing with another trailer and another dealer, and would use the money from that to pay back the money he took on the first trailer. He'd be working four or five dealers like that, and be staying two trailers ahead on the scam. The ruse wasn't necessary at all because D.J. could have made the same money if he'd just put as much effort into selling the product.

One time, he went to work for my buddy Doug Caruthers at Viking. Doug knew what kind of guy D.J. was, but Doug was in a spot and had some trailers he needed to get rid of. So

D.J. hauled a trailer off to Oregon and sold it to a dealer, got the money and kept the trailer too, telling the dealer it had some flaws, and that he'd bring him a better one from the factory. Then D.J. took the damn trailer down the road 100 miles and sold it again.

This was all going-to-jail stuff. Understandably, D.J. disappeared and Doug was stuck for the two trailers. A couple of months went by and D.J. came wandering in to Doug's place and said, "Hey, how ya doing? I've got some time. You need any trailers sold?"

Doug ripped into the guy, "You son of a bitch! Where's my money? Where are my trailers" and on and on. But within ten minutes D.J. had Doug eating out of his hand again, so that everything was alright and he was going to help Doug sell some trailers.

D.J. carried on like that for years, and I just got the biggest kick out of it. I'd see him, and he'd just laugh and laugh about what he was doing. There's a very thin line between a salesman and a con man.

There was a dealer in Kennewick, Washington with whom we did business who called himself the Mad Turk. That was pretty much truth in advertising. All he needed was a turban and a sword and he'd have been carving up infidels.

I first met him when I was driving around up there in a howling wind trying to unload a trailer so I could get on home. He bought the trailer, and I was glad for that, but it didn't take me too long to find out what he was about.

The Mad Turk had a bunkhouse on his sales lot and would offer showers and beds to the trailer haulers who delivered to him. Through cozying up to them, he'd get all the skinny about what was going on in Elkhart, which is where most of his trailers were coming from then, since Kennewick is in far eastern Washington. He'd find out which manufacturers had a surplus of trailers they really needed to unload.

When he'd call the factory, they'd think he was their

savior. He'd say, "Hey, a guy just happened through here who's living in one of your trailers, and I sure liked it. Is there any chance of carrying your line here in Kennewick?"

They'd say, "Sure, no problem." They'd send a trailer out and he'd pay for it right away, C.O.D. A day or two later he'd call up and say, "Oh, that's the greatest trailer ever! I sold that the next day, it's gone! Send me three more!" So they'd send out three more, but they'd seen the last of his money. He'd price their trailers below wholesale and blow them off his lot quick.

The manufacturer would want to get paid, but the Turk would bitch and moan about how defective the trailers were, how he had to dump them at a loss, and how he wasn't going to pay for them. It was a long ways from Elkhart to Kennewick, so the manufacturers would settle for 50 cents on the dollar. That was how the Turk typically ran his business, and how he sold his trailers cheaper than anyone in town and still made a killing.

I knew his act, but was selling him my trailers. I had been careful to set it up, so that when my driver delivered a trailer to the Turk, he'd go right to the bank and get the money. But somehow, as much as I knew how the Turk was, he got to me for a couple of trailers. He stopped payment on the check before the driver could get to the bank. I tried to collect the money and he stonewalled me. I hired an attorney in the county seat, Prosser, and sued him. I had to testify in court.

The judge awarded in my favor, attorney's expenses and the whole kiboodle. I didn't hang around to enjoy my victory, though. My attorney told me, "You'd better get out of here, because this guy is crazy. I think he might kill you." I don't know if he was a Turk, but boy was he mad. He was standing, glowering in the courtroom, turning so red that you could have glued claws on him and sold him as a lobster. I went out the back door of the courthouse and headed south.

The most crooked dealer I ever dealt with was one I

met up with much later, in the 1960s. Fleetwood always sold for cash and got the money up front, but somehow this particular dealer in Scottsdale, Arizona got into us for three trailers, about $12,000. We'd hired a collection agency, but they didn't get us any satisfaction. By the '60s, $12,000 wasn't that big a deal to the company, but it was a challenge to me because we'd never been beat out of any money. So I jumped in the car and drove to Phoenix, taking my friend John Cummings, who dressed for the trip in a trench coat and snap-brim hat, looking like a gunsel.

I hired a private detective to do a rundown on the dealer. In a couple of days he came back with the damnedest report. He found that in the following week the state was going to come down on the dealer for sales tax fraud, so that didn't give us much time to get to the guy. Handily, the detective also found that, though the dealer was married and lived in Scottsdale, he had a pregnant girlfriend in an apartment in Phoenix.

This was really good, because, in addition to selling trailers, the guy was a holy roller. Every weekend he'd pull a flatbed truck in front of his location and have a band play. He'd preach the gospel. Then he'd sell some units.

I went to the dealer's office, and his old pappy was there running it. I asked to see his son, and he said he wasn't in. I said, "Well have him drop by and see me," and I gave him a card. It had the phone number of the hotel where I was staying, but for the address, I wrote down the dealer's girlfriend's apartment.

I hadn't been back in my room five minutes when the phone rang. The dealer was in a rage wanting to know how I knew about his girlfriend. I told him I wasn't looking to cause any trouble: I just wanted my money or my trailers.

I learned from him that he had the trailers stowed at the edge of town, parked right alongside a row of houses, so you would have needed a helicopter to find them.

When this guy was prosecuted, it turned out he owned a manufacturing plant down in the south. He wouldn't pay for trailers, and would tell the manufacturers they'd been stolen off his lot. He'd ship them down to Alabama, have a new serial number stamped on them, and sell them as if he'd manufactured them new. He wound up in the slammer. He could have done well on the straight and narrow, but he was bent and that was that.

A night out, 1953.

On the Little Toot, with Johnnie, Harry Aides
and 145-pound friend, 1957.

RELAXING

When Fleetwood nearly went under in 1954, I learned my lesson about not taking care of business, but I was just as careful not to go overboard in the other direction. Ever since I'd started having jobs of responsibility at Blackhawk, I'd learned how to train people and turn over responsibilities to them. I wanted to be free of responsibility so I could come and go as I pleased.

Being able to delegate allowed me the time to troubleshoot problems when they arose and to come up with new designs when we needed a home run. It also left me a lot of time to screw off.

In 1955 I bought my first little boat, a 23-foot Owens single-screw cabin cruiser, named The Little Toot after "The Little Engine That Could." I kept it in Newport Harbor, and my sons and I were always down there together. We were all over the ocean in that little thing, marlin fishing from the coast of Mexico to Santa Barbara Island.

We also took a family vacation every year, up to a month, traveling the country. Life was so different from when I was a kid, when we didn't have the money to go anywhere or even a car to go there in. When my kids came along we had two or three cars, the boat, and money to buy the kids the things I never had.

Andy had been born in Dec. of 1950, about 18 months after Johnnie. Donna had that miscarriage in between, so in the first few years we were married she was pregnant most of the time. After a while we figured out what was causing it, and we made sure she didn't get pregnant again until 1957, when she had Emily. Donna had really wanted a little girl, and that made the family complete, or so we thought until Susie came along and surprised us in 1961, making us truly complete. It was a super family.

Donna and I almost never argued about anything. In the fifties I still had to go on the road a lot, on sales trips or visiting our plants, and could be gone for two or three weeks. I'd come home from those trips—or sometimes Donna would fly out to join me—and each time it would be like a second honeymoon.

As much as I was on the road, I always wanted to get back out there with the family. When the boys were just little guys, I built a crawl-in trailer with a kitchen on the back. We tied a boat to the top, hitched it up to our '55 Mercury and took off for a month to June Lake, Yosemite, Sequoia and up to Seattle to visit my uncles. This was before there were any freeways to speak of, so we had to take our time.

It was so rare to see one of our trailers on the road then, I don't think we even bothered looking for them. This was before the freeways. We'd camp a couple of nights and then spend a night in a hotel so we could shower. To camp then, usually you'd just pull over to the side of the road.

No one ever worried about security. Even now, you rarely hear about trailers getting broken into. It could be because campers are good Samaritans, but mainly I think it's because they're all armed. You see a lot of "Protected by Smith and Wesson" stickers on trailers and motor homes.

We took a big trip in 1956 through the South to the gulf coast, then through the Ozarks, up to New York and back through the northern part of the country. Air conditioners for trailers had just come on the market, and I built one into an old chassis we had at the plant. It was an oddball thing, and was way too heavy on the hitch. We dragged it as far as Yuma, where I left it with a dealer I knew and bought a Terry from him.

We also had a new car by the time we finished that trip. We'd left in a '56 Lincoln Premier, but in New York it burned a hole in a piston and turned into little more than a luxurious smoke bomb. Right at Broadway and 42nd Street in Manhattan, it started puking out blue smoke something awful. We'd been pulling a trailer, of course, and cops on horseback had to start diverting traffic around us. The New Yorkers looked as funny to us as we probably did to them. None of them had apparently ever seen a trailer in the flesh before, and they were all running out into the middle of the street to peer into the windows.

We got the car patched up enough to make it to Harrisburg, Pennsylvania, where we had it properly torn apart. I called the Lincoln dealer in Anaheim, because I had a few things to say to him. He smoothed things over by telling me that he had a new Mark II on his allotment, and that he'd take my Premier in trade at the factory and I'd get the new Lincoln.

We picked that up at the factory outside of Detroit, and it was a gorgeous car. Even then, it sold for $10,000. Lincoln had modified their production engine to get about 100 more horsepower out of it. The seats were all custom-sewn from hides imported from England. Lincoln only built the Mark IIs for two years, '56 and '57, which is too bad because it could have been the American Rolls Royce if Ford had stuck with it.

We took several trips to South Dakota to visit Donna's aunt and uncle on their farm, which was always fun for the kids. On shorter trips, our neighbor Ed Pash and I would take the kids fishing in the High Sierras.

I also used to go up there with my old sales manager Carl Jensen. He'd had a serious gambling problem, which he quit when he quit drinking. But one time we went over to Lake Mead, and stopped on the way at the Railroad Pass Casino to get a cup of coffee. We ordered, and then Carl wandered away. I drank my coffee while his got cold. Finally, I went looking and found him in the casino, shooting craps like his life was in the balance. It was the first time he'd gambled in three years.

I said, "Hey, Carl, we should get on to the hotel and claim our reservation. It's getting kind of late."

He tore himself away. We drove to the hotel, and settled down to dinner in the dining room. He immediately told the waitress, "Bring me a cup of coffee right now!" She come back first with the setup—the knife, napkin and fork—and he exploded, "Goddamnit, I said to bring me a cup of coffee right now! C'mon, John, let's get out of this place."

I couldn't figure why he was being like this, until he drove us back to the Railroad Pass Casino. He kept on there, gambling, while I went back and slept.

He just couldn't quit. Over the years, his habit reached the point that the El Cortez Hotel in Las Vegas would keep a room for him right off the casino. One night he was gambling there, and at two in the morning he collapsed on the craps table with a heart attack. They took him to his room and called a doctor, who came around and gave him a shot of something. His wife nursed him for a couple of hours, and before dawn he was back at the crap table.

The last time I saw Carl, he'd been having more heart attacks, and had both legs amputated. I visited him, and he started right in, "Lookey here, they've got an ad where if you buy a new Caddy at McLean's Cadillac, they'll give you an insurance policy where if you die the Cadillac's paid for. I want you to take my Cadillac over and trade it in on a new one." I did, and he got his new Cadillac. About ten days later he was dead. That was Carl, slightly shady to the end.

Orange County was still rather rural in the 1950s, without too much development. The main excitement was watching Disneyland being built. I drove by it every day on the way to the plant.

Disneyland didn't exactly open with a bang. The Bank of America had made some big loans to get it going, and they were worried because the park wasn't doing very well. We banked with Bank of America, and the branch manager used to call us up and ask us to go eat lunch at Disneyland just to get some people in the door. You could shoot a cannon through the place and not hit anything. Before long, though, Walt Disney had touted the joint enough on his TV show to start filling the park.

We really had a neat six years on Beverly Lane in Garden

Grove, having parties with the neighbors and enjoying the suburban life. Our house became a hub of activity, because we had a pool and a color TV set. That latter item was a rarity, since scarcely anything was being broadcast in color, and no one knew if it was going to catch on. As a trial, RCA sold 1000 sets in the LA market, and they cost $1000. If color broadcasts didn't work out, there was an agreement in which they'd give back your money.

The first time the Rose Parade was ever shown in color, our living room was packed with neighbors watching it. It amazed me, that you could have the Rose Parade in full color in your front room, coming out of thin air.

In late 1956, I learned more about the human body than I wanted to, like how there's a tube that runs from your kidney to your bladder, and how mine was all squiggley where it should have been straight. I had developed a pain in my back, and when they X-rayed me, they found the screwed up tube. If they didn't fix it, I was in danger of having a swimming pool-shaped kidney.

The problem was discovered in mid-December and they weren't able to schedule the surgery until mid-January of 1957. That was a nervous wait. The operation itself was a long, exhausting thing, and experimental at the time. If the surgery didn't work they were going to have to go in again and take out my kidney.

I was eight weeks recovering at home in a hospital bed, with tubes in me to drain my kidney. It hurt like a son of a bitch to laugh, but every evening I'd be waiting for my neighbor Eddie Pash to come by and tell me a joke on his way home from work.

For those weeks, I lay there and read Winston Churchill's books. Before that, I couldn't even really read, as far as my attention-span went. I never got into a book. But I was interested in World War II and devoured all six volumes Churchill wrote. That started a love of reading that's still with me. I only just read *Catcher in the Rye* at age 74.

As soon as I recovered that Spring, my family and the Pashes and their boys took a Caribbean trip on a freighter. First, though, we had to get our shots.

I'd had my first malaria shot when I was in Navy boot camp. It gives you a good touch of the disease. You get the fever and chills and feel like warmed over shit. They'd given everyone in the barracks the shots at the same time, and we had 160 guys lying there moaning and wondering if they were going to die. Some of the guys went off their rocker and went running up and down the hall screaming until they were tied down.

And before our Caribbean trip our family doctor did the same thing, giving the whole family that shot at the same time. That night Donna and I were so sick we didn't know if we were coming or going, and both boys were sick. Why not give the shot to us two at a time so we could take care of each other?

After we recovered, the two families took a pair of cars to Galveston, where we caught a freighter to Venezuela. There weren't any cruise ships then, just the luxury liners that crossed the Atlantic. Freighters would take on a limited number of passengers, and our comfort was far from their chief concern.

The one we were on was loaded with government-giveaway powdered milk called Klim (which is *milk* spelled backwards). It was also transporting a huge metal tank to an oil instillation. Until they off-loaded it, it made the ship list to one side. As I usually do when I travel, I took a tool box onboard, and I wound up fixing doors, cabinets, the ship's washing machine, you name it.

We didn't stop at any vacation spots, mostly raunchy port towns, but it was fun anyway. Then-Vice President Richard Nixon had been to Caracas the week before we arrived, and they'd thrown eggs at him. They'd also just had a coup, so there were people walking around everywhere with machine guns. It made you a little nervous. You could understand the unrest, though, because you would see one wealthy neighborhood with fantastic houses and marble driveways, and the rest of Caracas was just hovels.

The 15 miles between the harbor to the city was traversed by a beautiful four-lane freeway. There was virtually nobody on it, because it was a toll road, while there was bumper-to-bumper traffic on the old free road. You'd see a high-rise apartment building that was barely occupied, while people were camped out on the adjacent street. There were the very, very rich, the very, very poor and nobody in between.

When Donna and I were living in our trailer in Anaheim in the late '40s, it was often so hot that we'd drive our old Model A down to Newport just to cool off. I'd see the grand boats and houses and think "Where do these people get all that fucking money?"

Then, when I got our first boat in 1955, I started spending a lot of time in Newport with the kids, and started thinking about buying a home there. I'd seen several inland that appealed to me, but Donna insisted that if she was going to have a house at the beach, she wanted one on the water where we could dock the boat. That way, she said, she'd see me once in a while.

One day in 1958 a real estate agent showed me to a house at the end of Newport's Balboa peninsula, a frigging palace with eight bathrooms and six bedrooms on a 60-foot lot with a swimming pool, that J.C. Penney heir George Hoag had built for himself. His wife had caught him shacking up with another woman and divorced him while the house was being built. As soon as the divorce was final, George married the new gal, and she wanted no part of the house because she knew it had been built for the old one.

Hoag put it on the market for $150,000. There wasn't much demand for houses in that range then. The real estate man said it couldn't hurt to make an offer, so I offered $125,000, which was a zillion dollars then, but a real bargain for this palace.

About that time, old George was drinking an awful lot,

spending most of his time at a bar overlooking the water. When the real estate man took the offer to him there, George was swacked and he just signed it. So there we were with a fully decorated and furnished waterfront behemoth for $125,000. We could well afford it, but we were used to living on the conservative side, so it was a big jump for us.

The beach was a whole different lifestyle. We missed the neighborhood in Garden Grove, but the boys were crazy about Newport, because they spent all their time on the water, surfing and sailing and all that stuff. Andy Divine and Dick Powell lived in Newport then. Richard Boone did, too, but you'd never know it because he was holed up on his boat all the time. He hired a boat-painter friend of mine to look in on him once in a while and bring him his booze.

Newport was a lot smaller and less ritzy than it is now. The fishing was very good, and the town revolved around that. There was a cannery on the peninsula, and half a dozen tackle shops and still more boatyards along the Coast Highway.

When I had first bought the Little Toot in 1955, I was working on it one Sunday with my brother Kenny, when he looked up and said, "That looks like Harry Aides." Harry was a friend of Kenny's, who I'd first met when I was 13. He'd worked his way through law school by delivering ice on Catalina Island, and he'd taken care of Loretta Christofferson's divorce when I was running around with her in 1946.

We'd all fallen out of touch with him, and there he was, right in the anchorage next to mine. I'd always admired him, and even though he was at least 30 years older than me, we became close friends from that point on. Sometimes, we'd be out marlin fishing four days a week in the Little Toot.

We both wanted a bigger boat, and we got one in a roundabout way, by buying a Renault dealership. By 1957, the VW Beetle had interested Americans a bit in import cars. A fellow in Anaheim came to me wanting to sell his faltering Renault dealership. Harry and I bought it out for next to nothing,

Hard at work with Fleetwood president Dale Skinner, 1959.

Launching the Prowler in Newport Harbor, 1959. Charley
Raye is at the piano. Donna stands between aristocrat
hipster MC Lord Buckley and the Rev. Ed Smith.

Donna with Chuck Connors and his wife, Kamela, in Cabo
San Lucas in the early 1960s.

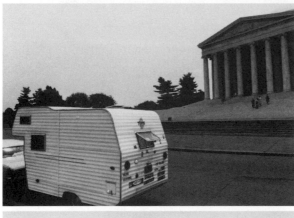

Seeing
America
by trailer,
1960.

and set up a system that worked for the place.

We were getting 15 Renault Dauphines a month and we were getting full sticker for them. The lot's problem had been its trade-ins, which just sat there, accumulating. Harry and I started a new policy where, if the salesman took a trade-in, he wouldn't get paid his commission on the Renault until the trade-in was sold. And if they hadn't sold it in a week, we sent it out to auction. That lit enough of a fire under them to take care of that problem.

We dumped the agency after a year and a half, because Renault started flooding the market with their stuff, but in that time Harry and I made enough to build a 31-foot sportfisher, which we named the Prowler.

We made it at a boatyard in Seal Beach where they'd construct the hull and house of a boat, and you'd build the rest. We put in the engines, electronics, cabinets, the mechanical things and everything else. It was a long project but it was a great family experience.

We had a big launching party on May 24, 1959, with hula dancers and my pianist pal Charley Raye and his combo (This was only five months before Charley died in a plane crash). Charley brought along a friend to MC the event, the hipster raconteur Lord Buckley, which was sort of like having Jack Kerouac officiate at your Kiwanis meeting.

In 1961 I wanted a boat that could better travel long distances, and built the 42-foot Prowler II. It was a twin screw diesel, employing new lightweight aluminum engines that had been developed by the P&H Company in Michigan. The idea of the engines was good, but they just didn't work. You'd find that out while stalled in the middle of the ocean. I spent the first couple of trips down to Cabo San Lucas in the engine room most of the time.

I've since learned that if you want to relax, you go to the desert, because that old ocean won't let you rest. It's always active, and there's always something going wrong on a boat.

I once was invited to go pheasant hunting with some fellows from our plant in Idaho. They gave me a shotgun and we went out to a corn field, where the stalks were all laying in piles. I was walking along and a pheasant flew up from one of these cornstalk piles, and I just up and, *blam*, hit the thing. The bird went down and one of the dogs dropped it at my feet. It was a beautiful cock pheasant and I immediately felt bad. What did I shoot a pretty thing like that for? It soured me on hunting.

That never bothered me at sea, though. I'll go out and kill fish right and left and never give it a thought. In 1957, I landed a 200 pound marlin after a four-hour fight. An experience like that hooks you as much as it does the fish. That marlin hung for years in the Balboa Market.

We had some pretty weird neighbors, like the Carvers. They lived in the house surf guitarist Dick Dale later owned. The old man worked for Ford Aeronutronics while his wife, Marge, was kind of a beatnik type. There was a hipster coffee house on the peninsula called the Prison of Socrates. She'd take her 11 year old kid in there to play guitar and sing folk songs.

Donna became friends with Marge and, with three other women, started going to a physical therapist who had them doing exercises and Tahitian dance three times a week. The therapist, Joiselle Brand, had worked for the Paramount studio in Hollywood, getting their starlets in shape. I went to her for a while, learning yoga stretches for my back.

It was a real wonder what she did for the gals. They each lost about 30 pounds and worked out until they really had great bodies. And all five of them got pregnant, with daughters. That's when Donna had Susie in 1961.

Things were going so well at the company that I didn't really have a lot to do, so in 1961 I enrolled at Orange Coast College, the local junior college, taking history, speech and English. That's where I started reading Steinbeck, which I think is some of the best stuff ever. It wasn't part of the studies. In one of my classes, a girl sitting next to me was giggling and carrying on so much over a copy of *Sweet Thursday* that I became interested in it. She loaned it to me, and I got such a kick out of it that I read everything Steinbeck wrote.

I took the speech class because I was scared to death to speak in public. It only helped when I was in class, though. I was 36 then, and most of the kids in class were 18 or 19. Debating them was a piece of cake. Out in the world, though, I could never bring myself to prepare for a speech, and I wasn't comfortable with it for years.

In 1961 I got into racing again briefly, driving formula junior cars. In April of '62, I raced against Steve McQueen, but I'd lost my edge. Those cars were too small and too fast, and it had been too long since I'd raced.

This'll stop you even faster than a parachute.
In New Mexico, after losing a race to a dust devil.

Conquering the Alps in a VW bus, 1964.

Donna in Greece (and a mini-skirt),
with Red and Virginia Caruthers.

Doing yoga in Austria in 1966,
as our new Porsche 911 awaits.

Trying to remember if this is my bait or my catch.
At sea in the 1960s.

THE CREAN, CREAN GRASS OF HOME

I was so good at delegating authority at work that I followed suit at home. Donna was in charge of the kids and most of the household decisions. The bigger decisions were mine, but I don't think I ever did anything drastic without discussing it with her first.

When we were living in Newport, Donna wanted to send the boys to military school, where she thought they'd get a better education and learn discipline. I would have rather had them at home, but I let Donna make that call. From junior high through high school they went to military school. There was one year when they decided they wanted to go to public school, so they came home for a semester, and decided they didn't like it any more than they did military school.

Johnnie and Andy had different personalities. Johnnie would rush into things like he knew what he was doing, and was always getting himself into trouble, whereas Andy was very cautious about anything he did. He'd examine a situation before he'd get stuck in it. Johnnie was always self-assured, to the point of being a smart-ass, while Andy was more humble. As a result, he didn't appear to be as sharp as Johnnie was, but he was, in a much quieter way.

Andy was able to keep his composure and stay out of trouble. If he got caught doing something, he'd calmly talk his way out of it. Johnnie would look and act so guilty he could never get out of it. Johnnie would actually pound his head on the pavement sometimes. If Andy stole money out of Donna's purse, he'd come home with stuff he'd bought and Donna would ask him where he got the money. "Oh, I found it in the street." You knew damn well he was lying, but you couldn't really nail him. I don't think I ever paddled Andy, but Johnnie got it a couple of times.

We didn't spoil them. Though we were well off we were

fairly conservative and didn't put on a lot of airs. The place where the boys did pick up some attitude was at military school. They'd call us saying they needed money for something or other, and we'd give it to them. What we didn't find out until later was that all the students had certain duties and Andy and Johnnie were hiring other students to do their chores. It was a bad thing for them to learn because they're still like that. If something needs to be done, the first thing that pops in their minds is, "Who can we get to do this?"

Unlike some parents, we didn't send the boys to a school to get rid of them. We loved having all our kids around, and you had better if you're going to live in a trailer with them for months at a time, which we still did every year.

Along with our cross-country trips and boat trips down to Cabo, in 1963 we expanded our roaming into Europe.

That year we arranged to buy a Porsche and a VW bus in England. The idea was that Donna and I would take the Porsche and the kids would be driven in the VW by their 18-year-old baby sitter. But she was such an airhead that she had no concept whatever of geography and it was impossible to give her directions to where we were going. So we parked the Porsche and all of us crammed into that bus as we traveled all over Europe.

I had no trouble driving on the left side of the road, but I did once decide to turn around on a narrow lane by driving through a hedge. At the cost of a bumper, I learned that it was one inch of hedge and ten inches of stone wall.

We took the ferry from Scotland to Ireland, and drove to County Cork, where my dad was from. I stopped at a phone booth to look in the book for a Crean, and found a whole page of them. I ripped the page from the phone book figuring that eventually I'd write to some of them and see if I could locate any relatives. We started north on the main route, but got off on a side road trying to reach the ruins of a castle we saw on a hilltop.

Instead, the road dead-ended in a farmyard. An old lady with big hairs growing out a mole in her face glared at us and asked "Are you English?" When we said, "No, we're from America," she brightened right up. It was clear she had no use for the English at all. We asked how to get to the castle, and she went into a tirade about Cromwell coming down through there and messing things up, like it had been yesterday.

I asked her if there were any Creans living in the area and she said, "Oh, mercy yes. There's Creans all over the place." She directed us to a pub that used to belong to a Crean. There, one of the old characters told us, "Con Crean lives right down this first lane here."

When he said lane, he meant lane. It was this overgrown goat trail a car could barely go through. After a mile of that we emerged to see a fenced farmhouse. When we drove up a red-haired woman was standing outside and we told her who we were.

Then the old man came in from the field, Con, which was short for Cornelius. He was 61 and it turned out he was my first cousin. When he walked up his wife asked him, "Can you tell who this is?" He looked me up and down and said, "You're from America?"

"Yes."

"Well you must be Andy's boy."

They were all tickled to death, and asked us in the house, which turned out to be the house my dad was born in. He had been one of ten kids, nine boys and one girl, and somehow they all grew up in this little house. There were two-rooms on the first floor, bedrooms upstairs, and no bathroom at all. They had a pot, or you could walk out in the field.

They had a phone, though, and called a couple more of my cousins, who came bouncing right over. They all went into the living room, pushed the women into the kitchen, and opened a bottle of whiskey to celebrate.

I told them, "The only one who does any drinking in my family is Donna." I opened the kitchen door and invited her in, which irked those Irish. Drinking doesn't work that way over there.

We wound up meeting several other Creans, like my cousin Ned who had a dairy and was a lot more up-to-date than Con was, meaning that he had a toilet.

It was interesting to me to find that, out of all those Creans, there wasn't one of them who worked for anybody. They were all in business for themselves.

On that same trip we also drove through Holland, Belgium, Germany, Italy and France. Then we flew to New York to see the World's Fair.

The James Bond novels were big then, and the kids would sit in the back of the VW bus reading those and not paying much attention to anything else. They liked getting Cokes and ice cream from room service too. That was Europe for them.

In 1964 Donna and I went to England by our selves. At the London Hilton, I came down to the lobby at about 11 at night, and a guy in a RAF uniform approached me. He had two tickets he couldn't use to a show starting at the Palladium at midnight. It was called the Night of 1000 Stars, and was some kind of charity event, with the Beatles, Laurence Olivier and all these other people.

I got Donna and we ran over to the Palladium. The Beatles put on quite a show—I remember them having a trapeze. But the most memorable thing that evening was that Judy Garland was in the audience. At the time she was just recovering from cutting her wrists in a suicide attempt. The MC introduced Judy, she stood up in the box and took a bow, and everybody just went crazy clapping. She'd start to sit down, and the instant the applause started to die down, she'd stand up again. It was amazing how she worked that audience. Then they insisted she come down onstage and perform, and she must have been on for an hour, setting back all the scheduled performances. It went until 4 a.m.

I had to go to Europe again the following year, 1965. Roy Clayton had retired to Cannes after I bought Terry Coach from him. From there, he'd ordered his attorney to sue us, demanding $100,000 some insurance company had paid to Terry Coach that Roy thought should be his. He had no case at all, because he'd signed an agreement that any money due Terry became ours after the sale. But our lawyers couldn't even get him to look at the documents. He was just pissed-off and wanted to sue.

I went over there because I was about the only person Roy was willing to talk to about it. The business didn't take long, because as soon as I showed him what was what, it was all settled.

Then it was fun time. I'd brought my friend John Cummings along with me. We rented a car and drove through the Alps to Stuttgart, where I bought a dark blue Porsche 911, which had just come out. We were really wailin' on the rest of that trip. John kept telling me how he always wanted to see the Rhine, and what little he saw of it was at 125 mph.

The following year I went over with Donna and bought a first-year 911-S. When it came time to ship it home, one guy we talked to suggested, "Why don't you buy a ticket on the Queen Elizabeth and take the Porsche as baggage? You'll have it home in five days." That sounded good, and, sure enough, a first class ticket home wasn't all that much, and the car was just a couple of hundred dollars more. That's a pretty good carry-on allowance.

In 1969 we did that in reverse. I had a Rolls Royce that I thought would be fun to take to England. We were living in San Juan Capistrano then, and had become friends with a musician, Arie Rozeboom, who was sort of a Dutch mariachi at the El Adobe restaurant. Eventually he came to work for me at the ranch. We'd been planning the Europe trip with Red Caruthers and his wife, Virginia. We decided to do the trip in a pair of little MGB-GTs, with Arie following us in the Rolls as the pack mule.

First, Arie and I had to drive the Rolls to New York to catch the Queen Elizabeth. At the time I was having problems with my manager at the Waco, Texas plant. I told him I was driving cross-country in the Rolls, and if he'd meet me in Denver, he could ride with us and we'd talk things over, which we did. That's my idea of taking a meeting.

Arie and I took turns driving, and whenever we'd stop he'd get out his guitar and sing "Gentle on my Mind" and a lot of Dylan stuff, which wasn't made any more intelligible by a Dutch accent.

In London, we picked up the MGB-GTs, which we had equipped with illegal CB radios. A parcel of mail had come to our house right before we left on the trip. We couldn't be bothered opening it, so Donna threw it in a suitcase with a bunch of extra junk, and we motored about with that in the trunk of the Rolls. After several days in England, I started going through the mail, and found that one envelope contained 15 $100,000 bearer bonds. They were as liquid as cash, so we'd been sleeping soundly in the hotels while $1.5 million was just sitting there in the Rolls.

I'd bought them to pay the $1.5 million in taxes I owed that year. The firm I'd purchased them from should have delivered them to us in a Brinks truck. It took forever to find a firm in England that would send them back for us. When I told Arie about the money he'd been hauling, he said, "Shit, if I'd known that, I'd have been gone," and he would have too, in a minute.

Those MGs topped-out at 105 MPH, and that's where we had them most of the time on the Autobahn. Then, at one spot in France we got in a race with a couple in a Ferrari. We'd pass him when we were going through a town or in the hills, but on the big, long straights, his car was good for way over 105. We kept passing each other for a while, until he passed us

No, we're not heading to San Francisco.
Arie Rozeboom and me traveling by Rolls Royce
to meet the Queen Elizabeth in New York.

My actor friend Pat Hawley and me, looking for someone to
kick sand on at Huntington Beach, 1966. Pat was one of the
stars of my third movie *Moment of Truth.*^

for the last time on a straight-away heading into Switzerland. The road took some sudden turns, though, and we came around a corner and could see these big black marks in the road from where he'd spun out, doing three 360s. The couple was out of their car by the side of the road and you could see the guy's wife or girlfriend there just screaming at him. We tooted as we went by.

The '60s was supposed to be a tumultuous time, but it didn't effect me much. I was upset about Johnson's Great Society and the way we were handling the Vietnam War, which I think should have been all or nothing. But mainly, I was working or out on the ocean.

Our kids were pretty good. A lot of their contemporaries, who probably had a better upbringing than our kids did, went off the deep end on drugs, but our kids never got into that.

To me all the hippie stuff was just funny, a bunch of wackos. I probably would have been one of them if I'd come up then. It was an adventure for kids, and I'm sure most of them came around, if they had any brains left after all those drugs.

Johnnie and Andy were both draft age, but they were in college for much of the war, and had the student deferment that everyone else did.

All my kids married young. Johnnie was only about 18, and his wife, Linda, was maybe 16, but they made it work. Andy met a girl from Pasadena while he was a student at Baylor in Texas, and they married. After a couple of years she got into the hippie culture and left him. That kind of ripped Andy up and he hung out single for a couple of years until he met his wife Charlene. They've had three children now and are doing just fine.

As I mentioned, by 1969 we were living in San Juan Capistrano, the place the swallows return to every year.

We'd moved out of the Newport house in 1965, because some woman had driven by the house and wanted to buy it in the worst way. In this case, the worst way was $225,000, which was a lot more than it was worth. All the furniture was worn out by then and the boys had pretty well banged things up. So we just went ahead and sold it.

Initially, we moved into a new apartment building on the peninsula, knocking out a wall between two apartments to make a single big one. I found I didn't like apartment living at all. I don't think humans were built to live like that. Everybody needs to have a little real estate. We felt like we were living in somebody else's house.

Donna had got into playing bridge with a bunch of gals out in Riverside where the plant was, and I was also driving out there all the time. So after about a year in the apartment, we bought a place in Riverside.

We immediately hated that, too. It was hot, nasty and smoggy out there, and we were burglarized three times. Donna had a housekeeper, and, as the police later told us, her son was bad news. He knew when we were gone, and he and his buddies would go through the place. Along with what they stole, they broke and tore up a lot of stuff, and that's a real intrusion on your lives. At least one of the guys got zapped pretty good, though. He'd taken a kitchen knife to slice through the stereo's speaker wires and cut into the AC cord as well. We found the knife lying there with the handle burnt.

Around that time we had some extra money and Donna didn't have much to do, so I asked her, "Why don't you go out to the Lancaster-Palmdale area and buy a bunch of acreage? The way development is going, it looks like a good investment." She contacted a real estate agent and, instead, he took her to a huge property named Rancho Capistrano. It was 93 acres with an old Spanish-style house built in 1925, a guest house, a five-acre lawn, a big pool and a lake.

When Donna saw the place she went nuts for it, and she dragged me down to look at it. I agreed it was nice, but wasn't that gung-ho about it. The woman who owned the place was asking $1.2 million for it, and I thought, "Oh well, we'll shoot her an offer." I offered $750,000 for it, cash, with no termite inspection, nothing, just a seven-day escrow and the woman would be done with it.

It turns out that this woman's husband had started a saddle club on the adjacent property and he'd got to playing around with some gals there. She caught him, and in the divorce he got the saddle club and she got the ranch. So she didn't exactly have fond memories of the property. She accepted my offer, and we became the owners of Rancho Capistrano in August of 1968. So, with that and the Newport house, I guess we just followed people around profiting from their adulteries.

Fleetwood's top management in the early 1960: VP Bill Weide, Executive VP Jack Dahl, Financial VP Dave Mariner, President Dale Skinner, me and Senior VP Dan Stretch.

Mobile home life in the '60s.

We always used tiny women
to model, to make the homes look bigger.

IN THE MONEY

By 1958 things were running smoothly for Fleetwood. We'd open new plants every year, and each would be a clone of the others. Every year the company would do comfortably better: grossing $9.5 million in 1962, $13.5 million in 1964, and so on.

Like in the car industry, dealers expected our models to change every year. I'd work full-bore on our new designs, but, aside from that, I would only turn up at Fleetwood when I was needed.

In late 1963 we moved our headquarters to Riverside, east of Los Angeles. We'd been landlocked on four acres in Anaheim with no room to grow, and property was cheap in Riverside. Though the new site was Fleetwood's home base, it was hardly any different from our other plants. I've never been big on lavish offices, or even on a place having more filing cabinets around than absolutely necessary. The more filing cabinets a company has, it seems, the more files they have.

When Andy was a little kid, I'd become involved in the Indian Guides in Newport. Another dad there was a stockbroker. He asked me about my company, and after I told him, he said, "You ought to go public. You can sell shares and take some equity out of it."

I'd never taken anything out of the company. I'd had a salary and bonuses and that was all. He explained the entire routine to me. You needed to have at least five years of certified statements by one of the big three accounting agencies, which we fortunately already did. I started a relationship with this guy's firm, Shearson-Hammil.

By the mid-'60s, Fleetwood had reached a point where we were doing about $16 million a year, and if we had another two or three million in annual sales, we'd be big enough to qualify for a public offering. We had also accumulated an awful lot of cash. As a privately held corporation, if you had surplus cash and hadn't paid out dividends, the IRS would come in and declare a dividend, and you'd have to pay tax on it. If we went public we wouldn't have that forced dividend.

That prospect hung in the air for a while, with the sales level we needed to go public just out of grasp. One day, I was on my way to LA, and passed the Great Western Showgrounds on Atlantic, and I saw they were setting up for a trailer show. We still weren't exhibiting at the shows, but I decided to stop in and see if any of my old buddies were around.

Walking through, I came upon my former partner Roy Clayton setting up the booth for his company, Terry Coach. He was moving palm trees around, putting carpets down, huffing and puffing. I'd barely said hello when he started griping, "Goddamn, for fifteen cents I'd sell this fucking company. This is just too much."

I asked if he was serious, and he said he had somebody interested in buying it right then. I knew it was a solid offer, because the same company had approached me about selling to them. But Roy said, "They want me to work for them for five years, but I've got glaucoma pretty bad and don't want to do that."

He wanted $1.5 million for the company and said his sales were between $3 and $4 million a year with earnings of $400,000. I told him, "If that's all accurate, *I'll* buy it." In no time at all, we consummated the deal, in November of 1964.

I went over to Terry Coach one morning to get acquainted with the personnel, who largely turned out to be a great bunch. The purchasing manager, though, was the same son of a bitch who had been taking kickbacks at Kit Trailers back in my Venetian blind days. When I went in to see the guy, he started laying this whole ego package on me, saying, "Before I agree to stay, I'm going to have to have this, that and the other thing…"

I said, "Tom, I have news for you: You ain't going to stay. In fact, get your ass out of here right now."

"What do you mean?"

"Well, I don't think I can use you." And that was that.

Buying Terry gave us enough sales and earnings to go public. In 1965 we did, and sold $2.5 million of stock, about 15 percent of the company, on Wall Street. I'd been the sole proprietor, so that meant Donna and I got $2 million dollars— $1.3 million after taxes—and we became official millionaires (the other half-million went to the company). That was really an exciting time. We flew to New York with Red Caruthers and his wife, and watched Fleetwood go up on the big board at the stock exchange as people started to buy the stock.

Later, from the high-rise Wall Street building where Donna and I were handed our check for $2 million, I was able to look out the window and see the Seamen's Church Institute flophouse where I'd stayed, drunk and broke, for two nights 20 years earlier.

After the stock sale, we started increasing production, because we grew like crazy. The price of the stock went up, up and up. We sold some more shares and, between 1965 and 1971, I received over $15 million from Wall Street.

Another factor contributing to our growth was that, unlike the rest of the economy, we kept lowering our prices. Between the late '50s and the early '60s, we decreased our prices 11 times. We were able to do that due to production efficiency and volume purchasing.

Not too long after the first stock sale, we started doing trade shows again and advertising a little more. We had ten plants at the time, and they all adhered to our policy of limited production. But that reached a point where our backorder situation was ridiculous: Dealers were so sold-out of Fleetwoods that they weren't even able to keep a unit on display.

Our Georgia plant was the worst. They were building

ten trailers a week and had backorders for 150. We finally gave the OK for them to increase production. Right away, they were building and selling 20 a week, and, boy, did we have earnings, because our overhead hadn't gotten any higher, and we'd doubled our production. We did the same thing at all our other plants, and then started increasing it above that.

Before long, instead of having a shortage of product all the time, we had modest surpluses that required us to start doing a little selling. It made sense at the time because the income we had from the extra volume paid for it. Our advertising brochures got a little fancier. Incidentally, to make our mobile home interiors look roomy in our ads, we'd always hire little, bitty gals to model in the photos.

Going public changed the structure of the company. Now we had a seven-member board of directors. The picks were my call. All I looked for in a director was someone I could trust, and who would trust me enough that I didn't have to convince them of every detail when I wanted the company to go a certain way.

I've sat on numerous corporate boards over the years, and I've tried to be that sort of member. I was on Georgia Fontiere's board for the Rams for years. Our job was to make it look like it wasn't a one-woman team, which it was. I think I may still even be on the board now that they've moved to St. Louis. Georgia told me that she liked that I was the only board member who never offered her any advice. I just went and ate the hot dogs.

The Fleetwood board didn't direct the company very much. Typically, the operating management would come up with programs they thought would be a good thing for the company, and we'd just approve them or disapprove them. About the only time we'd turn something down was if it was against company policy. In those cases, it was usually management coming up with new ways to cloak debt, because they really missed being able to borrow money the way other

Two years after going public, we went on the New York Stock Exchange in 1967. Nelson Potter, Red Caruthers, Jack Dahl, Dale Skinner, some stock exchange guy, me, Bill Weide, Dave Mariner and a total stranger.

companies did.

Since the mid-'50s, when I had bailed out of my partnerships with Speed, Carl Jensen and the others, Fleetwood had only been in the mobile home business, making the kind of units people used for permanent dwellings. With the acquisition of Terry Coach we were also now back in the recreational vehicle business, making travel trailers.

We kept making them under the Terry name (We didn't affix the small "By Fleetwood" logo to our various lines until 1978) at their El Monte factory because they had a good thing going. The Terry design guys had been tutored by Roy, and he was a terrific product man. They were from the old school, guys like me who had started on the assembly line and knew what you could and couldn't do and what was efficient. The Terry design was good, and they were responsible for a lot of the changes on our subsequent travel trailers.

The Terry plant in El Monte was doing so well that we decided to put in an Eastern plant. We bypassed Indiana—the traditional center for the trailer business—and went all the way to Winchester, Virginia.

Travel trailers did so well on the West Coast, I think, because most people here were nomadic adventurers, or else they wouldn't have been here. The business had started in the Midwest, but it seems most of the people who bought RVs there came west. It was like an extension of the covered wagon.

But the East Coast and the South were unproven territory. We knew we could make money on mobile homes there, but weren't sure we could on travel trailers. As an insurance, we made the plant big enough that we could switch it over to building mobile homes if we had to.

When the plant opened, we found there was a strong demand. We had the whole eastern seaboard to ourselves, and did a land office business. We ended up cloning the Terry plants the way we had Fleetwood, going into Ohio, Oregon, Texas, and other states.

The Terry was a mid-range priced unit, while our success in the mobile home business had everything to do with our making a low-end unit with a lot of value in it. I decided to make a low-end travel trailer. Dale thought we should name it Prowler, after my boat. I came up with the cat logo we've used for decades.

My original design for the trailer wasn't as long-lived. From all the model airplanes I'd built, I knew you could get a tremendous amount of strength out of wood if you construct it properly. I designed the Prowler without the steel chassis that trailers typically had. It was all wood except for the hitch and a dolly arrangement where the wheels were.

I built a prototype and tested it more strenuously than we did our other units, because it was so experimental. At one point, I needed to get some weight in there to see how the floor held while I towed it. I was at our headquarters in Riverside, so I volunteered some people, and loaded the Prowler with 2,000 pounds of executive. If the unit had failed, we would have needed a new management team.

It tested out fine. We went on the market with it in January of 1966, and it sold great guns.

The Prowler was inexpensive to make, was several hundred pounds lighter than similar trailers, and, as we found after we'd sold several hundred of them, lots of them split right in two.

The care I'd taken in the wood joining in the prototype made a strong structure. But the work wasn't as consistent in production, so glue joints broke loose and hitches started pulling up. About 25 percent of the units we sold went bad and we wound up having to retrofit a steel frame under them.

When you're the boss you can experiment and try new things like that, where if you're an employee you might hold back for fear of getting criticized or canned.

It all worked out for the best anyway, because with those first several hundred units we established dealers and a huge

The first Prowler, introduced in 1966. A great little trailer,
except for the little matter of it falling apart. Once we worked
the bugs out, it went on to dominate the industry.

Camping in style.

market share. The fact that we fixed all the problem units without giving anyone any hassle earned us a lot of points with the dealers and the public. Manufacturers were famous for not being very responsible with their warranties.

(By then we'd expanded on our bare-bones warranty of the '50s. Today Fleetwood buyers get a printed warranty that says everything works and will keep working. If they have a problem within a year, the dealer will fix it and bill the company. If it's after a year, owners bring them to a plant, and the plant will keep fixing them until they're five or six years old. It's a company policy that's kept Fleetwood in good stead with the customers.)

After my design had its problems, the Terry guys jumped in and designed a new Prowler that was more or less a low-end Terry, and they were fine for the price.

When people buy something inexpensive they think they're saving money. In most cases, they're not, they're just spending less and getting less. If a Terry had 5" seat cushions, the Prowler had 4". There's no magic in manufacturing. But the Prowler was still a lot of trailer for the money, because of the efficiency we'd learned from building low-end mobile homes. The floor plans were good, if nothing revolutionary, and we didn't leave out things that people would need, because then they wouldn't be saving anything, since it costs a lot more to retrofit.

We came on the market with the new Prowlers right on the heels of the disastrous model, and it was a huge success.

There was a large company near the Bay Area called Aristocrat that up until then had cornered the business in lower priced trailers. They had a huge production rate and a good plant operation.

We were just starting to get some of Aristocrat's business when they had a strike, a union organizational attempt. The owner simply shut the plant down and locked it up. His dealers had no merchandise, and they turned to us. We jumped to first place in sales right away. When Aristocrat's owner got past the strike and came back, he'd lost it. He was just making a comeback when some big company bought his business. In six months they put it in the toilet. The Prowler has stayed in first place in sales nationally since 1968.

In 1967 we also started another line of mobile homes, called Broadmore, that were an upgrade from the low-cost Fleetwoods. I took the bill of materials on the Fleetwood and added $300 to it, making changes that were all visible improvements. It was an immediate success and we soon had five Broadmore plants that did very well for a few years.

It was my policy to give my managers more autonomy than most CEOs have, and usually they were up to the responsibility. Every so often, though, things would get out of whack. The Broadmore line, for example, kept getting more upscale, and more expensive, and they kept adding different models. Before long, most of the plants were running at a loss, and Dale wanted to close them.

I took off in my Porsche 911 and went to the plants: Texas, Georgia, Ohio and all. By the time I was heading to the Idaho plant it was pretty clear in my mind what we needed to do, which was go back to where we first started.

On that trip I visited a lot of dealers. Over the years, trailers had gone from being 8'-wide to 10'-wide, and most of the people building them had merely added two feet in the middle and had basically the same unit, just wider. But I saw a few units on these dealer's lots that had a new side-aisle design, where the hallway went down the side of the trailer instead of the middle, and the rooms were off the aisle.

It was a pretty darn good design, so I drew up a floor plan for a side-aisle Broadmore on graph paper. I called Dan Stretch, our national sales manager, had him get a piece of graph paper on his end, and communicated the design to him by counting it out in graph squares: so many down, so many over. That got them started building a prototype.

I did essentially what I did when Fleetwood nearly went belly-up in '54. I had the plants get rid of everything that didn't fit this one particular model, which I had dressed-up with $300 in materials over the Fleetwood model. All five plants did that, the new model was a rip-roaring success and they were back in business again.

My adventurer pal John Cummings with his ever-present ukulele, in Cabo San Lucas.

ON THE BAJA

John Cummings (whom I mentioned in my Europe and Tucson travels) was someone I had met in AA. He was married and had two kids, but he was the most footloose and fancy-free guy I knew. In his early days he'd worked for the wealthy at Newport, Rhode Island, taking care of their boats, life-guarding, and mainly having a bang-up time with his co-workers.

When he married, he couldn't carry on that lifestyle, so he got a job selling door-to-door—and was good at it—while his wife quit her teaching job and raised the kids. After their daughter married and their son was in med school, John's wife went back to teaching, and John figured there was no point in him working anymore. He knocked around Mexico a lot, hitching rides down on cargo planes, or thumbing rides and riding in truck beds, sitting on a load of lobsters or whatever. He didn't see a hell of a lot of his wife.

When I met him, he was getting on in years, with thin gray hair. He looked very Irish, though I don't know if he was Irish or not. He had an East Coast accent.

One day he came down to my boat and asked if I needed a hand. I told him I couldn't afford anybody. He said, "I just retired. Can I just come along? I'll work for nothing." I did wind up paying him a salary, which he sent to his boy in med school.

I'd have the boat down at Cabo San Lucas at the tip of Baja Mexico for two or three months in the wintertime. Donna and the kids would fly into La Paz and I'd drive over from Cabo to pick them up in a Volkswagen bus I kept down there.

Like most of the Cape, the 130-mile road between La Paz and Cabo was an unpaved coccyx-crusher. The boat builder Dale Jeffries was living down there then, and he'd set a speed record between the two towns in an Olds V8-powered custom buggy he'd built, which he named la Mula del Diablo.

One day John and I had dropped the family off at the airport, and decided to best Jeffries' four-hour speed record on the way back to Cabo. It had rained a bit, out of season, the night before. The good part of that was it settled the dust, so we were racing along back to the cape. The bad part was that usually the only way you and another vehicle could know you were coming up on each other was by the dust you kicked up.

We were making great time, doing some 13 miles-an-hour better than Jeffries had, when we came around a corner and were headed smack at a one-and-a-half ton truck loaded with oil drums. The driver did everything he could to avoid us, going clear off the road, and I did everything I could, but the left-hand corner of the VW bus still smashed into the truck bed. We didn't have seat belts, and, without really thinking, I somehow had been able to slide toward the passenger side. I'd have been squashed flat otherwise, because the steering wheel was crushed into the seat. The door was folded double, wedged in between the truck's cab and bed.

The guys in the truck were scared, because when you have an accident like that in Mexico, they throw *everybody* in jail. They were afraid we'd want to get the authorities in on it, but we let them know we'd just as soon go on our way too. We tied the back of the Volkswagen to a big cactus, and then the Mexican guys put a rope around the front panel of the bus and used the truck to pull the dashboard away from the seat. There wasn't room to sit behind the wheel, but I could crouch halfway on the passenger side and work everything. It fired up, and I could steer it.

John only had a cut on his forehead from hitting the windshield, and I didn't have a scratch on me. As we were getting ready to leave, I thought I'd mark the spot by sticking the crumpled driver's side door up on a cactus branch. I hung it on a big one, and, as I let go, the branch broke and the whole thing—door, cactus and all—hit me square in the face. By the time John got all the stickers out of my mug I looked like I'd been through a war.

Later, I had a blacksmith shop in La Paz straighten out the bus and put in a windshield. I never did get a door, but that doesn't matter so much on the Baja. You can still see the shell of the bus at the Cabo San Lucas Hotel. The owner wanted it because there was always a shortage of vehicles there, and I traded it for our tab one year. They used it for years, and then started pulling parts off it.

After making several trips down the Baja in my fishing boat, John mentioned one day that he'd always wanted to go down there the hard way, driving. There was just a rocky trail down to La Paz then, really no road to speak of. The trail was mainly there to connect the local ranches and maybe only one or two cars a week would drive the entire distance.

In 1966, Andy turned 16 and I bought him a Meyers' Manx dune buggy for Christmas. (It was built on a '61 VW chassis, with a 1200cc engine.) He didn't have much opportunity to drive it, because he was off in the Army-Navy Academy most of the time. John saw that buggy, we agreed it would be a great thing to take down the Baja, and I said, "Well, why don't we?"

John made a big production of it, going to the Mexican Tourist Bureau in Tijuana and setting up a promotion with them in which we'd attempt to establish a speed record for driving from Tijuana to La Paz.

I didn't give that much thought until, on the evening of January 18, 1967, we pulled up at the Department of Tourism on Avenida Dieciseis de Septiembre in Tijuana and found a send-off ceremony awaiting us. When we took off at midnight, in a thick fog, they gave us a motorcycle escort out of town, with sirens and the whole bit. The authorities made arrangements with the radio station in La Paz to clock us in when we got there.

It was a grueling trip. Half the time we were working

on the car. We had a couple of flats and had to dig ourselves out of the sand a few times, but our main problem was with the suspension. It was bottoming out so badly that, after going only 200 miles, I became pretty sure we weren't going to make it. But I was able to get the torsion bars loose and turn them each one serration, and that gave the suspension more travel. We only had a couple of wrenches and things, so we mainly did the work with two tools: grunting and swearing.

We worked on those suckers for 14 hours, and were so bushed when we were done that we just slept all night. Next, when we got about two-thirds of the way down the Baja, the front motor mount broke. Both the motor and transmission were flopping up and down like crazy, and the gas and clutch pedals were being actuated every time that happened. I put some chunks of wood around the motor and used a rope with a trucker's hitch tied around the roll bar to hold it still. That worked for the 150 miles into Santa Rosalia, where we got it into a welding shop.

We got into La Paz at 5:03 p.m. on January 22. Just to get the last word in, the buggy's skid plate fell off just before we got into town.

We'd lost so much time screwing around with repairs that it had taken us 88 hours and three minutes to cover the 982 miles, but never-the-less it set a record, because nobody else had ever driven down there in much under a week. (We'd crossed a time zone, so the certification has it as 89 hours instead of 88. Our actual time spent driving had been 29 hours and 17 minutes.)

It was in the newspapers down there, and quite a bit of fuss was made over it. I absented myself from the festivities. I took a shower, crashed, and slept through until late the next morning. But John, who was 62 then, was so excited about having made the run that he was carousing around town all night.

The next day, the governor of Baja Mexico held a

John Cummings beside our dune buggy, en route to setting the Tijuana-to-La Paz Baja speed record in January, 1967.

A local youth pokes our buggy with a stick, as I try to fix the suspension.

Grabbing a moment's snooze on the hood.

Being greeted by some official in Pa Paz upon completing
our Baja run. Once we set the record, others rushed to beat
it, resulting in the first Baja 1000 later that year.

The official confirmation of our record.

DEPENDENCIA DIRECCION DE TURISMO DEL ESTADO DE BAJA CALIFORNIA

SECCION   OFICINA EN TIJUANA

NUMERO DEL OFICIO   T-043

EXPEDIENTE

GOBIERNO DEL ESTADO
LIBRE Y SOBERANO
DE BAJA CALIFORNIA

ASUNTO   " ACTA DE FE "

Tijuana, B. Cfa., a 17 de enero de 1967.

"ACTA DE FE"

En la ciudad de Tijuana, Baja California, México, frente a las oficinas de la Dirección de Turismo del Estado situadas en la Ave. Revolución (Edificio Foreing Club) entre las calles 3/a y 4/a, se constituyeron los Sres. ALFREDO LOPEZ GUTIE-RREZ, JOSE LUIS ROSAS QUIROZ, ALBERTO BAROCIO MOREL y JOSE HERNANDEZ DOMINGUEZ, cuyas firmas aparecen al margen, para "DAR FE" de la hora de salida de los señores JOHN CREAN y JOHN J. CUMMINGS, - norteamericanos residentes de la población de Anaheim, California E.U.A., los que se proponen efectuar un viaje a La Paz, Baja California por la ruta terrestre en el vehículo marca Volks Wagen, modelo 1961, tipo convertible, con placas del Estado de California No. JMG-403, motor No. 3526362, con el cual tratarán de establecer un récord de tiempo entre las mencionadas poblaciones de TIJUANA-LA PAZ.

Sufragio Efectivo. No Reelección

El Director de Turismo del Edo.

Alfredo Lopes Gutierrez

Día de salida: Enero 18 de 1967

Hora de salida: 00.00 horas

The La Paz newspaper account.

"Ultimas Noticias"

DIARIO DE LA MAÑANA

UN VOCERO AL SERVICIO DEL PUEBLO

Reg. Conforme a la Ley, como artículo de Segunda Clase con fecha 2 de Marzo de 1956.

PRESTAMO
CONST
2
CONSTRUCCIO
PROYECTOS
S.

ral Arturo Sotelo y Canett.— La Paz, B. C., Martes 24 de Enero de 1967.— Administrador: Arturo Sotelo Jr.

lones de Empadronados en
ernador Continúa su Fructífe

Implantan Record Automovilístico en B.C.

Los norteamericanos John Crean y John Cummings, de Riverside Calif., a bordo de un automóvil Volkswagen reformado, manejaron día y noche para implantar una marca.

——o——

El domingo pasado, a las 17.08 hs., arribaron a esta ciudad, a bordo de un automóvil Volkswagen, los norteamericanos John C. Crean y John Cummings, que venían de piloto y copiloto respectivamente, quienes implantaron un récord de .... 89.63 hs., manejando a través de la península de Baja California. Ellos salieron el miércoles pasado de Tijuana, B. Cfa., a las 12 hs., y se levantaron actas oficiales haciendo constar su salida. Hicieron un tiempo aproxima-

do de 53 horas efectivas manejando.

El día de ayer fueron recibidos por el Sr. Gobernador en funciones, Sr. Lic. Angel César Mendoza Arámbu-

De izq. a Der. Sr. John Cummings, Lic. Angel César Mendoza Arámburo, Srio. Gral. de Gobierno; Sr. John Crean; Sr. Isidro Jordán Carlón, Oficial Mayor y el Lic. Ricardo García Soto, Jefe del Depto. de Turismo. (Foto ULTIMAS NOTICIAS).

ro, Secretario General de Gobierno, el Sr. Isidro Jordán Carlón, Oficial Mayor, y el Sr. Lic. Ricardo García Soto, Jefe de la Oficina de Turismo, en donde manifestaron entre otras cosas, que el tiempo efectuado en el viaje no es récord oficial, pero sí para implantar un tiempo exacto de recorrido, para que futuros automovilistas traten de romperlo. Añadieron el gran entusiasmo que hay en los EE. UU., principalmente California por conocer nuestra tierra, asegurando además que en unas semanas más saldrán con este destino una caravana de 8 automovilistas que tratarán de romper la marca establecida por ellos.

Es de gran importancia señalar lo manifestado por el Sr. Crean, quien expresó elogiosos comentarios para las bellezas del territorio. "He viajado dijo el Sr. Crean, por

(Pasa a la Ultima Pág.)

Exitosa Operación de la Vista al Niño Vicente Rochín

Procedente de Los Angeles, Calif., arribó a esta ciudad la Sra. Esthela Amador de Rochín, en compañía de su hijito Vicente, después de haber sometido a éste último a una delicada operación de

Sesiona el Jalisciense este día

A partir de las 8.30 de la noche del día de hoy se iniciará una sesión ordinaria más del Círculo Social Jalisciense de esta ciudad, en el

Hotel Misión de La Paz, estando a cargo de la cena el gerente del mismo hotel Mayor Luis Palos Torres.

(Pasa a la Ultima Pág.)

Exhorto

Por medio de la presente se exhorta a los presuntos

reception for us at his palace, and then there was a party at the Hotel Los Cocos. I took the occasion to predict to the local press that I expected there would someday be a full-scale race down the peninsula.

That next morning, John and I decided we'd take a trip south around the cape and come up the other side, to visit people we knew. We went down the western side and spent the night camping on the beach. Wherever John was, if there was water nearby, you could count on him going swimming at the crack of dawn. He did that the next morning, but came out of the water complaining about not feeling very well, that maybe he'd eaten something bad.

As we headed east back toward La Paz, John began complaining about being cold. Though it was 80 degrees, I put the buggy's little top and side curtains up, and he was still just shaking with chills. We got to Rancho Buena Vista, a fishing village, early in the afternoon and I said, "John, we're spending the night in the hotel here. You've just been going too damn hard." He agreed, which was unusual for him, because he loved to camp out.

The hotel served dinner at a big, long table there, family style, passing the bowls of food around. They'd heard about us making the record run down there and the tourists and locals whooped it up over that.

Come nine o'clock, I went to bed, and John stayed up talking to people, and must have turned in around midnight. The next morning, a jackhammer started up right outside our room, along with other construction noises. I looked over and John was still in bed. He slept on his right side, in a curled position. I hollered at him and got no answer.

I went over and tried to shake his shoulder, and it scared the hell out of me. John was stiff as a board. He didn't even feel like something that had ever been alive.

He had died in his sleep. When the coroner got there from Santiago, he went through John's things and found unfilled prescriptions John had from the summer before from a doctor on the mainland. That previous summer he'd been missing for a month, which wasn't so unusual for John because he'd bum around Mexico a lot. But now we found out that he'd keeled over in the street in Culiacan with a heart attack. He'd been hospitalized during that missing time, and didn't tell his wife or anyone.

They loaded John's body into an airplane and flew him to La Paz while I drove the buggy into town. I had mixed emotions then, feeling sorry he was gone, and the next minute being madder than a wet hen that he'd gone on this trip and not taken care of his heart, and not said anything to anybody about it.

He was embalmed down in La Paz. I flew back to California with him. He was buried in Anaheim near his home.

A couple of months later John's widow called and said she couldn't get the death certificate from the coroner in Santiago, and needed it to get John's Social Security benefits. I was heading down there in my boat, and when I arrived I went to the coroner's office. The coroner acted like he didn't know what I was talking about, and kept on that way until I conquered our communication problem with a $20 bill. He went over to a file drawer and pulled the death certificate right out.

We had no sooner established the speed record down to La Paz than several off-road racers followed up on it. Within 60 days, they'd broken our record by a huge margin—one driver made it in 31 hours flat. Between our January run and September, at least 13 vehicles attempted the Baja run, and seven of those never made it the full distance.

As I'd predicted, but sooner than I thought, a group of off-roaders decided to have a race on November 1, 1967. That was the Baja 1000 (originally titled the Mexican 1000 Rally), sanctioned by NORA, the National Off-Road Race Association, with permission from the Mexican government.

It was well-promoted, and 70 cars competed in that first race, everything from a Land Cruiser to a Citroen. Donna did it

This fully enclosed, Porsche 1700cc experimental car was driven by the husband and wife team of John and Donna Crean.
(Jack Brady Associates photo)

VW-Powered Manx Tops 68 Entries During Tough Mexican 1000 Rally

By Jack Brady
Contributing Editor

LA PAZ, Mex., Nov. 4 — Vic Wilson and Ted Mangels in a Volkswagen-powered Meyers Manx took top honors in the inaugural Mexican 1000 Rally, covering the 903-mile grind in a record-breaking 27 hours and 38 minutes. The Manx crew split $2275 of the $13,775 total prize and contingency money.

The old record of 31 hours by Spence Murray and Ralph Poole, set in July in a Rambler American, fell without a whimper.

The new Conquistadores of "the Road" are, appropriately enough, Californians from Costa Mesa. Their route, referred to with awe by all those who have made the trek, has changed little since the Spanish soldiers and the mission-

aries started up the peninsula of Baja California more than three centuries ago.

Probably one of the toughest motoring events since the Redex Round Australia Trial, the Mexican 1000 started at Tijuana on the Mexican border at 1am Wednesday, Nov. 1
(Continued on page 8)

From *Autoweek,* November 25, 1967.

Donna with our re-built Porsche-powered dune buggy, just prior to running the Baja race.

Donna and I chowing down in Ensenada prior to the 1968 Baja 1000.

Ray Conniff and me in the 1968 Baja 1000. It's obviously
near the beginning, since we're not filthy yet.

With Parnelli Jones, 1968. He was part
of our Baja race team, and won that year.

with me, in Andy's dune buggy. It was hardly the same vehicle, though, because we'd had it rebuilt by Indy designer Don Edmunds, who put in a Porsche industrial engine. Donna was the first woman ever to do the Baja 1000. She's a great sport about trying things like that.

Only half the cars that entered made it all the way, and of those we were nearly the last. As long as we were on reasonably smooth ground the Porsche engine went like crazy, but when the terrain grew bumpy, it would crap out. I tore it apart as best as I could, but didn't discover what the problem was until after the race. The carburetor had a needle valve that let the fuel in, but when it was jiggling it was closed two thirds of the time and the jet wasn't big enough to keep the carburetor float full. It would run out of gas and we'd just stop. Then we'd start up, and away we'd go for another five minutes.

There was an old woman who had a ranch that was one of the checkpoints on the race. About 15 miles before reaching the ranch, we blew a front tire. It was totally shot and I'd only brought spare tubcs.

We crawled into the ranch late at night, and it was teeth-chattering cold. There were maybe 15 busted cars at this ranch, and the drivers were sleeping, sprawled all over the cement floor of the ranch house.

I told Donna that we might as well forget it, that we couldn't go any farther, and should find some way to get home in the morning. She slept in the car, while I found a cement shelf in the ranch house where I could lic down.

I didn't have a blanket and it was colder than hell. I was shaking and shivering so much that my elbow was rubbed raw from bouncing on the cement. I thought, "Fuck this," and found one of the guys in there, Bruce Meyers—who'd originated the Meyers' Manx—sleeping on the floor. The old gal who ran the ranch had plenty of beer and tequila, and Bruce, like most of the guys there, was stoned out of his gourd.

I shook him awake, and said, "Hey, Bruce, can I borrow

the tires off your car? I want to keep on with the race." He never quite woke up, but said, "Yeah, yeah, yeah, go ahead, John."

I blocked up Bruce's car and got his tires on the buggy. Donna and I were off and gone, making all of 15 miles before we hit some bumpy road and the engine started crapping out again.

The next day, we were behind two young fellas in another buggy, and ended up in a box canyon that didn't go anywhere. There wasn't room to turn, so I suggested to the two guys that the three of us lift the front end of each vehicle to turn them around. They just looked at me with these buggy eyes. I don't know what they were on, but they were stoned out of their minds. They couldn't even talk. Donna and I were slowly able to rock our car around, and we left them there, staring at the canyon wall.

No one especially noticed, but we finished the race. There was a big party winding down all over La Paz by the time we got there, after 72 hours and 32 minutes.

The next year Donna and I did the Baja again in a Ford Bronco prepared for us by Bill Stroppe, who had built up my little MG when I was into sports car racing. Bill was hot and heavy into the off-road racing with Parnelli Jones then. Donna and I did a little better time with the Bronco, though, by the time we finished, we'd had three broken axles and sundry other problems.

Through a mutual friend, we loaned the fixed-up Porsche-powered dune buggy to James Garner for a race near Vegas. Then we bought into Garner's race company, American International Racing. Jim was a super guy, though he was having back problems at the time. He was as nice as he could be for a guy who was in pain all the time. He was crazy about racing.

The company looked like it would be a fun venture. We got sponsorship money from Ford and Goodyear—and later American Motors—and nearly broke even because of that. We

After the Borrego Springs race, with Johnnie, 1969.

Our team in 1969 in Ensenada before the 1000,
which Bob Bondurant (to my left) won that year.

With our racing partner James Garner.

Donna with Garner at Daytona.

ran Daytona with Corvettes. Then we got three Formula A cars from Europe.

American International Racing turned out to be a fluky deal. From what little I saw of our company's mechanics, they didn't look to be qualified. With the equipment we had, we should have been winning the races we were entering all over the country. Years later I found out that Jim was filming all this for a movie he made called *The Racing Scene*, and all the people in our pit were more actors than they were mechanics.

Though it was a sports car racing company, we did the Baja for fun. In 1969 we entered a team of ten cars. With AMC as the sponsor, we built up a four-wheel drive Rambler that came in first in two categories, the four-wheel-drive sedan class and then the all-out race with the car Bob Bonderaunt was driving. We also took the 3rd and 5th place wins in the passenger car category.

After that, I drove a couple of races with my son Johnnie. One year I went in a Rambler with Red, while Johnnie and the bandleader Ray Conniff were in the Bronco. About halfway down the Baja, in the middle of the night, Red and I got lost and wound up on a remote farm road, with no idea of how to get back on track. We finally saw some headlights approaching us from the other way, and they pulled up alongside us. Impossibly, it was Ray and Johnnie, as lost as we were.

Even so, that year was the fastest I ever made the trip, 31 hours, and we came in around 40th amid 400 cars. I think later Parnelli made it down there in 18 hours, but the equipment and the logistics were a lot better then.

AMC was pretty good to us in some ways, but in others they were real dopes. In 1968 I tried to talk them into making a four-wheel drive station wagon. It stood to reason that there were people who wanted four-wheel drive, but didn't want to have to drive a Jeep to get it. We made one wagon up for the racing team. The AMC people looked at it, said, "That's interesting," and forgot about it. They could have cornered the sports utility vehicle market decades ago.

When AMC canceled their contract with us, we still had a zillion of their cars and parts. On one of my trips to Europe I'd been impressed reading about some college kids who had made a huge stone out of paper mache and taken it up and added it to Stonehenge. It was there for ages before anybody noticed it.

I thought it would be fun to do a big piece of art like that, welding all the AMC stuff we had into a tall tower and calling it the American Motors Shaft, or maybe Chromehenge. It would have made a hell of a monument, but I guess other projects got in the way.

Off-roading wasn't the same rush that sports car racing had been for me, but it was fun, and brutal. The worst of it was one year when Johnnie and I went in the Bronco on an 800-mile race called the 7-11 near Las Vegas. It just beat you to death. The third day we were right up near the winner's circle when we had an axle break, and we got bogged in sand 15 miles from the finish line.

I shoveled and dug for an hour, trying to get out of the sand. I utterly exhausted myself, on top of being beat from the race. I gave up and lay down in the back of the Bronco, with the hose from a jug of Gatorade stuck in my mouth. I must have sucked down a half a gallon of Gatorade. By the time we'd caught a ride to the pits, I was totally goofy, didn't know what was going on from taking in all that sugar all of a sudden after exhausting myself.

At Ontario, with a Formula A car we owned.
It was wrecked in a crash not long afterward.
We used the hull as a planter on the ranch.

GOING MOBILE

Back around 1960, when we had five or six plants, there was a company in Gardena named Modernistic that was building RVs. The company's two partners called me up and invited me to lunch. There, they told me they wanted to build a plant in the East, and wanted to know how Fleetwood had managed our expansion. I wasn't making RVs then and had no plans to, so I told them exactly how we did it, how to pick an area, how to wrangle the best deal from the chambers of commerce and so on.

They followed my advice, and one of the towns they wrote to was Forest City, Iowa. It was strictly a corn town. The town undertaker, a guy named John Hansen, was on the local industrial development commission. He was instrumental in pushing the town to get Modernistic to locate its plant there.

Modernistic had their Forest City plant going less than a year before they went broke. John the undertaker was embarrassed because he'd help talk his neighbors into financing it, so he took the plant over and tried to build and sell trailers. He couldn't make it work, and was readying to close up the plant, when he got a call from a company called Lifetime Homes. They were building motor homes on Dodge chassis, and were selling them faster than they could build them. They wanted John to start building units for them at his plant.

By the time he got up to full production supplying homes to Lifetime, John said, "What do I want to be messing around with these guys for?" So he just took the motor homes he'd been building for them, slapped the name Winnebago on them and the rest is history. One little side note to that history is that years later Lifetime sued him and Winnebago had to pay them $6 million.

If it hadn't been for the two guys from Modernistic having lunch with me, there never would have been a

Winnebago, which became a real pain in the ass, because when we went into motor homes in 1968, Winnebago had the business tied up.

Winnebagos were light and performed well, but they were just a cheap four-walled box on a Dodge chassis. The company was making huge margins on them, 10 percent after taxes, which is an awful lot to an RV manufacturer. When everyone else saw the margins Winnebago was making, they jumped into the motor home business too.

I'd wanted to start building motor homes two years before we did, but it was too risky to suit Dale. By 1968, however, we were in such solid financial shape, and our sales guys were so keen on having motor homes, that we started looking around for a company to buy. It speeds your start-up if, instead of starting cold, you can acquire a company that already has product on the market.

We found a little company for sale in Anaheim building a motor home called the Pace Arrow. I bought one of their units and Donna and I took a two-week trip in it, up Highway 1 to the Bay Area. We came back thoroughly enthusiastic about their motor home, so we bought the company right away. It was a decent buy because the owner wasn't in the best of health and was looking to get out.

We moved the operation to Ontario, California and it was very successful from day one. The old Pace Arrows were good, but they weren't much to look at, just big boxes. We built their old model for one year, then we transferred some of our travel trailer design staff into the motor home division. Within a year they designed a model you didn't feel embarrassed to be seen with.

The following year they designed an 18-foot Class C— meaning a small unit built on a chopped van—which we called the Tioga. We built that in Anaheim and it was an immediate success, with 35 units a week coming out of that single plant.

At first, to make the Tioga, we had to buy a van cab

and chassis, and then chop open the back end and top of the cab. Later, Detroit began making ready-to-use van chassis for the industry.

We pretty much had to take what the auto-makers offered us. We've had some luck requesting things we've needed, but supplying the RV manufacturers is not that big a business to them. It has been getting more important to Detroit now that their competition is so tight.

For years all we could build on was a 14,500-pound capacity chassis, and they wouldn't make a bigger one for us. Finally Ford came in with a chassis that would bear 16,000 pounds, and General Motors bested that. Some will handle up to 21,000 pounds now. That's what we need. A lot of the big houses we built on the 14,500-pound chassis weren't very good.

After the Tioga, we came out with the budget Southwind line, and we opened a second motor home plant, in Decatur, Indiana. Then we went into Texas, and then opened them all over the place.

On the Southwind, we tried a different kind of construction, using a steel frame instead of wood. It was a new idea for the industry and it sounded impressive on the showroom floor, but on the road it proved to have rattles and loose insulation that fell to the bottom of the wall and became useless.

Instead of going back to the wood construction, we devised an entirely new type of steel frame which Fleetwood still uses today. We used a welded tubular steel frame, with the inner and outer skins glued to the framework. We filled the space between the skins with block foam, and sandwiched it tight on a vacuum press. That resulted in a strong, well-insulated wall. It soon became the standard in the industry, and is what is still used today.

There has always been a friendly rivalry between Fleetwood and Winnebago. I'd see John Hansen at trade shows now and then. The guy did actually look just like an undertaker. The last time I saw him was at a show at Dodger Stadium.

Later that day, he told one of my sales managers, "This year we're going to outsell you." The manager said, "Well I don't think so."

Hansen said, "I'll bet you $100,000 we do," and he went on his way. This conversation got back to me, and I tried to chase him down. I just missed him, and he left the show and flew off to Hawaii. I was trying to get to him because I was going to cover the $100,000 bet. I'd have won it, easily.

GROWING PAINS

By the late 1960s, Fleetwood was growing at such a phenomenal pace that we couldn't come close to filling all our new management positions by promoting from inside the company. It was all we could do to find qualified people anywhere and pump them through our management training program fast enough to keep up with the plants we were opening.

A good case in point is Elden Smith. In 1968 at age 28, Elden had a secure management job in the tool industry. With no trailer experience, and with his first child coming, Elden gave up that security to come into our management training program for half the salary he'd been making, because he saw opportunity there.

Elden started in the program on Dec. 9. He impressed everyone and after six weeks was asked to go into our program where we trained plant general managers. In July of 1969 he was in Hancock, Maryland, staring at an empty shell of a building on a landfill, wholly in charge of turning it into a functioning Prowler plant. He did it, and their first unit rolled off the line in late August.

Despite the problems we'd had with the early Prowlers, by January of 1970 the plant was showing a profit and Elden was making a solid bonus. In January of 1971, 2 $\frac{1}{2}$ years after starting with the company, Elden was made general manager of the entire RV division.

With so many new people needed, every year we'd have fewer in management who actually had any assembly-line trailer-building experience. Most of the new crop were business school graduates. In fact, so many of our new people came to us from our accountants, Arthur Anderson, that they accused us of poaching their staff. What actually happened was that their guys would get a look at our books and see the potential for themselves. They were clamoring to join us, with no particular encouragement from us.

I think Fleetwood and the trailer industry followed the changes that happen in almost any growing industry: it gets more professional and structured. In the early days of the trailer industry there simply was no upper management. If you were the president, you'd better also have been handy with a wrench. As the saying went, you was the horse *and* the mule.

All of Fleetwood's growth was getting to be a little hard for our president, Dale Skinner, to keep track of. He was such a stickler to detail. When we had 15 plants going—ten mobile home plants and five RV plants—Dale had a ledger pad with 15 columns in it, and in each column, he kept track of one plant. When we got the 16th plant going and he didn't have a column to put it in, it really threw him for a loop.

That was about the time computers were coming into use. I told Dale he could get one and have someone punch in all that information for him. But computers struck Dale as just one more level of confusion, in a job that was already being made needlessly complex for him.

Dale's second-in-command then was a young whiz kid named Jack Dahl, a brilliant little guy. I didn't realize it at the time, but Jack was doing everything he could to unload Dale, because he wanted Dale's job. He was making things look more complicated to Dale than they were.

One day, Jack took me aside and told me a story about when he was a young fellow in Canada, saying, "I was raised on a ranch and had an old horse I'd had ever since I was a kid. I used it to run the cattle. I just loved that horse. But my dad took me aside one day and said, 'Jack, that's a nice old horse, but to take care of the work the way it is today, you've got to get a younger horse. This horse just can't keep up.'"

So, Jack continued, "I really hated to, but I put that old horse out to pasture and got myself a new young horse and, boy, it made such a great difference."

End of story, and I'm thinking, "What the fuck has that

got to do with anything?" It didn't sink in on me at all.

This was in 1972. I didn't give Jack's story much thought until one day, not much later, when I received a call at home from Dale.

"Hey, John, I think I'd better get out of here. It's just too much and I can't handle it any longer."

"When do you think you want to go?"

"Well, today's Thursday. I'd like to leave Friday."

"Boy, is it that bad?"

"Yeah, it's just too much for me. Jack can do a lot better job than I can."

So Dale left. Jack had certainly psyched him out.

I don't know what Fleetwood would have been without Dale. He was ultraconservative in business and on top of every detail. He was the perfect foil for me, because I tended to be a bit wild, shooting off in several different directions at once, and paid hardly any attention at all to detail.

When I established Fleetwood's policy in 1955, Dale saw the wisdom of every bit of it. He practiced it to the letter, while from time to time even I'd go off it, and he'd bring me back into line. I had an awful lot of respect for him, and we made a real good balance.

Dale was very likable, very reserved, a bit on the shy side, but he had a sense of humor if you listened close enough. He enjoyed his home life so much that he'd just as soon stay home and mow the lawn as go play golf. Once he was out of the hot seat, he got to do both.

Jack Dahl was a Canadian Mormon CPA who had been one of the trainees who came to us from the Arthur Anderson company. Jack was a quick study in our training program, and he did well in every position we put him in. He'd only been with us about five years before he was situated right under Dale.

As soon as Jack got Dale out of the way and became

president, he showed a lot of ambition, and for a while I thought that was fine. But he really got the hots to become a player on Wall Street. The price of stocks was everything to him.

About that time, the market was flying high, and Jack got off a $40 million public offering of Fleetwood stock, at a high price.

With that money, he started some 20 new plants in a year, but they had poorly-trained people in them and the plants were losing money like crazy. We had enough good plants to keep us in the black, but it was quickly turning into a bad situation.

I stepped back into the picture and told Jack, "OK, knock it off. No more new plants." And he said that was fine. Then within a couple of weeks he'd opened yet another plant in Canada.

I went to his office and said, "What the hell are you doing? You agreed you weren't going to open any more plants." And he said it was an especially good market and bla, bla bla, and fluffed the whole thing off. From that time on, Jack and I clashed on policy. He was merely trying to pump up the price of the stock and wasn't watching what was important to me, the product and its quality.

It finally came to a head in February of 1973. One of our top managers' wives had caught her husband playing with his secretary. Jack didn't know what to do about that. He called a meeting of the executive committee of our top managers to take a vote about what to do with the guy. They decided to fire him.

When I heard about Jack taking a vote on that, as far as I was concerned, that was the end. That's not the way it's done. When you're in charge, if a guy's done something for which you think he should be fired, you fire him. You don't call a meeting. What it came down to was that Jack couldn't handle that much responsibility. (And, in the case of this manager playing hanky panky, I don't think I would have done anything.

The affair was the wife's business and none of ours.)

I called Jack in and told him, "You're just not going in the direction I want to go. You have to get out of here."

Just to try to soften things a bit, I added, "It's never easy to fire anyone. You know how it is."

And he said, "No, I've never fired anybody." That pretty much told the story right there. He'd had to get the committee together because he couldn't take it on himself.

Jack wanted to hang around in the job a while, but I told him, "You can get out of here right away." That same afternoon I appointed Bill Weide president. In the next two weeks Bill closed down most of those 20 plants (we either sold them off or reopened them at a more opportune time) and pared things down to where we only had the profitable plants. Of the $40 million we'd taken in from the stock offering, we'd pissed away nearly all of it in opening and closing Jack's new plants.

Nobody, particularly those in the financial community, could understand why I fired Jack. Within a week he had another job that was just as good with another company, as CEO of Guerdon Industries, a mobile home company of about our size. Guerdon wasn't in good shape when he got there, but in six months he put it thoroughly in the toilet and got fired. Then he got a job with one of our suppliers, Roland Sahm, and he didn't last at that job either. He was a brilliant guy, but his ego was too big.

Our biggest business at that time was mobile homes. When we'd gone into motor homes, Jack (who was still under Dale then) had strongly opposed that, but I insisted, because I liked the looks of the business.

About the time Jack got fired from Guerdon, I got a nasty letter from him, telling me what a jerk I was. Motor homes were on a downturn—this was probably during the oil crunch— so Jack also wrote, "I was right when I said motor homes were not a thing to get into." He wasn't right for long on that, since motor homes have been a huge winner for us for decades now.

At the time I just stuck the letter in an envelope and mailed it back to him, writing, "Jack, you'd better re-read this letter and think about it."

Bill Weide was exactly what the company needed after Jack. Bill was gracious and much more human, a great people person. He was always very fair. If he had to scold somebody, he had a way of doing it in which it actually helped the guy. He made a huge difference in the company, where morale was low because Jack had been so difficult and hardly anybody liked him.

Everybody liked Bill and he did a dynamite job as president. He got Fleetwood back to the way it had been under Dale. Bill had been with us since 1958, and had done a tremendous job of setting up new plants, negotiating contracts and handling all our union problems.

He was president for ten years. When he decided he wanted to retire, he spent two years grooming an understudy, Glenn Kummer, for the job, so it seemed to make a smooth transition.

Posters from the two
Hollywood movies I
produced in the early
1970s.

HOLLYWOOD HAMMERLOCK

Since Donna and I were very well-off by the time the 1970s rolled around, people were always trying to get us to invest in one thing or another. We had a bookkeeper named Melba working at our Capistrano ranch. One day in 1971, Melba had a call from someone who wanted us to bankroll a Liz Taylor/ Richard Burton picture. I wasn't much interested, but Melba was, and she kept bugging me about it. I called the party, Alex Lucas, and talked to him. He made film making sound like it might be fun. But, it turned out to be an Oscar-sized pain in the ass.

Once I decided to become a producer, I started a company, called J. Cornelius Crean Productions. I used my middle name because I wanted to distance myself from it a bit, and because the·moniker was in keeping with the tarted-up company names Hollywood was using then. We wound up producing three movies.

The Liz and Dick one was a weird picture called *Hammersmith is Out* in which Burton was more or less the Devil, but a low-budget one. He gets Beau Bridges (Robert Redford had turned down the role), to let him out of a mental institution run by Peter Ustinov, promising to make him rich and strong. When Beau wants a snazzy car, the Devil doesn't make one materialize; instead they go to a drive-in and Burton snaps some guy's neck and steals his car. Beau gets to hump Liz Taylor on top of a pile of tomatoes, and that's about the most that can be said for the picture.

Hammersmith looked good on paper, though. One of the biographies of Burton said he had really high hopes for it, but Richard had high hopes for everything. He was just a guy with a positive nature. And he was right. It could have been an interesting film if Ustinov hadn't directed it and entirely screwed it up.

Burton was really charming, which was great considering that we didn't meet on the best of terms.

The guy who had orchestrated our involvement, Alex Lucas, turned out to be one of those people who couldn't even tell you the time of day without tacking on a couple of hours for himself. Virtually every thing he said turned out to not be true. For example, when he first talked to me, he told me he had the Burtons signed, when they hadn't agreed to the picture at all yet.

After I'd signed on, and Ustinov had already done some pre-production work, I found out that Alex had lied one more time about something big, and I made up my mind that I wasn't going to be involved with him in anything. I wanted out, and would rather have walked away from my investment than dealt any further with that liar.

I scheduled a meeting with Alex at the Goldwyn Studios at such and such a time. But just as my pal Don Stewart and I got there, Alex was driving out. As he passed us, he shouted, "Hey, we can't wait. The Burtons are waiting for us at the Beverly Hills Hotel!"

He took off, so we spun around and took off behind him. When Don and I got to the hotel, we rapped on the door of the Burton's bungalow, Liz answered. I was so angry by then that I walked right past her and lit into Alex: "You son of a bitch! I don't want anything to do with you, and if you don't get out of this picture, I'm getting out right now! I want no part of it."

I wasn't exactly star-struck, and, meanwhile, this was the first the Burtons had ever seen of me. Elizabeth was sitting on the couch just about having a cow wondering who I was and what was going on. Their pal Michael Caine was also sitting there, looking like he was next to a cow.

Alex was scared to death and had nothing to say. I stormed out. Burton followed me outside and said, "Let's wait a minute, Mr. Crean. I'm sure we can straighten it all out. Why don't we step out on the porch and we'll talk about it?"

So we talked a while. He thought they could straighten Alex out and it would be all right. But finally I told him, "I don't think so at all. I don't think there's going to be any picture as far as I'm concerned." And Don and I left.

I called my attorneys and told them to extricate me from the project. They informed me that I'd likely incur some heavy losses. The next day they met with Alex's and Peter Ustinov's attorneys to wipe out our deal. I didn't even want to go to the meeting. I sent Don.

He came back and said, "I don't know John, These people sure want to make that picture." He told me they were going to push Alex off to the side and that he wouldn't be any more trouble. My attorneys got on my case as well. They suspected the other side was going to lay down some nasty lawsuits if I backed out. So I got talked into going ahead with the picture.

There was a mountain of negotiating involved before the filming started. One fellow I met during the process, named Milton Pickman, represented the production manager on the picture, and he negotiated the pants off me, getting his client ten times what he deserved.

When the picture was done and everything had settled down, I called Milton up and said, "Goddamn you. You sure did a hell of a job negotiating for that son of a bitch. But the next time I have any negotiating to do, I want you on my side of the table."

We wound up becoming very close friends, and I got him to serve on Fleetwood's board of directors for a time.

I put up the money for *Hammersmith* but wasn't involved at all with the actual filming. I was busy with Fleetwood, while all the filming was done in Mexico. They couldn't shoot in Hollywood because the Burtons' US tax situation was such a mess.

They filmed at Cuernavaca, and *on* Cuernavaca—the bottled kind—which was evident in the finished product. The whole crew evidently had such a good time down there that they didn't pay attention to business. On the soundtrack, it sounded like there was a constant party going on in the background. It was worse than a home movie, and there was no way we could put it out with the dialogue so muddy. We wound up having to loop the entire picture. (Looping is when actors re-record their lines in sync with their lip movements on the screen. It can take numerous tries to get it right, so a technician loops short segments of film so it will repeat as many times as needed).

The Burtons always generated a lot of press in the tabloids, but it was especially choice during the *Hammersmith* filming. *Photoplay* magazine had a cover story titled "Liz walks out on Burton after orgy on film set," alleging that the set was swirling in pot smoke, and that the Burtons were furious with the "trailer king" producer who was counting each bottle of champagne and scotch consumed, which I never did.

Practically the only time I heard from anyone in Mexico was when Liz's birthday was coming and Richard wanted to borrow $6,000 to buy her a new Corvette. I turned him down, because they'd each already received a $100,000 advance at the onset. If they'd already blown through that, I figured I'd never see my $6,000 again.

The first time I saw the ostensibly finished film was the same afternoon I was supposed to go on the *Merv Griffin Show* to tout it. We'd hired the Rogers and Cowan publicity firm, and they got me booked onto a night when all Merv's guests were millionaires. They had me, Bill Lear (who made the jet planes), old H.H. Hunt from Texas (who, I found, had worked as a cowboy on the Irvine Ranch in Orange County in his youth) and two other guests.

Right before going there, I watched *Hammersmith* at Fox Studios and was appalled by what an amateurish, unwatchable turd it was. The Griffin show taped at 6 p.m. As I was making the turn off Sunset Blvd onto Vine, to the theater where the show was taped (once the El Capitan theater, now named the Hollywood Palace), I was hoping, "If I crash my car, I won't have to go on the show."

During the taping, Merv did everything in the world to get me to talk about *Hammersmith,* and I changed the subject each time. The shape it was in, I knew we were going to have to loop it, edit it and do a lot more to make it at least a professional-looking turd before we released it.

Merv moved on to another line of questioning and asked me what the first thing was that I bought when I became a millionaire. I misheard his question and thought he'd asked what I'd bought when I first got a job, so I'd said, "A Schwinn bicycle." The audience laughed like I was the biggest idiot on earth.

Elizabeth and Richard were working on another film in Rome when we needed to loop their parts, so Donna and I flew over for that. Rome was cold and miserable, and the process took two weeks. It would have taken even longer, but both Richard and Elizabeth were really good at looping, usually nailing it in one or two takes.

We hardly ever saw Elizabeth in Rome, but we saw quite a bit of Burton. Liz had fifteen or twenty hippie-type hangers-on who seemed like they couldn't even talk. I mean they were catatonic. One guy had long, curly red hair that came to his shoulders, and always wore a long, raggedy fur coat that looked like an extension of his hair. Liz was supporting this whole crowd. They weren't Richard's kind of people at all.

Donna and I were staying at the same hotel and one night Richard called and wanted to come up, just to get away from that bunch of freaks. The rooms were stocked with mini-bars. When I asked what he wanted he said, "Oh, no, I don't use the stuff anymore." And then half a moment later he said, "Well, maybe a little vodka wouldn't hurt."

So I poured one of these tiny bottles of vodka in a glass with a little ice and handed it to him. He walked over to the mini-bar, popped the top off another little bottle, poured that in there, and then sat down and started talking. That was his idea of not drinking. Getting to know him was the only good part of doing *Hammersmith*.

Ustinov had a certain wit, but it was all staged. I spent a lot of time with him, and after you got to know him, you realized that his banter was just one shtick which he'd keep repeating. You'd start off thinking he was clever, but ultimately realize he was only annoying.

The movie didn't play at all well in previews. We took it to San Diego, San Francisco, Walnut Creek and couple of other places, and kept editing it, trying to make it work. The preview cards audiences were giving us just ripped the movie up one side and down the other. I don't recall otherwise hearing the phrase "It sucks" until the 1980s, but some pioneer wrote that on one preview card. That was one of the milder responses.

Ustinov had written himself into the script so much that he really dragged the movie down. We'd sit in the theater with Peter, and when one of his corn ball-lines came on, he'd laugh "Ha ha haagh!," and was oblivious to the fact that he was the only one in the theater laughing.

I was a huge fan of Stan Freberg's, going all the way back to *Beanie and Cecil*. He had been doing advertising for a few years at that point—he did all those funny Chung King ads—and I got him in to help on the *Hammersmith* ad campaign. I don't know if anything would have helped, but the good part is that Stan and I have been friends ever since then. In 1997 he gave Donna and me parts on his *United States of America, Part II* album—I play Uncle Sam!—which was great because we'd been such fans of his *Part I*.

To get the Burtons involved in the film, Alex had promised them a ridiculous chunk of the gross, 15 percent. That amount that made it virtually impossible for anyone else to make

With Stan Freberg and Peter Ustinov at the
Anaheim YMCA gym dedication, 1971.

Everybody involved in *Hammersmith* had a great time,
except for the audiences and me.

America wasn't ready for a black comedian in a dramatic
western. Too bad, because Bill was great in this.

any money on it. Eventually we sold the film to the Burtons and they then sold it to someone else, who re-cut it and took most of Peter out of it. It's a much better picture now.

I lost about $2.5 million on *Hammersmith*, but since I was in the 91 percent tax bracket then, I only lost about $225,000 over what I would have paid in taxes on that amount. People were much more prone to making bad investments then, as long as they were deductible. You had people buying race horses, drilling oil wells and making all manner of terrible movies.

Not long after I got involved in *Hammersmith* I was approached with another movie, which was Bill Cosby's first picture, a black western called *Man and Boy*. Bill was really on the ropes. He'd put every dime he had in the film, some $300,000. It was budgeted for a million dollars, and the party who was supposed to finance the rest of that amount bailed out, with only ten percent of the picture shot. I bought out the project, so Bill got his $300,000 back, and we finished it.

It was a good story and I thought it would make a good picture. And, unlike "Hammersmith," it was a good picture. It was a serious dramatic role for Bill and he handled it beautifully. It had a strong cast with Leif Erickson and Yaphet Kotto, and the score was by Quincy Jones.

But the idea of a Cosby who wasn't funny, in a black western, just wasn't something the public was ready for then.

Because they'd started shooting before I was involved, *Man and Boy* actually came out before *Hammersmith* did. It fared a little better, but not much. It opened in California in 50 movie houses and didn't do well at all, so the rest of the country didn't even want it. I sold it to Jerry Pickman, Milton's brother, who was in the film distribution business. I'd spent about $1.2 million, and ended up losing about a million of that.

But Jerry was delighted when I sold it to him, saying, "This is going to put my daughter through college." He distributed it in Africa and foreign markets where there were a lot of blacks and it went big. It's still making money for somebody, turning up on late night TV.

Bill did a performance at a theater near here recently and he told the audience, "Crean's been footing the bill for me for my whole career."

That's hardly true. I chiefly remember the time I turned him down.

Bill's never had trouble producing a big paycheck, but he used to be a hooked gambler. He's talked publicly about this problem, so I'm not betraying any confidences here.

A couple of years after *Man and Boy*, I got a call from Bill while I was working on my boat. He was in a Vegas casino.

He said, "John, I'm out of money, but I'm on a hell of a roll. If I can get $5,000 I can get back."

"Bill, it's a Sunday afternoon. Where the hell am I going to get $5,000?"

"You've got credit here, haven't you? Can you call the hotel credit manager and transfer some of it to me?"

"I guess so."

I called the credit manager and he said, "God, Mr. Crean, we can't do this. Bill has borrowed all the money he can from practically everybody in the hotel. He's lost all the money he has coming from his gig here. It just doesn't make any sense."

So he didn't get the $5,000.

A couple of years after that, we took the family to the Hilton in Vegas. Bill was sitting in one of the lounges and saw us in the lobby, and hollered us over. We spent the whole afternoon with him, and he told us about all he'd gone through with his gambling and the end of it. It had reached a point where his wife arranged through his manager for Bill to never see the money from his shows. It was sent straight to her.

Even that didn't stop him. Finally he wised up one time in Vegas. He'd gambled all he could borrow, went over to the black side of town and borrowed a little bit more, and ran dry playing the nickel slot machines. He made the decision then and there to stop, and it was soon after that he made it really big, with the Cosby TV show.

Having sunk money into two pictures, I must have looked to Hollywood like a turkey on Thanksgiving. Before long, I'd been sent a stack of scripts three feet high. The entire industry was in turmoil in 1971, because only three movies made any money that year: *The Godfather, Love Story* and *The French Connection.* As losers, my pictures had a lot of company.

I got a call from Warner Bros. because they were looking for outside financing on some movies. I went to a meeting on their lot with four or five of their executives. One of them, Frank Wells, was a fellow I knew because he'd been Jim Garner's attorney, and he was OK. But the rest of them were all on drugs. I don't know what the hell they were smoking or shooting, but they were in the executive offices all bare-footed and wearing chains and beads and all sorts of weird shit, sitting on the floor.

Maybe that's how they thought you got things done, but they all fell by the wayside while Frank Wells went on to become chairman of the board at Warners and then the number two man at Disney. I don't even remember what the scripts were that day, they were so vacant.

Not long after that, I passed on buying the screen rights to *The Great Gatsby* for next to nothing, which wound up becoming a pretty decent movie. At the time I was so involved in *Hammersmith* and the Cosby picture, and not very happy about it, that I really wasn't interested in anything else.

I made a third movie called *Moment of Truth*, because, after spending millions on *Hammersmith* and *Man and Boy,* I was really curious about what the production costs actually were on a film. I could see where the above-the-line stuff—the actors and script—would cost money, but I couldn't figure why the production costs should be anywhere near as high as they were. I wanted to make a picture where I could see the actual costs.

My musician friend Arie Rozeboom, with whom I'd made my British Rolls Royce trip, had a bullfight story. I wrote a script from the story, using the pen name Fred Lintz. When I first met Cosby, he'd done a funny impersonation of me, and he called the character Fred Lintz. I used that name in the film credits, because I sure didn't want to put my own name on a piece of shit like that.

I hired the production manager from *Man and Boy* to direct it. He had made all the *I-Spy* episodes with Cosby and Robert Culp. I asked him if we could make a picture for $100,000 and he said "Sure."

He took the script and worked out a ten-day shooting schedule. We hired amateurs to play most of the parts and paid them union scale, so the film's cast and script costs were almost nothing. The only real actor in it was my friend Pat Hawley, who had been in *Paint Your Wagon* and a bunch of other pictures. We bought some stock bullfight footage. For the production costs—the cameramen, the set people, the technical people and such—we paid for first-class people, real professionals.

We ended up with a 90 minute movie that cost $105,000. In early '70s dollars, we could have paid perhaps $50,000 on top of that to buy a good script and another quarter-million for talent. So, for under $500,000, we could have made a first-class flick. At the same time, the Hollywood studios were charging $3 to $5 million to get an average picture done.

From that, I determined that the movie business is largely a rip-off. An independent filmmaker, then and now, would have to go to the studios because the studios have the distribution system tied up. By the time it's all over, the expenses the studios claim they've spent are so inflated that the filmmaker never sees any money. I suspect that the studios just pick a number out of the air for their expenses, and stick good money in their pockets, while the creative guy who made the film gets nothing.

What we ended up with in *Moment of Truth* was a terrible movie with great production values. The acting is so bad that the only way it might have worked was if we took the dialogue out of it and ran it as a silent movie. It was so bad I didn't want to preview it, but Jerry Pickman, who bought *Man and Boy* from me, tried to convince me, "It can't be that bad. Any film has to have some value."

I told him, "I don't think this one has."

But he insisted, "Send it back to me. I'll preview it and find out."

Boy, did he find out. The audience response cards told him what audience members were also telling him to his face, that they were incensed that he would waste their time with such a piece of junk. Compared to some of the TV movies I see these days, though, it's not so bad.

In my hippie period, which lasted no longer than it took me
to get a barber to undo this whim of a Las Vegas hair stylist.
Emily and Donna pretend it's the stage show
they're laughing at.

Fleetwood's board and officers in the early 1970s:
(back row) Glenn Kummer, Dan Stretch, Harry Aides,
Bill Weide, Bill Lear, Boyd Plowman.
(front row) Dale Skinner, Marilyn Dickensen,
Chuck Chamberlain, me, Jerry Biddolf and Elden Smith.

TWEAKING THE ENGINE

The 1970s wound up being a challenging time for the mobile home and RV industries. We had to contend with the Arab oil embargoes, smaller cars that couldn't pull trailers, government regulations, and simply insane interest rates that resulted from the well-intentioned efforts of President Jimmy Carter.

Of those changes, the raft of new government rules regulating our product was the least troublesome for Fleetwood. Other manufacturers were running around like the world was ending, but that was because so much of their product was substandard. I'm opposed to regulations and think the industry ultimately would have straightened itself out, just by public demand. But in this case, the regulations actually played in our favor. Because our standards had been higher than the rest of the industry, and higher than most of the new regulations, the rules leveled the playing field, where other companies had to try to make a competitive product that was up to our standard.

We coasted through the regulations, but the oil embargoes and the interest rates nearly did us in. I had been content to largely leave the company alone when it was doing well, but with the messes we had then, I had to come on like gangbusters. My level of involvement then took a lot of people in Fleetwood's upper management by surprise.

Glenn Kummer, who started with Fleetwood in the '60s and eventually became president and CEO, recently recalled that his early impression of me—since revised a time or two— was that I was "one lucky sucker, who didn't do anything and was fortunate to have managers who could make things work."

About the only time he'd seen me in the 1960s was at annual golf events Fleetwood held in Palm Springs, where his abiding memory of me was that I was barefoot, and playing the entire course with a single goofy club that supposedly adjusted from a wood to a putter.

(I never did care for golf. One year at the third hole my group started talking to some gals who were poolside at a house adjoining the course. They invited us in to have some sandwiches, and after a couple of hours we just filled in our cards and strolled back to the clubhouse.)

By the early 70s, Glenn was at our Riverside HQ as divisional general manager of the RV group, and he practically never saw me there. Even when I was at our Riverside facility, the management guys rarely knew it, because I'd be working on something in one of the plants instead of hanging around in the office. In all my years there, I probably wasn't in my office more than 15 times, and usually then it was just to fire somebody.

So the upper management boys were a little taken aback when I was suddenly active, making decisions and doing end runs around them.

And I wasn't any too subtle about it. I had learned a trick from reading Winston Churchill, that when you have a problem and no one has a solution, you give the order to enact some ridiculous, far-out solution. Suddenly, your people say, "Hell, we can't do that!" and are galvanized into coming up with something less drastic and workable. That was a trick Churchill used all the time, and I found it was a great ploy.

As an example, we've had plants that were troublesome or unprofitable, and I'd give the order to close the facility and fire everybody, which was ridiculous. We had a big investment in the people and materials there. But when I gave an order like that, management would figure out what was wrong and fix it right away.

I did things like that during the first Arab oil embargo in '73-'74. It was a hairy situation, and I didn't have time to go through channels. I'd override upper and middle management, go directly to the plants and do whatever needed to be done. In a crisis, you have to get right down in the front lines and call the shots from there.

That made the management guys feel I was undermining their authority, but, again, this wasn't a time for niceties. I wasn't going to fire them, but there was a good chance we'd all be out on our ass if I didn't make some decisive moves.

Though I might disappear for months on the road or on my boat, when I work, I *work*. The first week I started addressing our oil crunch problems, I was up before dawn every morning to drive up to Fleetwood, and working into the night. I kept on the same routine Saturday morning, and Donna says that when I came home hours later I looked like a kid who couldn't find anyone to play with. It hadn't occurred to me that our people would take the weekend off.

Obviously, our motor home and trailer sales were hit hard by the oil crunch, but even our mobile home sales were in a slump. People lived in mobile homes, they didn't drive in them, so those sales shouldn't have been that affected. I couldn't figure out what the cause was, until I went out into the field.

At the time we had three mobile home divisions: Fleetwood, Festival and Broadmoor. The Festival division was doing the worst. So I went to the Festival division office—at our Riverside HQ—and asked the division manager, Asa Whitfield, what his worst plant was. It was Hillsboro, Texas. I said, "Well let's go down and straighten the sucker out, and maybe we'll find what's wrong with the rest of the plants."

So Asa and I took off in my car. Hillsboro is about halfway between Waco and Dallas. We called on dealers the entire way out there and even went into Louisiana to see what dealers were thinking there. From Albuquerque onward, they told us the sort of people who once bought mobile homes were instead buying condos or renting apartments. I couldn't understand a trend like that, because it seemed to me a mobile home gave its owner a lot more privacy.

I visited some new condo tracts to see what people were buying, and it was a revelation to me. The places had big, bitchen master bedroom-bath suites, and hardly any kitchen or living room at all. They were designed for young married couples. Their lifestyle involved opening a can or getting take-out from a fast food place, eating on trays in front of the TV, and spending the rest of the time doing what young marrieds do in the bedroom.

That was totally different from what we were building. Our models had a big kitchen, a bath off the hall, and nothing at all sexy about it. So I designed a trailer that was more like these condos, with a huge master bedroom and bath that was really romantic—we had a big Roman tub, with a mirror on the ceiling, and some scalloped draping, with dingle-ball thingies hanging from it like a Tijuana taxi. The rest of the unit wasn't of much consequence.

I put a bar in the unit—not a wet bar, but just a place to store liquor, with a mirror behind it—with a wine rack above it. It was such a unique feature that when it went on the market people always referred to the model as "that one with the wine rack." The dining table was a rustic-looking thing that we made in the plant from shipping pallets, so our materials cost on it was nearly zilch. It went well with the house though.

At the time, the beds used throughout the industry were made of foam rubber only a couple of inches thick. The whole mattress couldn't have weighed more than a pound and a half. The supposed "box spring mattress" that some makers used was equally terrible. You'd sit on them and sink to the floor. Young marrieds were buying mobile homes equipped this way, and were probably buying a new bed the next day.

Several of our design changes were money-savers, and we instead put that money into supplying our new model with a top-of-the-line Serta box spring and mattress. It made all the difference in the world when customers looked in there and saw the Serta label.

When we had the basic design done, I had the company decorator outfit the model, and his decor didn't match the trailer at all. It was far too conservative. I wanted to change it, and as luck would have it, the decorator asked me for a few days off to attend a trade show in Chicago.

I told him that was a great idea, and the minute he got on the plane, I called a trailer decorator I knew in Alabama whose style was a lot more overt. They called the style "Alabama flash," and it was really far-out, exciting stuff.

The designer drove all night and day to get to Hillsboro, looked the model over, drove back to Alabama, had the drapes, spreads and all sewn up and came back and decorated the unit. It was really sharp.

We built a two-bedroom unit that was 72' long and 14' wide, and a three-bedroom 80' unit. They were the same except for the 8' for the additional bedroom. We called the model the Festival Series Seven, which didn't mean a thing. It was just something the marketing boys came up with.

Asa came down to Hillsboro when I had the model ready to go into production, and he asked, "Well, what about the rest of them? Where are the other models?"

I told him, "There ain't going to be no rest. This is it." He tried to convince me that a company couldn't make it with just one model, but I knew from past experience that you certainly can if you've got one good one.

Good though it was, the Festival Series Seven had a tough time getting started because the dealers had inventories on their lots that weren't selling, and they had very little confidence in us. Our model priced out right and our sales guys were excited about it, but they couldn't even get the dealers to talk to them.

I figured that if dealers had a chance to see the unit, they'd stock it, and it would sell. So we worked out a plan in which we told dealers, "We're going to ship one to you, and if you don't like it, we'll just take it back, with no obligation at all."

And we did it just like we had in the old days. Our drivers had a route, where if the first dealer didn't take the unit, we'd have another dealer a hundred miles down the road who probably would. I don't think anybody refused to take the trailer. Once customers saw it, sales took off.

We put the Festival Series Seven into production in Idaho, Georgia, California and our other Festival plants, and the whole division came back to life. In Texas, the Hillsboro plant was too small to keep up with demand, so we moved production to our Waco plant. We built and sold that same model for 11 years without having to change anything.

Throughout both the Arab oil embargoes of the '70s, we put out new models, came up with new designs and improved our product. Like a guy who gets cancer, you can act like a victim and sit on your ass waiting for it to consume you, or you can take charge and fight it every way you can. You can't merely wait for business to turn good again. You have to show a little faith and do the positive things that help make it good again.

We were running lean and mean, but we were running. And when we came out of the tough times, we were a lot better off than our competitors, because we'd been improving our product while they were lying low.

In 1973, before the first embargo, we had $346 million in sales. The next year, during the embargo, sales were down by some $50 million, and our profits were nearly cut in half. But, because we kept pushing forward, when things had fully recovered in 1976, we did $392 million in gross sales, and doubled our net to $10 million. Fortune magazine also ranked Fleetwood as 6th among the top 500 industries in growth of earnings per share for the ten years ending in 1976.

In that bicentennial year we had an ad slogan: "See America: It's close to home." It's a great slogan. I wish I'd thought it up.

One thing we did in response to the first energy crisis was diversify into making public transportation. In 1974, we converted a Southwind plant over to make a 22-foot, 19-passenger midi-bus called the Crosstowner. It was a good

The roof-mounted Dandy prototype, in the 1970s.
Still a great idea.

Appealing to the burgeoning flamenco dancer market,
in a 1970s brochure.

vehicle, in some ways one of the best products we ever made. Some are even still in daily use out there. But our guys weren't used to dealing with government agencies. Every municipality wanted their own custom version of the bus, and it just wasn't financially feasible.

We also made a camper van called the Santana, that we did up with snazzy paint jobs and thick pile carpet interiors. There was a heck of a demand for them, and they sold well for a year and a half. Then the finance companies started getting repos on them like you wouldn't believe. The kids who bought them would trash them and get tired of making the payments. It got so bad that the companies decided not to finance the campers for anyone under 25. Since that was the audience for the Santana, it killed the market, and we dropped the model not long after that.

Right after the first gas crunch, Detroit was big on making small cars, which couldn't pull a trailer the way an old V8 had. I gave myself the goal of building a trailer that weighed under 1000 pounds. When a trailer is under 1500 pounds, the manufacturer doesn't have to equip it with brakes, which saves a lot of money.

I started toying with a design that seemed pretty outlandish, but I built a prototype that worked. Instead of connecting to a trailer hitch at a car's rear bumper, my little trailer attached to a hitch ball mounted on a removable roof rack, which attached to the car's top with pop rivets. The center of gravity was on top of the car, so there was none of the sway you get with a bumper-hitch. The weight was evenly balanced. Without sticking out longer behind the car, there was about four feet more trailer, because it overhung the car.

I attached the prototype to a VW Bug, and it handled ridiculously well. Even inside the narrow plant building, I could make U-turns or drive in circles all day.

I named it the Dandy, and was genuinely excited about it. But by that time Fleetwood was going great guns again, and no one in the company wanted to touch anything as new and different as the Dandy. My son Johnnie had already started in the trailer business, and I tried to give it to him, but it was the same story. Andy had his sales lot, and I was keen on getting him to go into manufacturing, but Andy never gave a fig about manufacturing. He wasn't interested at all.

The Dandy is still a damn good idea, with all the small cars and their popcorn engines now. I expect that someday soon someone will come out with a similar model.

On top of the financial problems we had during the gas shortage, the government decided to go after the industry then as well. The Federal Trade Commission had several beefs, from shoddy construction to lax warranty service, and I pretty much had to agree with them. Business had been so good for so long that we and others weren't providing the value and service we should.

As usual, the government remedies were worse than the problem. In early 1974 I flew to Washington with some of our people to meet with FTC officials and other representatives from the industry.

I managed to piss a few of those guys off, because they were there to defend their practices and argue that their trailers weren't substandard. In fact, my guys wanted to do that as well. To me, what the industry had been doing was indefensible, so I copped to it. I said it was terrible what was going on, but that the remedies the FTC had set down weren't going to get the job done at all. I gave them an alternate list of suggestions, and that helped to settle things.

After the hearings were over, I was headed for Dulles Airport in the Hertz rent-a-car when I got to thinking about how much I'd hated flying out. I don't like flying to begin with, and the flights were crammed during the oil embargo.

I decided instead to drive out to our plant in Winchester, Virginia. Once I got out there, I figured, screw it, I might as well drive home. I made it to Tennessee before the Hertz car

Our home away from home. On the road in 1975.

Happy campers.

started to run out of gas. During the fuel crunch you could only buy gas on odd or even days, depending on the last digit of your license plate, and it wasn't my day.

I drove by a Porsche dealership with a big sign in the window, saying "400 miles on a tankful." I pulled in and they had a nice yellow 914 on the floor. I told the salesman, "If you can get this thing gassed up, arrange for payment through my bank, run this rental car to the airport for me and get me out of here in an hour, I'll buy it." The sales kid went to work, and he had me out of there in a hour.

It was a great trip home. There was hardly any traffic, and I was running that Porsche 100 miles an hour the whole way, until just before I got to Oklahoma City. I was getting lonely, and I'd called Donna to have her meet me there, so I was really anxious to get into town.

When I crossed into Oklahoma, the weather report on the radio said there was a snow storm coming down from Tulsa. I was 100 miles from Oklahoma City, so I thought, fine, I'll be there in a hour, doing 100 mph. Ten minutes later the snow started coming down, sideways in a heavy wind. By the time I passed a sign saying "Oklahoma City, 75 miles," I was doing 75. When the distance was 40 miles, I was doing 40 miles an hour. And, sure enough, when I finally got to a sign that said, "Oklahoma City, 10 miles," I was doing ten miles an hour. If there had been many more signs, I might still be out there.

I like to joke that the trip cost me $17,000 dollars. The Porsche only cost $7000, but Donna was into that turquoise jewelry then, and we wound up buying $10,000 worth of the stuff in Albuquerque.

Fleetwood had always specialized in low-end and then mid-priced product. In 1977, we acquired a company in Benton Harbor, Michigan called Avion, which was the third most successful of the three major high-end trailer makers. Airstream and Holiday Rambler were the two companies above it.

The high-end trailers were bought almost entirely by

retirees who were well-fixed, since the trailers cost almost twice as much as average models. Instead of a wood frame, all three companies used riveted aluminum on an aluminum frame construction.

That was supposed to make them superior, though the aluminum construction actually had a lot of drawbacks. To begin with, wood-framed trailers could be insulated far better, while aluminum is a terrific conductor of heat and cold—that's why it's so good in cookware. The rest of us in the industry referred to the aluminum trailers as "silver sausages."

In marketing, you can't always go by the way it is; you have to go by the way people perceive things. These older buyers were around in World War Two, when airplanes were considered the pinnacle of technology and riveted aluminum was used in aircraft construction.

Airstream had pioneered that market. The company had been started by a couple of guys out in the San Fernando Valley, but the person who put the company on the map was its second owner, Wally Byam.

Wally started out working at one of the dealerships that handled Airstreams. He was a real merchandiser, and made a display with moving lights, where, at night, it looked like he had an Airstream parked in front of a waterfall. During the daytime, he'd have a guy with a bicycle pulling an Airstream around.

He was the only dealer who sold many Airstreams. The owners didn't have enough volume to keep the factory going. Wally managed to get some financing and bought the company. He was one of my Venetian blind customers back when I had that going.

He made a good trailer—considering the aluminum— but the best thing he did for his customers was to create the Airstream club. The club would organize great caravans that probably added years of fun to his retired buyer's lives. Wally became the figurehead of the club, sporting a tam-o'-shanter and outrageous clothing. He took care of the promotion, while the plant was run by a fellow, Art Costello, who was a great production man.

After Wally died, Art ran the company, and did well with it. He eventually sold it to Beatrice Foods, and it went downhill. Meanwhile, the Holiday Rambler product was pretty much crap, but they had a strong dealer network.

Avion had been chugging along in last place for a long time. It came up for sale at what we considered a real bargain price, and Elden Smith, the VP of our RV division, negotiated our buying it. As soon as we acquired it, I stepped in to see what we could do about its third-place position.

Donna and I went on a trip with one and found that Avions were well-built and the quality was great, but the designs were ten years behind the times.

I moved into a Holiday Inn in Saint Joe, Michigan for two months to redesign the Avion. While we didn't buck the aluminum construction until about a decade ago, we made some major changes. I had learned about an automotive suspension system when I was racing, where some English fellow had taken a regular Ford chassis, split the front axle in the middle and hinged it, and wound up with an independent suspension.

I did the same thing with the Avion. Bill Stroppe, with whom I had worked on race cars, came to Benton Harbor and built one of those suspension systems with me. We tested it on a cheap trailer from one of Fleetwood's other plants, and it made an appreciable difference in the ride. The trailer just flew over bumps.

When the weight of a trailer went above a certain amount, manufacturers would usually just slap on bigger wheels and tires to raise it higher. That compromise never looked right to me. With the Avion, we handled the weight with our independent suspension and a triple axle, which was an industry first.

We came out with that design and it was a rip-roaring success. We soon equaled and sometimes surpassed Holiday Rambler and Airstream in sales. We didn't hold a commanding lead over them until years later, when both companies were bought by big corporations, which, as usual, put the businesses in the toilet.

When our Avion models finally got rid of the riveted aluminum, I supervised both the new construction and the marketing plans. The new construction still had an aluminum frame, but the outer shell was now vacuum-formed fiberglass. Since the older Avion buyers had liked the aluminum because of its use in aircraft, I had our marketing stress that our model changes were employing advances in the aircraft industry.

When Avions were still made of aluminum, we had started to use 1/16" of rubber to cover the roof. Before that, after a good hailstorm, your aluminum roof looks as pocked as the moon. I don't think we were the first in the industry to do that, but, whoever did, it worked and we carried that over when we went to the fiberglass construction.

While it wasn't nearly as big as the Airstream club, Avion had a club of aficionados, and still does. They have an annual rally in Florida where 600 to 1000 Avions show up with their owners. Donna and I bought an Avion and attended those rallies for four years. We'd mingle with the owners and find out exactly what they were looking for in the way of product, which was very helpful, and a lot of fun, too.

One of those times in Florida, Donna and I stopped at a rest area bordering the Okefinoke Swamp. I was walking around and came upon a ratty concrete bench shaped like an alligator. I thought that was kind of cute and sat on it. I was just looking out across the swamp, when I felt this bench move a little bit. I jumped up, and it was a goddamn alligator! It looked like cement! I hauled ass, but it really didn't pay much attention to me.

Me and the horse I rode in on, with Donna
at Rancho Capistrano.

I understand this hairstyle was later popularized
by Cameron Diaz.

I can dish it out, but I can't take it.
Manning the bar at Rancho Capistrano, 1971.

ON THE RANCH, IN THE HILLS

We were living on our ranch in San Juan Capistrano when our girls, Emily and Susie, were heading into their teens. They got into horses in a big way, and I can't tell you how many damn horse shows we went to at county fairgrounds all over the country. When you're involved in a scene like that, you're amazed at how much these far-flung places have in common: like heat and humidity and flies and horse shit. I hated every minute of it.

I have no business complaining, though, because the girls were so little trouble to us. They went to public schools and were good students, and had an adolescence blessedly unlike mine.

The ranch was tough on Emily and Susie, though. They had their horses, but on 100 acres with nothing nearby, they didn't have any friends around. Donna thought it would be a good idea for them to have neighbors, so in 1969 we bought a place in Monarch Bay, near Laguna Beach, and lived back and forth between the two places.

There had been something of an El Nino that year, and a lot of properties wound up with the ocean coming in their front door. Consequently, they were selling cheap. I had been doing a lot of fishing up and down the coast, and I'd seen the houses atop Monarch Bay being built. To level the bluff, they'd simply scraped dirt off the top and pushed it down the cliff, and it stuck there, with ice plant growing on it. In the big rains of early 1969, that dirt just slid down the side of the cliff like a toupee, and all the people living on the bluff were scared to death their houses were going to go.

Nearly every house was for sale. I knew the cliff itself was solid, so we bought a five-bedroom oceanfront house for $190,000. As we'd hoped, the girls made lots of friends in the neighborhood, including the kids of our next door neighbors, who turned out to be bank robbers.

Two families had rented the house and were living in it. When Susie and Emily would come back from playing there, we'd hear that they didn't have any furniture, just mattresses on the floor. We didn't think that much about it.

It turned out that the adults were only living there long enough to make their hit. On the weekends, they staked out the bank at Monarch Bay Plaza. It was right below the flight path of the jets from the El Toro Marine base. Whenever the jets masked the noise, the robbers went at the roof with jackhammers. They bored a hole through the roof and cleaned out the vault. Then they just disappeared for two years, when they were caught trying to sell some registered bonds they'd stolen.

With us only living there half the time, the 93-acre ranch seemed a bit wasted on us, so we opened it up to youth groups, letting just about any organized group have camp-outs there. The kids were great, but some of their adult advisors were a problem, getting looped and driving into washes and such.

In 1973 I helped Johnnie get into the trailer business. It was his own business, not a position with Fleetwood, because I had an anti-nepotism policy. When I had first started in business, I'd hired my brother-in-law, Mary's husband, who turned out to be worthless. Before I caught on and fired him, his failings were obvious to everyone on the shop floor. It had to be bad for morale, everyone wondering why I had an idiot like that on the payroll. After I fired him, my sister and most of my family didn't talk to me for a year. Then I hired my brother Kenny, who was a good worker when he wasn't shit-faced, which wasn't much of the time. It was also uncomfortable firing him.

So I adopted the anti-nepotism policy, which was good for Fleetwood. One reason why we didn't lose people to other companies was that the upper management of much of our competition was locked up by the boss' family members. Our guys could see they had much more opportunity for advancement with us.

And, on the parental side, I had seen where some of my friend's kids weren't amounting to anything because they knew they were going to have a cushy position handed to them, and I didn't think that was healthy.

So I just helped Johnnie get his own thing going, a company called Alfa Leisure. His start-up wasn't much different from when I started, except that, instead of Donna's dad's garage, Johnnie had a huge ranch on which to situate his operation.

We started an assembly line in a building on the property, and I pretty much taught him the business. Before long, he was building five trailers a week. He had some 15 young guys his own age working there, some of whom had been dopers and such. Now, they were all straight and working, and building a damn good trailer.

Then some county building inspector came by and said the land was zoned for agriculture (I was letting a friend raise some 400,000 juniper and Italian cypress saplings a year on the property), not manufacturing, and that Johnnie's business would have to clear out. The Arab oil embargo had started, and there was no leeway for something as major as a move then. It was a tough time, and I didn't have much time to help him. It was all I could do then just keeping Fleetwood afloat.

I did call Orange County Supervisor Tom Riley, and asked if there was some way we could get a special dispensation so Johnnie could stay at the ranch until the oil embargo was over. Riley arranged for us to meet with the fire marshal and other county government people, who proved to be arrogant autocrats, not to mention assholes. They were entirely unimpressed that this was a young kid getting started in business, and that he had these longhairs off the street and working. They issued an order that he had to move immediately.

Fortunately, Johnnie ran across a fellow with a plant in

Brea who was also struggling, and he moved in with him. They ran their businesses in the same building until the embargo ended. Then Johnnie moved his company to Chino, and he's been doing well there ever since.

About a year after Johnnie began making trailers, Andy started a business selling trailers on a lot in Irvine, and he did well at that.

Over the years, I've met several US presidents, and some would-be ones as well, but usually you'd talk to them for no longer than it took to take your photo. In January of 1974, though, I was invited to a closed-door meeting with Richard Nixon at his Western White House.

He was going on TV in two nights to announce his strategy for halting inflation and kick-starting the economy, and he was still working that out. I'm not sure where he came up with my name, but the others there included the CEOs of Hewlett-Packard, Levi Strauss, General Mills and Atlantic Richfield. With the exception of me, it was like they'd only invited guys whose companies had two-word names. Also in attendance was Teamsters head Frank Fitzsimmons—a noisy son of a bitch—and a young Alan Greenspan, who had just been named Nixon's top economic advisor.

I was able to get my two cents in, telling the President, "We don't need legislation to fight inflation. We're already being legislated to death. What we need is some strong leadership." He'd already used his leadership to get the country to voluntarily comply with energy-saving measures, and I thought he could do that again.

The Watergate mess was reaching a fever pitch then, and it was only months before he resigned. That seemed to be the farthest thing from his mind, though. He was just thinking about the country, and I was deeply impressed by his intellect and by his capacity to have all the details of the global economy memorized.

Johnnie and me with Richard Nixon. I don't know how he got out of having to wear a name tag.

It's a good life when you get to meet several U.S. Presidents *and* Col. Sanders. At the 1976 Golden Plate awards.

With the Reverend Bob Schuller at Rancho Capistrano,
sometime before we gave the place to him.

Johnnie, Andy and I drop in on John Wayne at his
Newport Beach home, August 1978.
He died less than a year later.

Around the time we bought the place in Monarch Bay, I sold my boat and did without one for a while. In 1973 I got the hots to be on the water again, and I had the Prowler 76 built. It was 76 feet long and we launched it in '76. We made a lot of trips to Cabo San Lucas in that. (I sold the Prowler '76 in 1987, but Emily bought it from the new owner a few years ago, so it's back in the family now.)

A friend of mine was doing a lot of international trading—I'm not sure what he was trading—and he called me one day in 1978 when he was going to be entertaining the heads of the Sudanese government in Newport. The Sudanese wanted to go out fishing and also meet John Wayne. They were all jet-black guys who had been educated in England and had proper English accents. My friend had me take them out fishing—it was a good time for swordfish—and then I docked at John Wayne's house.

In all my years in and around Newport, I'd never met him before. He turned out to be a fun-loving guy, and *tall*. Johnnie and Andy were along, and Wayne towered over us. What surprised me was his language. Every other word out of his mouth was "fuck," some really salty language, and I was embarrassed because these Sudanese guys were ever so proper. But I later found out that they were all a bunch of murderers. They had come to power and killed all the people they'd taken over from. Some time after I met them, they were killed by a new batch of SOBs seizing power. Meanwhile, cancer killed John Wayne less than a year after we met him.

I recently came across a poem I wrote for Emily's 13th birthday:

My little girl is thirteen—a lady now with her life before her. She's pretty, giggly and father's jokes aren't as funny as before.

She's busy now with friends her age, for only they can share that boundless teenage wisdom. Mother doesn't know, for how could a mother be so wise?

Brothers and little sisters are sometimes fun but how little do they know? That certain boy kind of makes her tingle, but at thirteen who could admit to such mush?

She wonders why the world can't perceive her train of thought. But, the world was thirteen so long ago.

My big girl is thirteen now and she finds it silly to sit upon my knee but this is how it is and always was.

And, though I'll miss my little girl, I'll find joy in knowing that her world is new and fresh and each day a bright horizon.

For dad was thirteen once and the pages of my book of life were each one a mystery simply solved.

So, dear Emily, though you'll find it hard, try to remember that Mom and Dad, brothers, the world and all, once knew the joy of being thirteen too.

It seemed hardly any time passed at all before my little girls were grown up. In keeping with the family trend of marrying young, Emily married a race car driver when she was 18. In high school she became interested in race cars, buying all the magazines, and watching all the races with binoculars. I was still fooling with off-road racing cars, and one day Emily went with me to a shop in Anaheim where a young fellow building cars hit her up for a date. The next thing I knew, they decided to get married. I knew his dad and that bothered me, because I didn't like the guy at all.

When Susie graduated from high school she moved out and rented a place in West Newport. She wanted to be out on her own. She had a rock singer boyfriend, and they were thick for about four years. I went to a couple of his shows, and it was horrible damn music (Not too many years later we ran into her old rock singer boyfriend. He was clean-shaven and working as a stockbroker).

I was hoping to get Susie to go to UCLA, and thought maybe if we moved near there we could entice her to enroll.

Emily and friend, 1972.

Susie, going faster
than her horse.

With Susie and Emily on the Ranch.

"Hey, look at the funny pants on that guy over there!"
Visiting a plant in 1975.

Our Beverly Hills demolition party, July 15, 1979.

Donna and I had been at the ranch for over a decade and we wanted a smaller, more manageable place. We'd also never lived in a big city and were curious to see how that was.

We found an old English Tudor style house on $^3/_4$ of an acre on Canon Drive in Beverly Hills and bought it for $750,000 just before the real estate prices really went crazy. We weren't that hot on the house, so I had an architect draw plans for a new house and applied for a permit.

Beverly Hills would only issue a limited number of permits per month, so the town wouldn't be entirely torn up with construction projects. A new application goes to the bottom of the pile, and it can take a year to reach the top. While I was waiting, somebody offered me $850,000 for the property, then a million, then whatever I wanted. I told him I wasn't interested.

Another fellow also liked the place, and took a more direct approach. Donna and I drove up to see the house one day, and found a squatter living there. He was a very sophisticated looking guy, with nice clothes, but he was living out of a backpack, in *our* house. He told us he was just coming through town and didn't have a place to stay, so he'd let himself in.

After that, we decided it would be better to tear the house down and have a vacant lot while we waited for the permit. Donna thought it would be fun to have a demolition party. We bought sledgehammers and axes and other implements of destruction, hired a caterer to put on some food, and invited about 80 people over one Sunday afternoon. It was a wild event. People were painting murals on walls while people on the other side were taking sledgehammers to them. It's a wonder no one was injured.

Once our permit was approved and started construction, Donna and I lived in a trailer on the site. We might very well have been the only people in Beverly Hills living in a trailer. The first thing finished on our new house was a little garage apartment. We then lived in that for about a year.

We were already friends with the fashion showman Mr. Blackwell—who we knew from benefits we'd hosted at the ranch—and he introduced us to loads of people in town. Some of them, like Milton Berle, are still good friends. Donna is a real movie fan, and was delighted when we met Jane Withers.

Jane was part of a celebrity charity event for which I was roped into providing the transportation. The only vehicle I had that would hold Jane, Regis Philbin and the other celebrities was one of my motor homes. After the event, the thing wouldn't start. The celebs were already bemused to be riding in a motor home. It was just icing on the cake for them to see me getting under the hood in my tuxedo. I did fix the thing, though.

Jane came by the house a couple of days after that. I was working in the garage, so she and Donna got to talking, and they've been talking ever since. They've been the best of best friends for years now.

When our new house was finally finished, we only lived in it for about six months, because we were tired of the whole place by then. Beverly Hills was fun for a while, but I just can't live in a town that doesn't have a hardware store.

The whole Beverly Hills routine is that if you look fairly presentable and have a clean tuxedo, everybody wants you to go to their events. Society people always need to wrap their good times in a noble excuse, so we were invited to a lot of what Donna and I called "Disease Dinners," that benefited one charity or another.

One night, we were at a fund-raiser for some marine conservation thing. Among the items being auctioned was a big, beautiful parrot. I could see him from across the room, and at one point early on, he fell off his perch, going *thunk* on the cage floor. That should have told me something. Later that evening, a fellow had the parrot out on his shoulder, and he was as good-natured a bird as you ever saw in your life.

The auctioneer that night was a total jerk, just in love with the sound of his own voice. When the bird was auctioned, he worked it up to $1,500 and kept yakking, "Do I hear fifteen twenty-five? Do I hear fifteen twenty-five?" I stood up and roared, "I'll give you $2,000 for the bird if you'll shut up!"

"Sold"

When we got the parrot home we found they must have had it drugged, because it was the nastiest son of a bitch that ever molted. If you got anywhere near it, it would bite you, especially me. They say parrots live to be really old, but that one wouldn't have if I'd been left alone with it.

We had him for a while before we gave him to a Mexican gal who worked for us. She lived in LA and her house caught fire one day. In all the excitement the bird dropped dead from a heart attack.

Donna and I would be out on the Beverly Hills dinner circuit four nights a week, and that really got old. You go out to lunch and dinner and talk about the same things. I'd always enjoyed the beach, boats and people down in Orange County a lot more.

Meanwhile, Susie had run off to Michigan to go to college because she'd fallen for some kid on the horse circuit who was going there—she wound up marrying him—so she wasn't going to UCLA and that was the end of that.

We had gotten rid of the Rancho Capistrano property when we were living in the guest house in Beverly Hills. Donna and I had decided, though, that it was just too beautiful and green a spot to sell it to anyone who might over-develop it in the same soulless way every place else in Orange County has been.

I had been to several weekend retreats at Manresa, a Jesuit retreat in Azusa. They had a very effective alcohol program, helping a lot of boozers who hadn't been able to shake the bottle elsewhere.

So we thought it would be good to give the ranch to the Jesuits for a retreat. I contacted them, and they were excited by the prospect. We nearly had the deal done with the Jesuits in Azusa when the head of the order, up in the Bay Area, put the kibosh on it.

He came down and I met with him, and he was a nasty old cuss. He showed me statistics, though, on how many priests were retiring and how few new ones were coming in. They realistically didn't have the manpower to take on a project as challenging as the ranch would be.

Instead, we gave the ranch to the televangelist Robert Schuller. Donna and I knew him, and had donated to various of his other projects. We thought that, with his hustle, Bob could probably get a pretty good retreat going there, and that's what he ultimately did.

In 1982 we sold the Beverly Hills place and moved into a house in Newport Beach on Bayside Drive, with 125 feet on the bay. What it didn't have was any parking to speak of, so entertaining there was tough.

Just before we moved from Beverly Hills, Johnnie decided to run for Congress. Some political consultants got hold of him and got him pumped up to where he thought he was going to go to Washington and save the world. It would have been fun having him in Congress, and he felt like he could really do some good.

But the consultants, Bill Butcher and Arnold Ford (the same consultants who put together Howard Jarvis' direct mail campaign), were just the worst opportunists you ever saw in your life. Johnnie pissed away almost two million dollars on the election, and most of it went to Butcher and Ford, buying ads and God knows what.

Johnnie meant well, but as the campaign went on, he fell into that politician's mood where the only thing that mattered was the votes. He won the primary, out of something like 15 candidates. There had been one strong candidate against him, and right before the election Butcher and Ford sent out a mailer that was the rottenest hit piece you could imagine. I nearly threw up when I saw it. But it worked. It just blew Johnnie's opponent right out of the race, with innuendo and untruths.

Due to repercussions from sending out that slimy mailer, Johnnie's popularity had sagged by election time. Meanwhile, a write-in candidate—Ron Packard, who had been mayor of Carlsbad—had joined the race. Write-ins usually don't garner many votes, but Packard would have drawn enough votes away from Johnnie that the Democrat on the ballot thought he had a lock on the thing.

Bright and early on election day, however, Packard supporters went to polling booths, breaking the voting machines so people could only vote by writing in the candidate. I guess people didn't like Johnnie or the Democrat enough to actually go to the effort of writing their names, and Packard won the election. The Democrat complained to Congress and they held an investigation, but nothing came of it. Packard's still in office.

Two good things came out of the race though. Donna and I became friends with the actor Buddy Ebsen and with a newspaper columnist, Jerry Kobrin.

Johnnie's campaign consultants had told him that Buddy was very popular in his district and that it would help if he could get his endorsement. A friend arranged for me to meet Buddy at a party. Even though he said he'd been run ragged campaigning for Reagan and others and didn't want to get involved, he met with Johnnie and wound up as his biggest booster. He appeared at loads of events, did everything he was asked to, and, after the primary, stayed up all night until the vote count was in.

Buddy and I saw a lot of each other after that. He'd just finished the *Barnaby Jones* series, had separated from his wife and was lonely.

Over lunch one day he told me a great story about how in his early days he'd been a contract player at MGM, and was doing pretty good for the studio. When his contract came up for renewal, they didn't offer him any kind of raise. He went to

Louis B. Mayer and said that if he didn't get paid more he'd leave the studio. Mayer told him not to let the door slam on his way out, and then blacklisted Buddy with the other studios.

Buddy wound up having to leave Hollywood to find work and teamed up with his sister on the East Coast in a song and dance act. They were driving to a gig in the Poconos in the snow and freezing wind in an open car, when Buddy busted out laughing. His sister asked what was up, and he said, "Boy, I sure told that son of a bitch Louis B. Mayer where to go."

At Christmas, Donna and I gave Buddy a wooden briefcase made of some exotic African hardwood. His marriage had reached the divorce stage by then, and he went to meet with his wife about the settlement. He came to see us afterward, and said to me, "John, that briefcase is really great. And do you know, it floats?" His wife had thrown the briefcase at him and it had landed in the pool.

Donna and I sat with Buddy at his table at his 90th birthday party recently. Sitting there, you'd swear he was on the verge of sleep. But when they called him to the microphone, he was as alert as anybody could be. He recited Lincoln's Gettysberg Address off the top of his head and followed that with a miraculous tap dance to the "Battle Hymn of the Republic." Then he came back to the table and started snoring. We really felt honored to be with him.

We met Jerry Kobrin when he was covering Johnnie's campaign for his newspaper. Jerry came from the old school of journalists, meaning he was about the cheapest guy you ever saw in your life. He never paid for a meal. Jerry loved to gamble. I booked his bets, and he always lost. When he'd get so far in the hole that there was no way he could ever pay up—and he never would pay up—I'd suggest that he just bet double or nothing and eventually he'd win. At one time he owed me $8000 before he finally cleared the slate at double or nothing. He'd bet just about every pro football game on a Sunday. He'd never bet with the Raiders, because they bugged him, and he'd always

On the road to Pennyslvania with my journalist friend
Jerry Kobrin. We towed a Jeep behind us, which is where I
made Jerry ride if he wanted a cigar while we were moving.

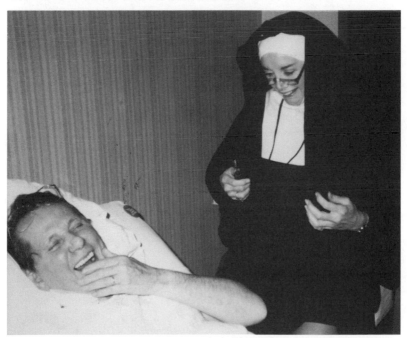

A "nun" gives me some. Jerry Kobrin's friend Jan Knowlton
cheers me up after my first carotid artery surgery.

bet with the Buffalo Bills because they had a Jewish coach.

Though Jerry loved a free meal, he hated having to dress for it, which so many of the society functions called for. He had a quick wit that I loved. One night we'd gone out to eat at a Thai restaurant, and as soon as we sat down, a black waiter walked by. Jerry exclaimed, "Jesus, John, not another black Thai dinner!"

I once had a junky souvenir boomerang that I gave to the Goodwill charity along with a pile of other things. Jerry called Goodwill's local headquarters, tracked down the area to which the items had been sent, and dug through heaps of junk in two of their stores before he found the boomerang and bought it back. Jerry did all this just so that, on my birthday that year, I'd open my gift from him and find it was that dopey boomerang. Jerry was standing there, and with a straight face, he said, "John, don't you know boomerangs always come back?"

In the area, Jerry was the magnet that brought everyone together. He was a real mixer. He'd call me up and say Joe Blow was dying to meet me, then he'd call Joe Blow and tell him the same thing. He added a tremendous amount to the social community, getting interesting people from all walks of life and social strata together. Since he passed away a couple of years ago, that doesn't happen anymore around here.

Launching the Prowler '76 in, conveniently, 1976.

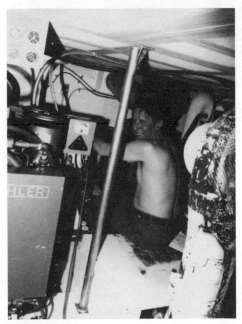

A typical scene of me relaxing at sea.
In the engine room of the Prowler '76.

This is the best a photographer could do with me.

GLAD TITHINGS

When I was a kid in Compton, the Eisenbeisz family across the street from us always went to church and Sunday school, and their kids all turned out pretty straight. They were just a nice family, and I always admired that. It put the idea in the back of my head that if I ever had a family, I'd get into a church. Donna felt that way too.

In 1955, one of my workers was involved in starting a Lutheran church in Anaheim. He and his wife called on us and invited us to attend. Our boys were getting to an age where we thought they might get some good out of Sunday school, so we went. To join the church, you'd attend a pastor's class one night a week, in which he'd explain the Lutheran faith. That's where Donna and I first heard about the notion of tithing.

At the time we only tithed to the church, because they were just getting started and needed help. I was taking a weekly salary of around $125, and we lived within our means, like working people. We started our tithing by giving $10 a week to the church. Then we made our giving a consistent 10 percent, and the percentage just kept going up from there. The money we tithed always came first, off the top of what we made, not from what we had left over after spending on ourselves.

What we get out of it is simply the fun of doing it. As thrilling as it was for Donna and me when we saw Fleetwood go public on the stock exchange in 1965, the big thrill was what came on the heels of that. After a day of frenetic hubbub at the stock exchange, the two of us ended up sitting on the floor back at our hotel, figuring everything that we could do with our $2 million windfall.

Our church had hopes of building a new sanctuary, and was trying to raise the $200,000 needed to build it. They'd raised $60,000, and Donna and I decided we had the rest of what they needed, phoned the preacher and told him they could get going on the construction.

That was a high point in our lives because we never imagined being able to do that. It still feels great to be able to help people out. And it may be coincidental, but the preacher had told us in 1955 that the more you give, the more you get back. That has been absolutely true in our lives. That's just the way it works.

But here's the catch: if you give in order to get, you won't get anything. It's got to be without any expectations, and you can't fool yourself on that. You can tell when you're giving for the joy of giving and when you aren't.

The first genuinely large contribution we made was after one of our stock sales in 1970. The Anaheim YMCA was nearly broke after starting a building project it couldn't afford. We gave them $1,170,000, which got them out of the hole and completed construction on their gymnasium. That made the newspapers because at the time, and perhaps still, it was the largest contribution, world-wide, that the YMCA had ever received.

Donna's and my notion of giving was still the one that my dad had taught me when he anonymously left the bag of groceries in the old woman's tent at Hobo Hot Springs. Charity is like sex: it's best done in private. That, however, has proved almost impossible to do, because the charities all plead with you to let them use your gift as an example, to get other people to give more.

The gym was named for Danny Caruthers, one of Doug Caruthers' sons. He was an excellent, fearless midget car racer, who died in a race in 1971. When the gym was finally finished in March of 1972, the Y got us involved in making a big thing of the dedication ceremony. *Hammersmith is Out* wasn't *quite* out yet, and I got Peter Ustinov and Stan Freberg, to attend.

The YMCA is a Christian organization and there was a lot of rah-rah patriotism in the ceremony, while Ustinov was neither Christian nor American. He was uncomfortable with the whole thing, but he was a sport, not to mention a ham, and he delivered the dedication speech.

I can't even tell you how much Donna and I have given away since then, but for years now it has been 50% of what we make. We'd give away even more if it weren't for the fucking income tax.

It was entirely our money we were giving away, not the company's. I have always felt that giving is a personal matter. My notion of a company's civic responsibility is to pay your people a good salary, and if they wanted to personally make contributions, that was their business. It wasn't our business to give away the stockholders' money.

The problem with giving money away is that everybody wants some. There are always people who are scamming you, or whose charity is inefficient or ineffective. There are a zillion charities whose main concern seems to be providing a nice income for the people running them. There are some where only five or ten cents on the dollar actually goes to the cause. Not all of our money has necessarily found its best use, but our big contributions have generally had good results. While we check out most of the folks we give to, we also rely on intuition a bit, and it has usually steered us right. Donna and I tend most often to help children's charities, because we believe the most good comes from that.

While it was a church that started us on tithing, we've grown to be a little cautious of religious organizations over the years. In our experience, they haven't misused the funds we've given them. The pastors weren't lining their pockets or anything. But the guys get *monumentitus*: they no sooner build a new church or tower than they need to start in on another glorious huge project.

It's practically an occupational hazard that seems to go with the territory, if the territory is the pulpit. These guys walk around and everybody tells them how wonderful they are, and soon they start to believe it and get a tremendous ego. It's like being a rock star. They may still be getting a lot of good work done, but they could do it without all the trappings.

Granted, Donna and I have people telling us we're wonderful all the time, and in Donna's case I have to agree with them. But if either one of us started to get a swelled head over it, the other one would stick a pin in it pretty quick. We know that we're only doing what we do because it's fun and because we've been blessed enough in our own lives that we're able to help others.

Organizations give us plaques all the time. They mean well, but Donna and I just have to joke about it—remarking at how we've subscribed to the Plaque of the Week Club—because trophies and monuments to our wonderfulness isn't what it's all about.

Jeez, at Fleetwood they tried hanging a portrait of me in the boardroom. I got one look at it and said, "Put that son of a bitch away until after I die." Who the hell wants to see something like that?

DOWN AND UP IN THE '80S

In our 1980 fiscal year, Fleetwood showed its first and only loss. That was during the second energy crunch, and it was also the tail-end of the Carter years, when interest rates were up over 20%. In 1979 we'd had an $800 million gross, and netted $23 million. In 1980 sales dropped to $472 million, and we ran a loss of $8.4 million.

Despite that, we still paid our stockholders a dividend of 13 cents a share. Our financial VP then, Boyd Plowman, pushed for that to protect our stock price, which it did. Boyd's an absolute genius, a hard worker and a good man, and Fleetwood was lucky to have him.

The second energy crunch was the same song, second verse: we did what we'd done before, running lean and smart while also pressing on with improving our product. In 1981, sales were down another 9 %, but we showed a $2.4 million profit.

I'd never been too worked up about politics before that, but Carter was just killing us. That was the only time since the mid-50s when I was really concerned about the business. The nation was just grinding to a halt with those interest rates.

Hence, the first political campaign I donated to was Ronald Reagan's. The day of the election, Fleetwood was taking part in a trade show in LA at Dodger stadium. The show was poorly attended, and the dealers that did come weren't buying any new product at all. To stock anything at 20 percent interest, they'd have to make a whale of a profit just to break even.

I was staying in a hotel in LA on election day, and I walked into my room just in time to see Jimmy Carter and his wife standing there on TV with long, long looks on their faces. I let out a war whoop. It was obvious they'd just thrown in the towel. It was a landslide for Reagan, and it was amazing how fast things turned around after that, starting even before he took office. The interest rates came down, and we got back to business. I still don't know what Carter could have done to screw things up as much as he did.

When downturns like that are over, the demand for product is staggering. If you can get back in business quickly, that's when you can really make your strides.

Because of Fleetwood's policies—because we ran the business with the knowledge that things weren't always going to be rosy; because we were debt-free and maintained a pretty good bank account; because we owned our properties and didn't have big lease bills—we were poised on the starting block when things began to pick up. It's easy grabbing market share and making big margins then, because the rest of the industry is struggling under its debts to get current.

Most of the industry ground to a halt with the 20% interest of the Carter years, and we did too. But we went ahead and completed our unfinished inventory, so we had lots of completed units. The plant in Riverside alone must have had a couple of hundred sitting there.

One day in the fall before the election, we had a visitor at the plant—I forget who—and he saw all our units sitting there and said, "That's kind of scary isn't it?" And I said, "No. We own them, so we're not paying a nickel on them. When this is over we're going to be glad we've got that product, because nobody else has it."

And, sure enough, after the election when interest rates came down, dealers were tickled pink to find we had that ready inventory. By spring it had all been sold and we were back in full production.

1982 was Fleetwood's first billion dollar year, and, boy, did we have a big party. The guys in management wanted to get an expensive portrait done of me. Instead, I told them what I really wanted was a piece of paper with the names of every single Fleetwood employee on it. I got that, and for the party, they had Sidney Miller—who was Donald O'Connor's old partner in Las Vegas—write a song, wherein he used the name of every soul in the company.

Not too long after that, I canned some of those souls. We had a plant in Visalia, north of LA, making a line of mobile homes we called Sandpointe. The San Joaquin valley was a booming market at the time, but in the plant's two years it hadn't been able to make a profit.

I designed a new Sandpointe unit in our Riverside prototype shop. It had a slightly different floor plan and a bright yellow exterior with white trim. They came to be called "banana trailers" in the industry, and you could see them from a mile away.

I went up to Visalia and threw out everything they were building and put the one new unit into production. Then I found that the foremen and a lot of people in the plant just couldn't do anything right. They'd make a jig to build a wall, and somehow the wall would always come out two inches too long or too short. They couldn't even put a light fixture on a wall straight.

These guys simply couldn't do the job. Several of them were bikers and I found out later that a lot of them were on some kind of dope. I fired them, just like that, and we proceeded to turn the plant around.

Not long after I fired the bikers, they all turned up in front of the plant, with their cycles, leather jackets, beards and all. The plant manager told me they were menacing the workers. I was out on the floor with a shop apron on, with a good-sized hammer on the belt. I was furious that these low-lifes who couldn't do the job would be getting on the case of those who could. I went straight out to the bikers and said, "What do you fuckers want?"

Maybe it was because I was still carrying that hammer, but they turned wimp right away. I told them to get out of there before I called the fuzz to run them in for vagrancy. And that was that.

Once I put a decent crew in there, we built production up to ten houses a day and shot to number one in sales in California. There was a company called Champion that had been number one, and one of my motivations was to beat them. Goals like that are fun.

After I moved on, the design staff had them start building the Sandpointe in more conventional colors. Eventually, the unit fell by the wayside. They'd improved it until it was no good anymore.

We started making another mobile home in the '80s that eventually turned out to be great for the company. Like everyone else, we'd been making our house trailers with aluminum sides, steel roofs and plywood interior walls. Starting during the Carter years, though, we had a double-wide trailer called the Chadwick that had sheeted plywood on the outside and a new product that looked like stucco on the exterior, so it looked like a house. We had a regular wood shingle roof on it, and the interior was wallpapered drywall. It was practically like a stick-built house.

The Chadwick had a lot going for it, but it was priced higher too, and it went nowhere with the interest rates of the Carter years. When things eased up after the election, we started building a couple of other models that were like the Chadwick. They just didn't catch on with the public, and we phased them out after about a year and a half.

But five years later, the rest of the industry started to turn in the direction of more house-like trailers. From our experience with the Chadwick and the other models, we were primed for that trend, and got in there long before anybody else claimed much market share.

We also started building a deluxe motor home in the '80s. In our Pace Arrow plants, we made a model called the Limited, into which we piled as much high-end junk as we could think of. The market responded to it, so we dedicated one of our plants in Decatur, Indiana to building Limiteds, and brought in the best people from our two nearest plants to staff it.

After a few years, the model name was changed to American Eagle, and we boosted the quality and price again. I say "we" but I actually had very little to do with the Eagle's success. That plant was nearly autonomous from our other operations, and its manager, Dick Parks, is the man who developed the product and made it soar. At this writing, he's the head of the RV division, and a great asset to the company.

The Eagle has been a big, big winner in the high-end market. We've had a lock on that market for a long time. You need volume to sell at the price we do, and no one else has been able to build up to that volume, because they'd have to sell at a loss to be competitive with us. The wholesale price of the Eagle line ranges from $160,000 to $225,000, and there's a new model that might be up around $450,000. In that market, the only way to make something sell better is to put more junk in it. The market for a high-end motor home is the wealthy retiree who wants to show off.

In the 1980s and earlier, it was hard for a buyer to get an RV financed. Mobile homes have traditionally been bad financing risks, but the people who bought RVs were solid citizens. There were no repossessions to speak of, and RV loans were really good paper. But for some reason the finance industry didn't see it that way, and it was hard to get financing.

So in 1986 we started the Fleetwood Credit Corporation. I put Larry Pitroff, who had been our personnel manager, in charge of the operation, and he did a tremendous job, building it into a substantial business with ten offices nationwide. Over a decade, we proved to the entire financing industry that RV paper was excellent paper. Consequently, a lot of other finance companies started handling RVs.

By 1996, Fleetwood's then-president, Glenn Kummer, was really hot on making the company look good to Wall Street, and one of the things that impresses the Street is a high earnings ratio. I've always felt that any black ink is good ink, but Glenn's view was that, because the credit corporation was less profitable than our other operations, it was bringing our earnings average down.

At Glenn's urging, we sold the Fleetwood Credit Corporation in 1996, at what seemed like a gigantic profit at the time. Two years later, though, the new owners sold it for three times what we received.

Instead of using the money we got from the sale to expand our manufacturing, Glenn used most of it in an effort to buy back Fleetwood stock, another ploy to make us look pretty to Wall Street, which I'll address later.

General Motors had been hassling us for just as long as we'd been ignoring them over our using the Fleetwood name, which they felt belonged to them because of the Cadillac Fleetwood. That resolved in the mid-'80s when, as I'd mentioned earlier, GM screwed up and gave one of their new motor homes a name we'd already trademarked.

GM's motor homes turned out to be remarkably unsuccessful. Automotively, their basic design made for a good, nice looking vehicle, but there were two things very wrong with it. It had windows that curved up over the top, and you simply couldn't sit in the thing if the sun was up, because it would cook you. The models were also designed with front-wheel drive, when all the home's weight was in the back, so they got stuck everywhere. GM was never even able to cajole motor home dealers into carrying their models. They had to foist them off on GM car dealers.

The entire motor home industry got a big laugh out of it. It was a terrible house, and it was always my opinion that a motor home had to be a house first and a vehicle second. That was always obvious to me, but it seemed like the rest of the industry didn't design that way.

Customers will ignore little lumps and bumps in the linoleum if you give them a unit that really works for them. When I'm testing out a motor home, I move myself into it. Where am I going to have my clothes? Where do my socks go?

Does the kitchen layout work for me? Those are the simple things that matter.

In the mid-'80s, Glenn Kummer had the idea that we should contact all of Fleetwood's customers to see how satisfied they were. We asked if they would recommend our products to others. Only 76 percent of the customers in our housing said they would, and only 82 percent of those with RVs.

Those are great approval ratings if you're in politics, but not if you're in business. Your customers are essentially your sales people. If a guy buys something and he's satisfied with it, he'll tell 20 people. If he isn't satisfied, he'll probably tell 30 people. So a satisfied customer is really what it's all about.

Our findings helped knock out any sense of complacency we may have been feeling amid all our success. We went to work on addressing their complaints, and got customer satisfaction up above 90 percent.

It wasn't until the late '80s that we began putting the Fleetwood name on all of our various divisions' products. That makes it easier to count all the Fleetwoods you pass on the highway, but otherwise it was a mistake for us. It gave customers the idea that the only difference between the lines was the name.

The reason for having different lines is that you then can have different dealers for them. The guy in town who has the Terry dealership has an exclusive on that product for a certain area, but if you also have a Prowler line, you can sell that to the dealer across the street.

I liked the idea of serving different dealerships, but felt we should supply them with different product. The Prowler, for instance, was initially totally different than the Terry, and the dealers across the street from each other would be happy.

But over the years the product lines tend to intermarry. Some of that comes from standardization being a more efficient way of manufacturing. Also, if you design a good feature into one model, everybody wants it. You know your competitors are going to copy it, so you pretty much have to copy it yourself in your other lines. As a result, though, before long the only real difference between your lines is the nameplate. In the industry, we call that "the nameplate game." I never did figure out a way to prevent it.

As fed up as my old boss Roy Clayton had been with the trailer business when he sold me Terry Coach in 1964, he eventually moved back to California from Europe and started another company.

Roy originated the idea of the fifth-wheel trailer, which is what the industry calls the now-ubiquitous design where trailers are hitched to the middle of a pickup truck bed rather than the rear bumper. Roy had been a truck driver, and his fifth wheel design was similar to the way trucks are hitched.

Roy began building his fifth-wheel models in Irvine around 1983. When I first saw one, I thought, "Hell, folks aren't going to buy pickup trucks to haul those things around." It wasn't three years after that that we had to start building fifth-wheel trailers ourselves, and they've now almost entirely replaced standard pull-trailers. So much for me always being right.

'80s LIFE

In 1987 I quit smoking and started painting, both as a result of having carotid artery surgery.

I had started smoking when I was 19, to accompany my drinking. If you drank, you smoked, and you only quit one. At AA meetings there would always be a pall of smoke over everything. It made you wonder if there were Smokers Anonymous meetings where they were all boozing it up.

I smoked Pall Malls until the last two years before I quit, when I switched to Kools. They were supposed to be not as bad for you, but I smoked twice as many of them. I never liked smoking, but, God, I was hooked. I couldn't do anything without smoking.

I was in the hospital for four days for the carotid artery surgery, and, of course, I couldn't smoke. When I got out, I thought, "I've got a head start on not smoking. I'll just keep going." And that was it. My last cigarette was on St. Patrick's day, 1987. That also is when I stopped being skinny. When you don't smoke, food tastes really good.

I was a long time recovering. The surgery itself wasn't so bad, but the doctors were giving me medication that was making me ding-dong. When I finally quit the medication, I got well in a snap. In the meantime, Donna hired an artist friend of hers to teach me to paint.

She'd come over with an easel and sit beside me while I worked at it. After a couple of weeks I was on my own. It was a great way for passing the time. When I first started I'd tire quickly, but before long I was sitting at the easel all day. I did about 30 paintings, of the hole in the rock at Cabo, the Dumont Dunes by Death Valley, and other landscape scenes. I gave most of them away, and haven't painted since, but I sure would if I were wracked up again or disabled.

Years before that, in Capistrano, I was recovering from something or other and had a go at making gold jewelry. I had a friend who made jewelry for Van Cleef and Arpels. He brought a bench, torches, acid and all that to the house, and gave me some lessons. I made necklaces and such for all the kids for Christmas, and a ring from 18 karat gold wire that I still wear. My favorites were a pair of earrings I made for Ray Conniff's wife, circles containing the lines of the musical staff, holding the first five notes of "Somewhere My Love."

We've been friends with the Conniffs since the '60s, and once Donna, the girls and I even did an entire European tour with the Ray Conniff Singers. Our job was to clap, and to find restaurants that were still open after the shows.

I had bought a new Rolls on that trip, while Ray was being chauffeured in a mere Daimler. The show promoters would see the Rolls, assume it was Ray, and motion us to pull up to the red carpet. Meanwhile, they'd be gesturing to Ray to get out of our way.

Something a lot of people don't know about Ray is that he's huge all over South America. Maybe it's because there's no language barrier, what with his singers always going "la la la" instead of singing the lyrics. Ray was down fishing with me in Mexico once, out in the very middle of nowhere. Two Mexican fishermen came up near us in their ponga boat, spotted Ray, and exclaimed, "Meester Coneeef!"

We've done a lot of traveling with Ray, and he's always doing something. One time, he got his trombone out, had all the kids in the campground grab pots and pans, and led them in a parade. Another time we heard a commotion, and it was Ray, standing on the roof of the motor home, playing the trombone, in his Jockey shorts.

"I shall return!" Piloting out of Cabo San Lucas.

Ray Conniff calling the fish to breakfast, on the Bounder in the '80s. Ray has made dozens of boating and RV trips with us.

The Bounder prototype in its larval stage,
in my workshop, 1985.

THE BOUNDER

It is always amazing to me to see the ways businesses find to throw money away. Instead of hiring consulting groups and commissioning endless studies, why not just get out there in the world and see what works? I got most of my ideas for what our product should be by traveling around the country, talking to people who own Fleetwoods, and experiencing the product first-hand. That's where our best known and most influential product, the Bounder, came from.

In the '80s Donna and I made a lot of plant tours across the country. I've always hated flying, and loved traveling by RV, so we virtually always used the latter means for our tours. On one trip in the Northeast and Canada it got so cold that all of our motor home's plumbing froze. We couldn't use the toilet or sinks. That was just an accepted fact in motor homes then, but after you've experienced it a few times, you start to think that maybe it isn't so acceptable.

When we came off that trip, I went to work developing a unit with a basement floor, where the water tank and pipes were enclosed, insulated and heated. The design I arrived at has since become the industry standard. After its introduction, you couldn't sell a motor home anymore where the plumbing froze up. That was the result of our simply *using* our product, which cost us nothing. So many people in business are unwilling to trust their own common sense, though, and end up chasing their tails with studies, polls, focus groups and such.

At the time, 1985, Fleetwood was doing exceptionally well with our Pace Arrows, Southwinds, Tiogas and Jamborees, and I didn't want to disturb a good thing. But I had a zillion ideas for a motor home, to make it different from the basement floor on up, so I decided to make a brand new model.

I've never been able to fully communicate to others what

I want in building a product, and I have no patience for engineers who will only look at something on paper or a computer screen just so they can tell you why it won't work. My thing is just to *do it*. Something might look fine, or utterly unworkable, on paper, but there are scads of unlooked-for factors that come into play when you build the thing in three dimensions. You'll hit snags you never imagined, but you'll also probably think of ways around them.

So I decided to develop the motor home on my own, away from the bustle of Fleetwood. I bought a building in Costa Mesa—about ten minutes from our home in Newport—set it up with some tools and started in on the new model, which we ultimately named the Bounder.

The major design innovation I came up with was to raise the height of the floor in the unit. Along with enclosing the water system, the higher floor provided lots of new storage space, which is what dealers and customers could never get enough of in a motor home.

On most motor homes, the storage was on top, which was particularly inconvenient—and downright dangerous—for our older, retired customers. The new design was a real mind-blower, because there was even room enough in our basement compartments to stow surfboards. There were storage compartments going most of the way around the unit, and they were all easily accessible from outer doors.

Conventional motor homes had other disadvantages people were accustomed to living with. On most, there was a step-down of ten or more inches from the driver's section to the rest of the unit, so unless you were sitting up front, you couldn't see out the windshield. With my raised floor, the entire unit was on a level with the driver's area and the view was better all around.

A lot of the new features I designed into the unit were just common sense. On most dashboards, if anything went wrong, it was a bastard to get up underneath the dash to fix the problem. I simply hinged the dash so you could lift it, and then fix things from above.

In most motor homes, you could scarcely find a horizontal surface on which to lay anything down, so I also made the dashboard flat, except for the control area, so that it doubled as a table. Throughout the unit, I gave nearly every flat surface a "keeper edge" to stop things from rolling off when you're traveling.

At the time, nobody in the industry was making much provision for a TV set. As standard equipment, I designed two TV sets into the unit, one in front and one in the bedroom, along with a VCR and a switching unit so you could watch the antenna feed on one set and the VCR on the other.

Most of the RV industry is situated closer to Detroit, and, perhaps because of that, they seem to design their motor homes like automobiles, while to me it's a house. It may be out in the woods or in an asphalt parking lot, but it's a house for whoever's in it. For the Bounder layout, I adapted the floor plan from a 28-foot Terry travel trailer, and it made a great house.

I had a kid from the Riverside plant come down to help me a bit, but I practically built the first Bounder by myself. It doesn't take that much to knock one of them together. When you're manufacturing an RV, you typically fabricate the walls on a big vacuum table, but you can make a wall yourself in four or five hours simply by using contact cement and a linoleum roller.

Dave Russell, the head motor home design person at Fleetwood, has signs posted in his shop that read, "The most valuable tool in the prototype shop is the dumpster," which I think is very true, and not just because he's quoting me.

It's my experience that the first prototype you build of anything is no damn good. It only gives you a little idea of how to do it better. So you build another one, and throw that first one in the dumpster, probably followed by the second, the third and more. I designed and built seven hinged dashboards for the Bounder, and threw the first six away.

So many people let their ego get in the way, where their pride of authorship won't let them think anything they come up with is less than pure genius. So when I see a dumpster filling up in the design shop, that's the healthiest thing around, because it means the guys aren't afraid to try stuff and aren't so proud that they don't recognize when it sucks.

I almost put the entire Bounder in the dumpster before I had it finished, though. I'd got it to a point where I had the floor built with the tanks enclosed and the cabinetry sitting on the floor, but it didn't have any walls yet. When you viewed it that way, it looked totally awkward and too top-heavy to go down the road, though it was only eight inches taller than what we'd been making.

That's how the Bounder looked when the management from our Riverside HQ came down and see how the project was going. I could see them giving each other looks and scratching their heads, like they were afraid the old man had flipped.

After that, I took a fresh look at it the next day, and thought maybe I had better just tear it up and forget about it. It was that ungainly, a word which, if you take out a couple of letters, means it was ugly.

But I was still curious to see what it would look like completed. So I built the walls and roof on it, and it was a whole different picture, though still not exactly *Gone With the Wind.* Donna threw a party when I finished it.

Then the plant assembled a 24-foot prototype (which we soon decided was a real dog) to accompany the 34-foot one I'd made. A gang of us took them on the road to show them to dealers. This included the head of our RV division—Elden Smith—Dave Russell, some of the sales staff and myself, and we had quite a time out there, driving 2000 miles and visiting some 15 dealers in Las Vegas, Salt Lake City, Sacramento and down through the San Joaquin Valley.

It was funny watching the dealers' reactions. They'd been told the chairman of Fleetwood was coming in with a new product, and then they'd see this four-wheeled atrocity pull up with me at the wheel, and start sweating over what they were supposed to say to me.

When they got down to it, the dealers agreed that it was the ugliest fucking thing they'd ever seen in their life, but they were really impressed with its features. As one dealer in Reno, Dennis Durant, put it, "It's no Christian Dior, but then that sonofabitch never went camping."

We'd take the dealers for a walk around the outside of the thing, and before we'd made the circuit they'd be sold. Even though, at that point, they were assuming the inside was ugly as the exterior, the design had already solved so many of the functional problems of motor homes that they were really excited.

Even the doors were a new design. Most motor homes had awnings, and the usual door's squared edges would catch on the awning and rip the material. My doors were rounded at the top, so there were no more rips. It was also less flimsy than most doors and had a different locking mechanism. The rest of the industry wound up copying it, and it's what they still use today.

With features like that on the outside, it was just icing on the cake when the dealers went inside and found the Bounder also had a surprisingly good-looking, functional interior.

One thing we learned on the road that I hadn't even planned on was that the basement floor construction radically cut down on road noise. But we also found that the vehicle had a few bugs, literally. I'd designed the windshield with something of an eyebrow overhanging it. When bees and other insects were headed for us, this brow caught them in an air vortex, where the bugs would keep spinning and spinning in front of the glass. I thought it was kind of neat, because it kept them from splatting on the windshield, but Dave Russell argued that it was distracting, and maybe even hypnotic, to have bugs swirling around like that all the time. So that eyebrow was short-lived. One other thing we learned on the trip is that when you use red oak for a cutting board, it smells like cat pee.

When we weren't visiting the dealers, we were camping, and we had a ball. One of the guys was a knife collector, as I am, and we had a one-upmanship thing going, until I got out a custom-made samurai-style knife I had, whacked through a tree limb with it, and then used the blade to shave the lettering off the guy's business card. There's nothing like a good knife.

In Reno, we decided to take in the show at the MGM Grand. It was sold out, but just before show time, I called my friend Milton Pickman, who was friends with the head of MGM. The next thing I knew, we were being ushered to the CEO's personal box, front and center. That really impressed our waitress, up until the point when she asked who we were. "We sell house trailers," I told her, and we just weren't important after that.

The response the prototype motor home got on the road was good enough that we decided to take a chance on it and put it into production. It was so radically different, and still pretty ugly, that we didn't want to put it out as a Pace Arrow or one of our existing lines, so we opened a new plant to build it.

I'd reached a point in my mind where I was pretty stuck on the Bounder's ugly duckling design, thinking it would make people focus that much more on its practical advantages. But Elden Smith and his marketing guys argued that they didn't want to have to drag people into it to get them to appreciate it. They wanted a rounder Bounder. Elden had the Riverside plant make up another prototype, which was given a good going-over by the design crew. Their new design cost about $600 more to manufacture and was a lot more presentable, though its looks were still a hard sell.

I had made the prototype's sidewalls the way we built

The "rounder" Bounder, that went to market.

My original drawing for the Bounder logo,
on a Denny's napkin.

travel trailers then, with a wood frame construction. It made for a cheaper unit, but didn't hold up well in a motor home, so the production models used a steel frame. We kept the wood floor, though, which contributed to the Bounder's quiet ride. The design folks came up with a better-looking front end, which got rid of the bug swirl effect.

We also switched to using a longer "stretch" chassis, which I'd avoided on the prototype because a stock chassis was cheaper. It's shorter wheel base maneuvers better, but it also will weather-vane in high cross winds, because the overhanging back end pivots on the rear wheels. When we had the prototype on the road trip, I once had to scoot under that overhang to fix something. I was wearing a pancake-sized, gem-encrusted belt buckle that I quite liked, and it caught on a doohickie under there. I was stuck beneath the thing until the guys lifted the rear end enough for me to slide out. Perhaps that's why I didn't put up much argument when the design team wanted to go with the stretch chassis.

Aside from those differences, the production Bounder was unchanged from the prototype, even down to the drawer sizes.

When we'd been casting around for a name, my journalist friend Jerry Kobrin gave me a list of names he thought up, and Bounder was the first one on his list. I thought it was a great name, but our marketing guys said, "We can't use that. We looked it up in the dictionary, and it means an unsavory character."

We were discussing this at a Denny's out in Riverside, and I said, "No, that's not what we mean," and took a napkin and did my best to draw a jumping kangaroo on it, bounding from one place to another. They thought that might work and took the napkin to a real illustrator to make it look less like a starving rodent. He drew the logo we have now, with the smiling kangaroo. It was a winner, a symbol Bounder owners really bonded with. They collect kangaroo mugs, kangaroo pillows and all manner of marsupial merchandise.

I wanted to try something new for the brochure too, to clearly illustrate the differences between the Bounder and everything else out there. I asked the marketing guys, "Why don't we make it a comic book, where we have neighbor families with a Winnebago and a Bounder, and have them compare them?"

That's what we did. We showed the guy with the Winnebago having a hell of a time getting his stuff stored, and having all the other problems that had been designed out of the Bounder.

For one thing, the Bounder's power supply included two great big golf cart batteries. A normal motor home only had one small battery, and if you weren't running the generator your lights typically would dim and go out in no time. So the comic depicted the Winnebago people stumbling around in the dark.

Fleetwood has been putting those comics out for over a decade now, and people collect them! It's a big deal for them to have one from each year.

The comic book wasn't the only place where the Winnebago didn't fare well. Here's a great example of how other companies throw money away. Concurrent with my making the Bounder, Winnebago was developing a new unit. They spent a year and a half and $28 million developing their product, while I spent $65,000 and my time, which was nothing but 90 days of fun for me.

I heard that when the folks at Winnebago first saw the Bounder, they all laughed and thought it was the stupidest thing they'd ever seen, except for one guy, who could see that we'd aced them. That was Dave Parton, who was also smart enough to come to work for Fleetwood not long after that.

We hit the market at the same time in 1986, and the Bounder left the Winnebago in the dust. The Bounder has remained number one in sales nationally ever since.

The plant manager, Loren Schmidt, was a big part of the Bounder's success. He'd worked as a plant manager for a

The first Bounder comic book, 1986.
Collect them all!

A page from a
Bounder comic.

Pace Arrow and a Southwind plant, and was a high-energy guy, with tons of enthusiasm. The Bounder was a strange product, and I knew it would take someone with those qualities, and a lot of faith, to get it off the ground.

I asked him to take the job, and he accepted, even though it meant a pretty good cut in pay at the time. Like all the managers, Loren was on a bonus system where he'd get a cut of the plant's success, and his old plant was very profitable. We gave him a deal where he'd participate in his old plant's success for a time, but it was still a big risk for him.

He got the Bounder operation going and really made it spin, and in no time at all it was more profitable than his other plant had been.

That first Bounder plant was in Riverside, and still is, with Loren still managing it. He does a great job, and it does well by him. He hasn't shown any interest in getting back into division management—where he had been at one time—because he's more of a hands-on guy. Also with his plant as successful as it is, his bonus probably allows him to earn a lot more than the division manager above him.

Once the Bounder was on dealers' lots, they started selling right away, even if one of our East Coast dealers did advertise it as "an ugly duckling with the heart of a swan." Meanwhile, the rest of our competition were as derisive of the Bounder as the folks at Winnebago had been. They gave us a solid year of bad-mouthing it, and that was fine by us.

Elden told his marketing and sales staff to do everything they could to make the other manufacturers think our basement floor design was a failed novelty, rather than something we were entirely committed to. By the time the competition's registration studies let them learn what a winner the Bounder was, it was headed right into first place in sales. We were also well on the way to converting the Southwind and Pace Arrow lines—which had strong sales already—to a basement floor design.

After about a year, some of the smaller companies started to copy us. We had patented the basement floor design, but it is a pain in the ass to enforce a patent, so we let them get away with it. Their copying us was actually to our advantage, because it lent more credence to the basement floor design. Meanwhile the major competitors such as Winnebago started to hang luggage compartments from their regular floor and do other things to work around our patent, because they knew we would sue *them* if they copied us directly.

The entire industry has since followed our lead, but we had the design all to ourselves for a long, crucial time. So the Bounder was a big home run for us all around.

Even with everyone copying the below-floor storage, the Bounder has stayed number one. That's because a lot of manufacturers don't realize that there's a whole lot more to the Bounder than just the basement. The only ones who do realize it are the savvy buyers, who have had motor homes before and can appreciate what works and what doesn't. That's who buys the Bounder. They are dedicated motor homers, and real proselytizers for the Bounder.

Donna and I bought one of the first units off the line. We took a lot of trips in it, and whenever we'd pass another Bounder, the people in it would be waving to us like crazy. We'd been driving the Pace Arrows and Southwinds around for years without that ever happening.

A bunch of Bounder owners soon got together and started a club, without Fleetwood having anything to do with it. Now there's two clubs, one on each coast, and each has about 5000 members. They have rallies, where guys run around in kangaroo outfits and everything. In 1997 I went to a rally near Seattle held by the West Coast club. Five hundred Bounders showed up, and most of them arrived right at the check-in time, so they were lined up, backed up onto Interstate 5 for a mile and a half. It's pretty swell to see a whole traffic jam made up of something you've created.

With Buddy Ebsen at our second demolition party,
making way for Village Crean.

Donna and me surveying the wreckage.

WE MAKE A VILLAGE

After we moved out of Beverly Hills, we spent the rest of the '80s living in the house we'd bought in Newport. Though we had 125 feet on the bay, it was a shallow lot, too small of a house and there was no parking to speak of.

I'd still owned and tinkered around in the building in Costa Mesa where I'd developed the Bounder. Donna had an office in Irvine where she took care of our charitable work. We wanted a place where we could fit all our interests on one piece of property, and there just wasn't that kind of real estate around anymore.

I checked out a two-acre lot above Upper Newport Bay, and it was useless, but we saw another place down the street on four acres, which was mostly a weed-filled lot. We drove in and saw that there was a house, with a pool being put in. A construction worker there told us the owner was fixing the place up to sell it. He also told us the owner was running out of money.

That's what I liked to hear, so we bought the property in 1989. Everything the owner had put in or fixed up, we bulldozed out and started with a clean sheet of paper.

Like we had in Beverly Hills, we had a demolition party, but this time it was covered in the *National Enquirer*, which ran a photo of me driving a big bulldozer, with Buddy Ebsen by my side. (That wasn't my only time in the *Enquirer*. Another time they wrote about a "perfect non-attendance" award I'd received from the Exchange Club in Newport because I'd paid my dues for 29 years without ever attending a meeting.)

I laid out the compound design on my drawing board, where we wanted the house, shop, pool and guest houses. Then I hired a draftsman and engineer to draw up proper construction plans for the permit. We never had an architect in on the project.

My son Andy had come down with cancer, had surgery

and then a year of chemotherapy. Andy had got the idea that he was probably going to die, and lost interest in everything. He'd sold his RV retail business and was doing more or less nothing when we started construction. He came to work for me, and supervised the building of the whole place. I don't know if that's what helped him come out of his funk, but I know he did a great job for us.

I did the interior work on the mansion with a guy named Larry Miller. He had first worked for me in Beverly Hills when he was a hippie wood-carver and surfer. He did a bang-up job on the interior in Beverly Hills, and has been busy ever since doing custom woodwork.

If you pulled the wood panels off our new home's mansion walls, you'd see the sketches on the drywall of the designs we did. I did a lot of the wood-working myself, the oak trim and paneling. We set up a wood shop in the garage and wound up making a lot of our own furniture out there too. The garage, I should explain, is more like a small aircraft hanger, since I built it to design motor homes in.

Newspaper articles keep saying the mansion was designed after Tara in *Gone With the Wind*, but it's actually based on the other mansion in the movie, Twelve Oaks, which had the pillars and the staircase. Donna always wanted a house with pillars, and for that to look right you need an open expanse. Our lot overlooking the bay gave us that.

The construction took nearly three years. There are ten bedrooms in the main house, then two bedrooms in each of the four apartments above the normal garages, along with a one-bedroom apartment, an ice cream parlor, a gym, a movie screening room with a $100,000 sound system I've never learned to use, and all the usual big rooms you find in a mansion. All in all, the interior space is about 40,000 square feet.

We have secret rooms on the third floor. With two of them, you have to pull a bookcase away to get to them. The other one is really secret, where you have to push on a panel

Our
little
grass
shack.

Our
daughter,
Emily

and slide it over.

One of our new neighbors is a fine writer and newspaper columnist named Joe Bell. One day we found a note from him in our mailbox welcoming us to the neighborhood, and suggesting the name Village Crean for our new spread. We liked that, and it stuck.

We were living there long before the construction was finished. Donna and I only live in an apartment in the house, which, along with our respective offices, takes up maybe 3,000 square feet. We never officially moved in. Every time we'd come over from the Bayside Drive house, we'd bring a few more things along, until we were living more here than there. The construction was finally completed in 1991.

I still love cars, which accounts for all the garages we have. There's a '49 Plymouth identical to the one Donna and I had when we first married. Then there's everything from a 1923 Chevrolet fire engine to a big Hummer that Donna likes to drive in the desert. We've got Mercedes and Porsches and all that, but our favorite car to drive lately is the new VW beetle. Everybody waves at you when you're in one of those.

Since Donna and I live in the apartment, the main thing we do with the rest of the property is host benefits, either for charities we support or for organizations who ask to use the place. We used to host three or four functions a week here, but we've recently cut back to one event a week, because we were barely getting cleaned up from one event before there was another. It was just too much for us.

We've had very few security problems, considering that we've had so much of the public flowing through the place. The Santa Margarita Catholic high school used to have their graduation parties here. One year, their party wound up at midnight, and, around two in the morning, Donna and I were in bed and kept hearing sounds from upstairs. I called the Sheriff's office, and they were a long time showing up. It turned out to be just a couple of kids playing hanky-panky in one of the bedrooms. They were long gone by the time the Sheriffs got here.

I enjoy the society things once in a while, but between our Beverly Hills days and now, we've pretty well burnt out on them. They're all the same, with the same people doing the same things.

We love being here at Village Crean, but we also love getting away from it sometimes. We still take off for months on our boat or in a motor home. There have been a couple of occasions when Donna and I have arrived home from a trip in the Bounder, and then realized we wanted a little more of that uncomplicated life. So we just go camp in the Bounder for another week at an RV park at the other end of the bay, where there's a nice view of our mansion on the hill.

My cooking show co-host Barbara Venezia and me
on the cover of PBS station KOCE's magazine.

RELEASING MY INNER JULIA CHILD

When I was a kid, with my mom working and my dad usually sick in bed, I did a lot of the cooking at home. I was making beef stew by the time I was seven. My dad showed me how to chop up a bunch of potatoes, carrots and an onion really small, to sauté hamburger in the frying pan, add water and the vegetables, thicken it with some flour and spice it with salt and pepper.

Up at the Kern River, I made a lot with eggs and Spam, which I still like. My dad was always praising me for my cooking, and you're proud to be able to do that when you're a kid.

Back then, people could buy hundred-pound sacks of sugar or flour for about a dollar. I learned to do a lot of baking, and what I made the most of was angel food cake. That was a Depression delicacy, because it was really nothing but egg whites and sugar with a bit of flour. Everybody in the neighborhood had chickens, so there was always a surplus of eggs, even though we had no chickens of our own. After the farm in North Dakota, my dad didn't want anything to do with animals.

In the seventh grade they had a school carnival, a fund-raiser where every home room put on a play or something to make money. I was out sick the day my class organized the play. When I came back to school, the teacher said I should figure out something to do in the back of the classroom. I went home and made 20 darts out of wooden kitchen matches, needles and paper—cross-hatching one end of a match and sticking in pieces of paper to make fins. Then I made taffy, making the pieces all different colors using food coloring, and wrapping the pieces in wax paper.

At the school I hung the taffy on threads. I made a sign with shoe polish on butcher paper advertising that throwing the darts cost so much, and that you'd win whatever candy you hit. I don't think my customers ever hit one, and I wound up making more money for the fund-raiser than the whole home room.

I learned most of my cooking skills when I was a galley man in the Merchant Marine. I got into that hot and heavy, even helping the chief cook butcher whole sides of beef, which I never became very adept at. But he also cooked all the meats, and made all the gravies and sauces, so I learned a lot from him.

The ship's baker would go to work at midnight and work through breakfast in the morning. There wasn't much else to do onboard, so on many nights I'd stay up with the baker and help while he made bread, which was very physical work. A big treat for the crew was when we'd make donuts every two or three weeks. We'd put out 300 donuts at breakfast time, and the 60 crew members would finish them off by noon.

Between that and all my cooking as a kid, I got good enough to really enjoy being in the kitchen. To me, cooking is always fun because there are no limits. You never run out of different things to attempt, and that's without even trying to eat a snail or a kangaroo, which I wouldn't do. I don't even like trying kidney pie.

I improvise a lot in the kitchen. My friends kid me about how, when we go out to eat, I almost always take them to Denny's. But the thing I like about Denny's is that it is consistently mediocre. Whatever you get, it will be just like it was the time before. I've had good meals in five star restaurants, but then gone back three other times and it's not the same. They're not consistent at all. Those cooks cook the way I do. If I was to cook what I made for dinner last night again tonight, it would be entirely different.

Through the years, it got to where I wasn't doing as much cooking as I would have liked. Donna is a good cook, and she does most of the cooking at home. So it's only when we're on the road or on the boat when it's her relaxation time and I do the cooking.

Then one day in 1992 a friend called up and said a reporter friend was stuck for an entrepreneur to interview and asked if I was willing. I made an appointment and promptly forgot all about it, until just as I was going out a couple of days later this woman, Barbara Venezia, came banging on the door with her cameraman. Along with having completely forgotten about the interview, no one had told me it was for television, and I had to change clothes to look halfway respectable.

So we did the interview—her show was just on local-access cable—and it was nothing earth-shattering. After the thing was over, we got to talking about this and that, and I mentioned how much I enjoyed cooking.

Barbara now claims that I'd said I'd like someday to do a cooking show on TV, but I sure don't remember that. The next thing I knew, she'd made an appointment to come the next week to video tape a cooking show in our kitchen. I don't even know how the hell that happened, but that's Barbara. She's a sneaky little broad.

We shot it in the kitchen of the house, and it was just impossible, with everything cramped, bad lighting and cords running all over the place. But there was *something* there.

I'm serious about my cooking, and like a lot of cooks, don't like someone in my kitchen when I'm working. Barbara's something like half my age, and from a generation that apparently doesn't know jack about cooking. The only thing Barbara knows how to make is reservations. She was in my way, distracting me with all sorts of asinine questions, while being so vivacious you wanted to turn a fire hose on her.

But it worked. For some reason, it was a hoot to watch, and we decided to tape some more.

I installed a kitchen set in one corner of the big garage at Village Crean that I build motor homes in. And Barbara and I just went at it, with one cameraman and another camera permanently mounted over the range. I'd cook and Barbara would stir and get in my way, and we'd just wing it, without a script.

For the first few shows we had guest celebrities cook with us, friends of mine like Mr. Blackwell, Stan Freberg and Joey Bishop. That didn't click—there was just too much personality crowded around the stove. Joey did give us our name, though. We were originally calling the show *The Village Cooks* but Joey said we were more like the village idiots, and then came up with *At Home on the Range* for us.

We'd shoot one night a week, live to tape, with an audience in folding chairs. Barbara bought time from the local cable companies and found advertisers to sponsor us. I'd built a Fortune 500 company and done all these other things, and suddenly, because of this dumb lark of a show, I started getting recognized everywhere I went. Old people would stop me in the supermarket to tell me recipes. College kids claimed they'd all get together to watch the show—zonked out of their gourds, I'm assuming. Newspapers and magazines started writing about it.

And it was just us fucking up food. Honestly, there were weeks when I'd slide the featured dish straight from the pan into the trash. We made onion rings once that looked like melted plastic, and we had some of *that* too once, when we left a plastic plate on a hot burner.

Another time, a pile of tortilla grease-soaked paper towels caught fire. Linguine came out looking like a big hair ball. It being the garage, a spider wandered onto the set and I inadvertently made a salad with eight legs more than the recipe called for.

None of that was staged. That's all stuff that usually happens to me when I'm cooking. Sometimes I'll crack an egg, throw the shell in the recipe and the egg in the garbage.

So I'm just being myself on camera. I'm barely even aware of the thing, or the studio audience, who—and I really don't get this—laugh even when I'm just opening a ketchup

Get a load of those bell peppers! With my "At Home on the Range" co-host Barbara Venezia.

Why is this man smiling?

My new look for the new century. With Barbara Venezia as the Mayor of Seville and wife in "Carmen."

With California Governor Pete Wilson and his wife,
on the set of "At Home on the Range."

"George, may I recommend the broccoli?"
With George Bush in 1998.

bottle. But I know that I'm cooking with a time constraint, and Barbara's distracting me the whole time, so I get flustered and sometimes just flat-ass forget to put ingredients in. There's a lot of joking between Barbara and me, and we're fine friends, but I also get genuinely exasperated with her when we're cooking. I think that may be what worked for some of the old comedy duos, that they sort of got on each other's nerves.

Orange Coast magazine asked Milton Berle why he thought the show worked and he said, "It reminds me of the early days of live television. It has that 'anything can happen' quality. They're funny enough; John's a hell of a cook; and it doesn't hurt that he owns Orange County." Did I mention that Milton's a friend of mine?

After we'd been on about a year, the *LA Times* did a story about the show, and then CNN, CBS' *Eye to Eye with Connie Chung* and ABC's *Home* show followed with pieces on us. The ABC producers liked what they saw enough to sign us up to be regulars on the *Home* show, with a six-minute segment every Wednesday.

I think he was laying it on a little thick, but the producer of the *Home* show, Woody Fraser, told *Orange Coast* that Barbara and I were "the Burns and Allen of Orange County. They're cute as hell together, and good teams are very hard to find. You can't build them: there's either a chemistry there or there isn't."

ABC would send a camera crew with a satellite link-up to the garage and we'd just do what we normally do, except now it was going out nationally to several million viewers. Barbara thought we should go for broke on our first show with them, since we weren't any too sure they'd want us back after that, so we cooked our most popular recipe, which was for dog food. Donna and I had been on a Slim-Fast diet a few years before and I'd found I missed cooking more than I did eating, and I started cooking for our dog.

You may as well get something useful out of this book,

so here's the dog food recipe:

> *Cook four cups of instant rice. Boil one pound of navy beans and drain. Shred two carrots and two potatoes in a food processor. Combine all that in a large bowl, with three pounds of 30% fat hamburger meat, four eggs, four teaspoons of beef bouillon, one teaspoon of salt, and—just so you can call it health food—one-quarter cup of wheat germ. Put on a pair of gloves and mush it all up until there are no lumps. Put it all in a large baking pan and bake it in the oven at 350 degrees for 45 minutes. Serve it at room temperature. If you serve it to your mother-in-law, add ketchup.* *

One thing different about being on network TV was that when we were doing the show ourselves we didn't have a Standards and Practices department getting in a tizzy over every little thing we did. I mean, so what if I blow my nose on-camera? We hardly had a week on ABC where we didn't get a call from Standards and Practices complaining about something we said, whether it was Barbara remarking that my oily sesame chicken would slide right through ya, or me mentioning that my starched chef's hat is the only thing about me that's stiff anymore. But the show was going out live, so there was nothing they could do except bitch about it afterwards.

One week, Hanukkah was coming up, so we decided to make matzo ball soup. I got a recipe from my friend Jerry Kobrin, along with some of his humorous take on the history of Hanukkah.

So, fine, we're going along cooking and the host, Gary Collins, asked me how Kosher salt was different from regular salt. I just said, "Kosher salt costs more."

---

* Barbara has put together a book of our favorite recipes and jokes from the show. It's available through the show's website—www.hotrange.com—or by phone at (949) 851-3922. Be advised that we are not responsible for lost or stolen articles that might appear on your plate.

A couple of days later, ABC got a three-page letter from the Anti-Defamation League, saying that my remark was perpetuating a conspiracy claim some southern racists had made against the Jewish people, alleging that Kosher food was priced to rip off the Gentiles. They demanded a retraction. So the next week, as Barbara and I were standing there, Collins apologized on the air. I told my friend Jerry about us getting that three-page letter, and he was incredulous, saying, "That's ridiculous! *Hitler* only got a one-page letter!"

We got a lot of response from other viewers as well. My favorite reaction might have been a caller from Kentucky who said, "I wonder if you two really eat the food you cook, because it doesn't look like you know what you're doing."

The *Home* show people themselves were a good bunch, especially considering that I'd rib them on the air about what a rip-off their $2 newsletter was. But some of their people didn't have any idea about continuity. Once they put us on right after a segment about a 17 year old girl who was dying of AIDS. How are you supposed to follow that?

Unfortunately, the *Home* show was on its last legs by the time they signed us, so we only did it for a year before the show was canceled. Then it was back to local cable for us. I've occasionally started getting tired of doing the show, but Barbara's always hustling up a new angle. Three years ago, she got us on cable all over Australia, and there was such a surge of interest from there that Rupert Murdoch's satellite network in England has been running portions of the show over there. Here at home, in 1998 Barbara got *At Home on the Range* onto the local PBS station, and we're waiting to see if other PBS stations fall for it now.

We're in our sixth year of doing the show now. Donna loves watching it, and I still enjoy doing it often enough to keep on doing it.

Tonight we're making a warm chicken salad. The recipe calls for all these chopped herbs and olive oil that I can't bother with. I just buy a bottle of salad dressing.

"Gee, I don't feel any smarter."
Getting my honorary doctorate from
Cal Lutheran University.

On the road again, again.

HOW TO SUCCEED IN BUSINESS WITHOUT PROBABLY DYING

My grandson Billy recently asked for my advice about going into business for himself. At least I think he asked for my advice, because I was certainly giving it to him.

When you reach my age you think you know everything, and that attitude is only fueled by the fact that you do. Everything changes, but if you've lived through enough of those changes, you see how much it's all the same underneath.

For instance, people talk about how there's a bigger gap between rich and poor now, and how it's supposed to be harder to bridge that gap. I don't really think it makes a lot of difference. People can be born into wealth and put it totally in the toilet. There are other things you're born with that make a lot more difference.

Everyone I know who has made it in business or any field did so because they have just a super level of energy. There's a lot of things a person can learn and skills you can develop, but if you're not born with this abundant energy, there's not a lot you can do about it. I always had bundles. When I drank, I could go on a tear for days, wearing out three sets of buddies before I crashed. After I got straight, I directed that same energy into my business.

Something else some people have and others don't is being visionary, being able to see a thing before it exists. It's imagination, the thing a little kid does when he's daydreaming. I think that's a must, because if you were to take things on their face value, without that visionary attitude to imagine a different future, you wouldn't do anything. And most people don't. It's a natural gift and if you don't have that, you're not going to make it big.

If you have those gifts, you don't sit around waiting to

start big, though. The most important advice I gave Billy, and that I'd give to anyone, is to go to work, anywhere and everywhere. You learn a lot from that. I'd work at a place until it got boring and then I'd go off and do something else, until I started building trailers and that never did get boring.

That's what you look for, and in the meantime, pay attention. With almost every job I had, I'd try to figure out how they did everything, and how I might do it better or more efficiently. Even working for Douglas and North American during the war, it didn't look to me like there was all that much to building an airplane.

You can mope your life away, sitting wondering what you really want to do. Instead, if you're trying out all these different jobs, you have a hell of a lot better chance of finding what it is you like and are good at. And there's nothing like having done a bunch of crappy jobs to spur you to make a success of the one you like.

Even when you know what you want to do, keep working for someone else, learning all you can on his dime before you go off on your own. College probably wouldn't kill you, but there's nothing to replace the experience you get working for someone who knows the business, and doing that on his money and clock.

That's why I don't think the minimum wage should apply to kids. It used to be that businesses would hire youths for well below what an adult would make, but that's because a young kid who doesn't know anything isn't worth much. While you're training him, he's even a resource drain. If we didn't have that minimum wage, I think young people would be hired more, and would learn a lot. A few of them might be taken advantage of, but I think what's worse than being exploited is not being exploited. If you're not, you're just sitting there on your ass and not getting anywhere.

By the time I was working for Viking, I knew almost every aspect of building a trailer except cabinet building, because we bought those from outside suppliers. So, during one of the times I had fallen out with Doug and quit, I tried to get hired by a cabinet maker. When the boss said he didn't need anybody, I told him that I really wanted the work, didn't need much money and was willing to put in long hours. Then he hired me.

Not having a car then, I hitchhiked from Compton to Bellflower and worked from seven in the morning to eight at night. He got his money's worth out of me, but in that 60 days I also learned everything about building trailer cabinets. I can't think of any way a person can learn as well, other than getting in there and doing it like that.

I realized most of what it takes to make a business work back when Fleetwood *wasn't* working in the mid-1950s, when we nearly went bankrupt. I'd refer you to the earlier chapter, *Recovery*, for what I learned then about profit-sharing, controlled production, promoting from the inside and advertising. Most of it still applies, some of it more than ever.

Probably the biggest mistake people make when they go into business for themselves is thinking they have to come up with something bold and new. That might service your ego, but your odds of coming up with something necessary and new are awfully slim, and the odds of selling the world on it are even slimmer.

What you should do is go into a business where there is already a great demand, and figure out how to get a piece of someone's else's business by building a better widget, or at least a cheaper one, or by offering a better service. You always can find ways to do those things.

A similar area where people let their ego get in the way is when they run up against a problem in their business. The best way to get over the hump is to find somebody who's already doing it well, and go copy them. Why try to invent something when almost everything has already been invented? You might as well make use of what others have learned. You'll find most people, even your competitors, are anxious to share the benefit of their experience. If your ego won't let you go learn from somebody who's doing it well and take their advice — good luck.

Early on, when I was building the Dixie trailers, I was having endless problems with roof leaks. The whole industry was, with the exception of one company, Pan American in Monrovia. I called Jerry Golden, the man who was running the plant, and asked him, "Goddamn, you guys never have any leaks. What the hell do you do for your roofs?"

He asked "Why?" and I said, "People talk about how good your roofs are. I just wonder what you're doing." He laughed, and said he thought it was kind of ballsy of me to ask. But then he said, "Well, if you want to know, why don't you come on out and I'll show you."

At Dixie, we were using metal roofs that had seams every four feet, like everybody else, and the seams would expand and contract with heat and cold, and leak. Jerry showed me that Pan American was using 3/8" plywood, tarpaper and tar, just like a residential roof. I went back to my factory and started doing the same thing.

Jerry was a tough competitor, but because I asked him, he took me out and showed me exactly how he did it. I've done the same, giving advice to competitors, but seldom do they take it.

One thing I've preached all my life is that when business is good, it's going to get bad and you'd better get ready for it; and if it's bad, it's going to get good, and you'd better get ready for *that*.

I've been criticized a lot over the years for being too conservative in business, with experts claiming Fleetwood could have grown much faster if I'd been willing to borrow against our worth. To me, I wasn't being conservative, I was just being a businessman instead of a gambler.

When I was reassessing my business practices in the mid-'50s, I took a tally and realized that most of the companies in business when I started weren't around anymore. Some had merged, but most just went bankrupt. They'd had it good, so they just spent and spent, borrowed money, and spent more. Then, when the business took a downturn, they probably weren't able to make their payments and went bankrupt.

At that time, I decided that the idea of business isn't to make a lot of money; it's to stay alive. I've run the company with that idea from then on. There's no such thing as bad black ink. You might only show a very small profit margin, but as long as you have a profit margin, you'll never die. If you're not leveraged and don't have a bank debt or leases to pay, when things hit a downside, you can throttle down and live through it. What's the point in making it big if you don't live through the downsides? It's all for naught. So all through the years I was careful to run the company with no debt.

Relative to that, I'd advise any new company, no matter how big your ideas, to start small, borrow as little as you can, and grow with the capital you earn. There's a lot of learning involved in going into business and you can't race that process. If you grow with the capital you've earned, that just about links the speed of your growth to the pace at which you're learning best.

If you take in a lot of outside capital, you get ahead of yourself. You haven't learned how to handle that capital and you start to piss red ink. You've also, of course, got a bigger debt to service, and that's just more red ink down the drain.

I can't stress this previous point enough, because even after Fleetwood had been running great for years, there was that time in the early 1970s when we took in $40 million in outside capital, and ended up blowing that amount. We went right back to growing with what we've earned, and stuck to that during my years at the helm.

You've got to ask yourself if you're willing to start small, not look very important, and get your ego out of the way. That's tough, because the human ego is the biggest thing that holds people back. If you can push it out of the way, your chances of making it are pretty good, but that's not easy.

The thing you really have to keep in mind, more than anything else, is that you're there to do a service for somebody else. You're not there to do it for yourself. If you're just in business to make money for yourself, at the expense of somebody else, you'll never make it. You might make it on the short run, but it just isn't the right motivation.

It's not so much dishonesty as it is an occupational hazard, and it's what takes you down. In the half-century I was active in my industry, I think there is only one other company, Kit Trailers, that lasted as long and is still alive. Meanwhile, I saw hundreds of others come and go. It's the same story from the ancient myths up to the recent White House: the kings and people in positions of trust screw up when they put their personal desires ahead of everyone elses'.

Whether you're in the bronze age or the information age, something that is always very important is getting along with people. For example, when I was out selling on the road, I found that when you walk in to see a dealer and are anxious to tell him about your product, he really doesn't give a hang. Chances are he's got his own problems and his own things he wants to talk about. If you get him going about what he wants to talk about first, then you get on common ground. The chance of him being interested in what you have to talk about comes around. When it gets to the point where he asks you, you're making really good headway.

When I used to call on a dealer with a trailer, I'd never park it in front of his lot. It would be around the corner, out of sight. When the conversation came around to him asking me what I was up to, I'd say, "Well, I'm building this trailer. It's 27 feet long and has a dinette, and a unique floor plan."

I'd describe it a little more and pretty soon he'd say, "That sounds pretty good. I'd like to see it."

"Well, gee, I've got one right around the corner. Want to take a look?"

He'd say, "Yeah, let's go." Whereas if I'd parked it right

in front of his lot, he'd have a negative feel about it before he even stepped into it. Once you've piqued his curiosity, it's a whole different attitude.

I also was sold on my product, and that's what makes a good salesman. I never sold anything that I didn't think was good for the guy. I knew he could make money on it. That's why I went into business for myself with the Venetian blinds, because the unit I was selling for the other guy had no advantage to it.

When you're in business for yourself, you have to have a team who you trust to do things for you. Otherwise, you're wrapped up in details you think are too important to cede to somebody else, and you keep yourself buried for 40 years.

I never did that. But I always did a thing long enough to find out how it was done before I'd teach somebody else how to do it, and then I got out of the way. Trust is a big part of the equation, because if you can't turn something over to someone and trust them, then you haven't really turned it over.

One of my competitors once was four times my size, with multiple plant operations, and his whole thing was to go from plant to plant, sometimes in the middle of the night, and rifle through everybody's desks to see what they were doing. His plant managers and other employees resented the hell out of that, and any time they could shaft him, they did. Sowing distrust is one of the worst things you can do. If it gets to a point where you have to distrust someone, you fire him. If a guy throws a couple of ringers at you and you can't trust him, he's out of there.

When they don't delegate, many people in business get themselves so tied down to day-to-day activities that they can't really see what's going on with the whole picture. And if they did see something wrong, they'd be so bogged down they wouldn't have time to fix it.

Eventually, my role at Fleetwood became pretty much like that of a fireman. As long as there weren't any fires to put out, I stayed relatively hands-off. But if something needed to be done, I was available to jump in there and do it, and knew how. To do that, you have to stay aware of what's going on, to stay in touch with the product and the customer response to the product. You can pretty well tell that by keeping track of retail sales, yours and everybody else's.

If we had production problems, where a plant wasn't productive or the labor costs were too high, I'd go in and reorganize them. There's a lot to running a production line and getting the maximum out of a certain number of people efficiently, but most of it is common sense.

When an assembly line operation isn't clicking off to the speed that it ought, you can usually go through the line and see that there's one department holding up the whole thing. You either put some more people in that department or move some of its work to another department that's getting ahead of its workload. When you get that done, you'll probably find another slowdown somewhere else once the line starts moving along. You locate it and do the same thing there. You keep fine-tuning the line until it's moving as it should be. For some reason, it was sometimes difficult for plant managers to see where the problem was, where for me it was really easy to step in and see it.

It helps that I've done virtually every job that every worker on the line is doing. That's not bad for employee relations either, to have a CEO who can understand and appreciate the job each of them is doing. Since you've been where he or she is, you also know what makes them feel good about their job and what they want.

That's why I instituted the profit sharing. This is where the work you put in at the beginning—learning and growing slowly—pays off over the lifetime of a company.

We haven't had any labor problems at Fleetwood, except for the union organizational attempts which were brought in from outside. Unlike so many companies, we believed that employees have to know what the company is about, how well it is doing and how we operate.

In order to keep the plant going, we have to have so much volume, and to have that volume we have to have a better deal than the competitor, and to have a better deal than the competitor, we've got to keep our labor rates at a certain place, just like the materials and overhead. That assures the employees of their job security. If people understand that, and they do at Fleetwood, then you won't have a problem.

Then, of course, you have to have some plan for them to share in the success. Then you won't have any labor problems. But the typical business guy, particularly when he starts to get successful, is jealous that the employees are going to find out how well he's doing, because if they find out they're going to want more, and he doesn't want to give up any more.

With the internal accounting system Fleetwood uses, the management people and production people can see if they had a bad week or a good week, and know if they need to put more effort in it the next week to make it different. Everybody in the company is striving for the same goal, so it makes a cohesive team. Most companies don't even allow a lot of their management people to know what those numbers are. We'd send a memo around, so everybody knows. We'd try to keep it confidential from our competitors, and did pretty well, because the employees have a stake in keeping it from the competition too.

One reason I got into the mess I did in 1954 was that I was relying on outside accountants for my information, and the routine accounting systems don't give you the information you need accurately enough and soon enough for you to act on it in time. So I went back to the internal system I had before, which I'd come up with only because I couldn't afford an accountant in my early days.

What I came up with, which Fleetwood still uses, is what they call a WUPCA: weekly unit production cost analysis.

Every week you divide your overhead figure for the plant by the number of units made, so you know how much per unit the overhead is. You divide the labor cost by the number of units, and then the unit material cost, on which your purchasing department keeps you current. When you do the arithmetic on that, you wind up with your net profit for the week. The managers can just look at that figure, multiply their share of it by 13, and have an idea of what their quarterly bonus will be.

Accountants like to use percentages, dollar volumes and things like that. They don't use the unit cost thing at all, which to me means everything. It all comes out the same on the bottom line at the end, but the end is a long ways down the line and it's too far down to act upon. The whole idea of an accounting system, as far as I'm concerned, is to know how well you're doing currently.

Is it harder to start a business now than when I started? Probably, but that just means you have to be that much sharper at your game.

It was almost like the frontier times when I started out: you just didn't have to think much about government regulations because there hardly were any. Government has since made doing anything a million times more complicated, and you know who has benefited from that? Big businesses.

People who know me say my politics are somewhere to the right of Attila the Hun. I don't like the size or intrusiveness of government one bit, and I think it has eroded the natural checks and balances of the marketplace.

My biggest complaint is that ever since Uncle Sugar created all these regulations and departments to watch over everything, the consumer just assumes the government is going to look out for him. He's not a careful buyer. When I went into business, he was. You really had to make sure that what you were offering was up to snuff, because the buyer would really look it over.

As I've mentioned, when I first started, most of the other

companies were wiring their trailers with lamp cord. I wired mine better, the way you would a house. Dealers saw that and pointed it out to the public, and in no time at all, the rest of the industry had to improve their stuff, too. The marketplace took care of that on its own. It didn't need the government stepping in.

I think that if a guy wants to go out and buy a car made of toilet paper that will flat-out kill him in a fender-bender, it's his own goddamn business. I really think so. If a guy's going to buy a car, he should educate himself enough to be a responsible buyer. That's what they were like before Big Brother was there to take care of them, and it's too bad now, because the government sure as hell isn't going to do the job well.

When all these regulations came rolling in during the 1970s, I wasn't having the fits the rest of the industry was. That's because, industry-wide, the product was sub-standard, and suddenly they had to catch up to what we were already doing. The laws, even if they're stupid ones, applied to all of us, so from a competitive standpoint, it's still equal. The only one who gets screwed is the consumer.

But all the regulations make it hard for anyone new to get in the business, and that throws another of the important checks and balances off-kilter. As I found with Fleetwood in the '50s, when you become big and successful, you get complacent and don't do justice to the product, the consumer or your employees. That leaves you ripe for a small, hungry company to come in and pluck away your business, and that's the way it should be.

One reason I'm against big government is it promotes big business, at the expense of the little guy.

It used to be that anywhere you'd drive in the US there would be independent mom and pop service stations in every town. Then the Feds passed a law where everyone had to dig up their tanks and test them. The only ones who could afford that were the major oil company chains, and, bam, the tens of thousands of mom and pops vanished from the picture. Now you've got nothing but those big chains' stations, with one bored minimum wage guy sitting at the cash register.

You see things like that all the time. Cities will offer all manner of incentives and tax breaks to bring in a Walmart. They'll even use eminent domain to force little businesses off the property. Then the giant Walmart opens with all this government help; the little businesses who have been in the community for decades—and whose taxes probably helped pay for the Walmart—go under, and suddenly the well-being of the community is dependent on some executive several states away hopefully not making the wrong decision.

One thing I wish the government *would* start doing is enforcing the goddamn antitrust laws. Something that's big right now, and boy is it dangerous, is the proliferation of consolidators. These companies raise money by selling bonds on Wall Street, then they'll come into an area and buy up all the drug stores or all the Ford agencies or whatever.

In a town, they might have one drug store with their company name on it, but they've also bought up the three other stores operating under their old names. So if you buy something from any drug store in that area, you're buying the same product, from the same company, at the same prices that they want to set. The consumer really gets screwed.

Fleetwood is doing it in the mobile home business right now! The company recently bought up dealerships all over Texas, Oklahoma, Louisiana and Arkansas, so we set the prices there. People have been buying Fleetwoods in that area for 40 years, so a lot of them just automatically buy a Fleetwood product. But when they go to buy one now, they can't shop back and forth and get a deal like they used to.

We didn't start that. A couple of other mobile home companies did and Fleetwood got into it more in self-defense. That doesn't mean I like it one bit. But it is going on in so many fields, and no one is stopping it at all.

You can't convince me that there's less of a problem

than there was when Teddy Roosevelt first saw the need for the antitrust laws, but the Justice Department has not been enforcing them. If they'd do their job, it wouldn't be like this. We and everybody else would have to divest, and it would open up again. If it keeps going the way it is, a new person entering the business won't be able to find any dealers. If you walk into a dealer owned by a competing manufacturer, he isn't going to talk to you.

All this might sound grim, but even without the Justice Department stepping in, I don't think it will get to that. All that these consolidations and mergers mean is that these companies are getting a whole lot bigger and that they are going to be that much less efficient and more out of touch.

With the trailer dealerships it's almost a rerun of what was going on when I started out. Then, there were big dealers around who pretty well controlled the manufacturers. If you couldn't sell to those guys, you just weren't in business. They had the sales lots and were controlling the manufacturers.

When I started, there was no way I could make it onto one of those lots, so I started selling to little independent lots. Those dealers were a lot more efficient and could sell for less, and gave better service. Every one of those big guys went by the wayside, and those little independent dealers grew and became the big ones.

That will happen again. It's a great time for some manufacturer to do the same, which he could do by helping to set up independent dealers. That's what I would rather Fleetwood were doing. They'd have to be super-efficient and keep their margin down, but it can be done.

Hell, it has to be done. The idea of having competition is the only thing that keeps everybody honest. It is the lifeblood of the economy and the country. Without competition this country would have been nothing.

Fleetwood president and future CEO Glenn Kummer
enjoying his favorite hobby.

Man struck by airplane. News at 11. Me enjoying the model
planes that are still *my* favorite hobby.

FLEETWOOD PEOPLE

Whenever I've had to make a speech about my success, I try to spread the credit throughout the company, because all I did was create an opportunity where good people could do their best.

I can talk for days about my curious friends or about people who were peripheral to Fleetwood's success, while it's much harder for me to talk about those who were directly responsible for it. There were honestly so many of them that I could mention a hundred and slight hundreds more in the process, because it really has been a great crew, all down the line.

There are some individuals I absolutely have to mention, though, and I hope they give you some idea of the character that ran all through the company.

I've already talked about Dale Skinner quite a bit, but I can't overemphasize how important he was to the company. I was only able to flit around the way I did—trouble-shooting, designing new product, or just goofing around—because Dale was there holding things together for so many years.

Dale was a staunch advocate of Fleetwood policy, and an example of how well it worked. With our expansion and our promoting from within, he rose from hick accountant to president of the company. He was so humble that every time he was promoted he was sure he was in over his head. And then he went in and did the job like gangbusters.

I always trusted Dale's judgment, but the one place where I really should have argued with him was when Jack Dahl had him convinced he was so old-fashioned that he needed to get out of the way. It was a genuine loss when he retired.

Bill Weide was another giant in the company. He had the responsibility of locating new plant sites, negotiating for

368 ✳ JOHN CREAN

them, getting them built (and he really got run ragged under Jack Dahl, with all those damn new plants). He was super at negotiating contracts, and when we had union troubles, he took care of that, 100%. And that was hairy work.

He's the one, you might recall, who had driven down to interview with us in the early '50s and nearly kept driving when he saw our tiny office in Anaheim.

As president, Bill gave the company a tremendous amount of stability. Jack Dahl's Wall Street ambitions had thrown us off-kilter and Bill stabilized things. He did a hell of a job for the ten years he ran things. Bill and I did a lot of socializing and traveling together, and I still love getting together with him.

Someone else who went way back with Fleetwood was Cliff Breitweg. I actually met him right after the war, during my brief tenure at the Supercold company. After that, he went to work for a trailer company in South LA, and then Doug Caruthers hired him when we were building those government contract trailers in the late 1940s. Cliff came to work for me in September of 1950, and stayed with me right straight through.

He was the fastest sidewall man I ever saw, but he quickly worked his way off the line and into management. When we first branched out, with our Waco, Texas plant in 1956, I picked Cliff to be the plant manager there, and he did a hell of a job. We became close friends over the years.

Years later, in the early '70s, the company appointed a division manager, Jon Nord, over Cliff's plant, and they never got along at all. Cliff's numbers and results were far above our other plants, but he never filled out reports. Jon was an MBA, so he was always demanding detailed reports, while Cliff didn't think those mattered. That wasn't his style. Where Cliff came from, you just got the job done and the result was all the report that was necessary.

Remember the time I drove the Rolls to New York to put it on the Queen Elizabeth to England, and had a plant manager ride part-way with me to smooth out some problems he'd been having? That was Cliff, and his problem was Jon.

I managed that time to talk Cliff into hanging in there. But two or three years later, Cliff just got pissed off at Jon again and he quit. He owned a lot of Fleetwood stock, and had made a killing on it, so he just retired and spent the rest of his life hunting and fishing. He used to go fishing in Mexico with me.

We were close until he died. He had a heart condition and was wracked up on all sorts of medication. Then he came down with cancer, and he figured, "What the hell, I'm dying anyway, what do I want to take all this shit for?"

He threw all his medications in the trash can, and he got well. Doctors in Houston had just started doing heart bypass operations, and Cliff was one of the first to get one. He tried to show me Polaroid pictures where they had his heart out on the table, to which I naturally said, "Get those the fuck away from me, Cliff!" Who needs to see that? Anyway, the operation was a success and he went like a tiger for a decade before the cancer came back and did him in.

Clint Dorsey was another one of the originals who first came to work in Anaheim. He was a very good hands-on guy, and wound up being general production manager. Dan Stretch came to us a little bit later, when we opened our Douglas, Georgia plant in 1958. Dan worked his way up the line until he was plant manager in Douglas. Then he was plant manager in Carbondale, Pennsylvania, and went through a horrible strike there in the early '70s. He had to move his family into a motel because the strikers were throwing rocks and bottles at him. As soon as we needed a divisional sales manager, we brought him out to Anaheim, and he kept climbing the ladder until he was general sales manager and senior Vice President under Jack Dahl.

Dan was a firm believer in Fleetwood policies. He'd preach it to employees, except Dan had been in the Marines, so it was more like barking orders than preaching. The company was his whole life, and he would have been good material for president if he hadn't sounded so much like a drill sergeant.

We were growing so fast in the late '60s that we were opening plants faster than we could promote people who were ready for the job, so we recruited management from outside. During that time a lot of good people came to Fleetwood.

One was Jon Nord, who, despite Cliff Breitweg's differences with him, was great for the company. Before Jon came to us in the '60s he'd been Assistant Dean of Students at Cal State LA and he had a '60s academic's typical distrust of businesses. I guess he found that Fleetwood didn't fit his idea of most businesses, because not long at all after he came in as a trainee, Jon became a Fleetwood regional manager. While I could sympathize with the plant managers like Cliff who didn't share Jon's affection for reports, Jon really got things done.

We had three mobile home divisions in the '70s—Broadmore, Festival and Fleetwood—and Jon was promoted to head the Fleetwood division. That was at a time when I was working very closely with their product design people on new mobile homes, so I got to know Jon well. From there, he went on to be vice president in charge of the whole mobile home side of Fleetwood, and he took sales from $150 million a year up to the $1.5 billion it's recently enjoyed.

Elden Smith did very much the same thing over on the RV side. The growth in dollars was about the same, and that meant a change from something like a 6% market share up to over 25%. Since I love designing RVs, I spent a lot of time working with him too.

Both he and Jon kept their nose to the grindstone, though Elden would let up long enough to get some gin rummy in. So I had a lot more social contact with Elden, and we took some great trips together. I could never remember how to spell his name, though, whether it was Elden or Eldon. Fortunately, he had been with a tool company before he joined Fleetwood, and he'd given me a promotional pocket screwdriver with his name embossed on it. It was a handy tool, so I always carried it in my pocket. It was doubly handy, because, whenever I needed to spell his name, I'd just pull the screwdriver out.

I've considered Elden a friend for years, but he is such a straight-arrow that when someone recently asked him when he became friends with me, he said "in August of 1997, when I retired." Up until then, he said, he thought it would have been presumptuous and improper to consider himself a friend because he was my employee.

Both he and Jon were so up on the doings in the industry that their reports at the Fleetwood board meetings were great. They were very detailed, practical reports that would really let us know where we were. I didn't really notice how good the reports were until they retired and Nelson Potter took over delivering the reports, and they're a whole lot of nothing, which Nelson is excellent at. He's a genius at rattling off rhetoric.

Fleetwood's current president and CEO, Glenn Kummer, also came to the company during our expansion in the 1960s. He'd been a CPA at Ernst & Ernst and took a cut in pay to become a trainee with us at $135 a week. He became plant manager at the Pendleton, Oregon Prowler plant, and excelled there, setting company sales records at the time.

He came back to Riverside and ultimately became vice president of the RV side, and Bill Weide tapped Glenn to become his successor (that's when Elden became VP of RVs). Glenn became president at a prime time in company history, 1982. Under Bill, we came out of the Carter years just roaring, hitting $1 billion in sales for the first time, and becoming No. 1 in all our fields.

With Elden Smith and John Nord running their divisions so well, Glenn did a largely ceremonial job, and the company continued to grow, up to its recent $3 billion level.

My take on Glenn was that he was super-trustworthy, ambitious but not overly ambitious. He was very analytical, not the sort to jump to conclusions. When I finally retired, I thought I was leaving the company in good, steady hands with

Glenn, though, as you'll read later, I've recently had to reassess everything I thought I knew about Glenn.

Because Fleetwood gave its people a lot of authority, and rewarded initiative, the company developed real depth of management. For every good guy who rises to the top level at Fleetwood—like Dick Parks, who made the upscale American Eagle such a success, and is now the RV general manager— there are several equally deserving people who likely would have done as well, if we had enough positions for them to rise into.

One such talent is Pat Scanlon, who we gained when we bought the Coleman tent camper company. He's been a great, well-liked manager, even while he was battling cancer.

One of my very favorite Fleetwood guys is Dave Russell, who is the head motor home design guy. He's very hands-on, and understands that's the way to win arguments with me. We had a confrontation right after he joined Fleetwood in the early '70s, when he redesigned the Prowler and took away the distinctive brow it had up to that point.

I told him, "That's sort of the Prowler badge. You shouldn't be messing with that." But then he explained, point-for-point, how his swept-back design was better, and he was right. I liked that this guy who had just started with us was willing to stand up to the boss like that.

He did a Bounder redesign once, and I walked right by the scale model without even recognizing it. He directed my attention back to it, and I was aghast, exclaiming, "That looks like a bread truck. That can't be it." But, again, he was able to demonstrate that his new vertical, un-sloped front end made a better product for the customer. His redesign had more storage, and more headroom, so users wouldn't bang their head on the TV.

Dave is also a lot of fun. One time his product design group was meeting with the sales people. The sales guys were always trying to influence the product in ways the designers didn't necessarily appreciate. So, at this meeting, the sales team came in, and did a double-take, because Dave had his 30 guys all sitting there wearing masks made from Xeroxed photos of my face. Dave then told the sales guys, "Just because John Crean comes in here and works on the product with us quite a bit, I don't want you sales guys to feel intimidated by that when you're trying to influence the product."

Dave would be a lot further up in the company's ranks if I had been ordering the promotions. I liked that Dave would argue his points with me, but his forthrightness doesn't sit well with the sort of upper management who only want to hear a simple "Yes sir."

Another reason why I've been sober for 49 years—
Donna smashes all my bottles.
Launching the water-going Bounder.

STILL SOBER

Back in 1950, not long after I quit drinking and started building trailers, a fellow came into my plant with a little travel trailer asking if I knew anybody who could repair its smashed front end. "I can fix that," I told him, and said it would be about $250.

I got it done, and before the guy came in to pick it up, I wrote an invoice up for $250. But when he came in, he sat down and wrote out a check for $350. I thought, "Wow, I can really use this."

I went into my office, flipped past that $250 invoice and wrote up a new one for $350. But I no sooner had it written before I thought, "Goddamn it, I shouldn't do that. That's not the way to do things." So I brought him the original invoice and said, "Hey, you made a mistake on your check here."

He wrote out a new check. Then, as he was driving away, I thought, "What the hell did I do that for?" because that wasn't like me at all. But I'd quit drinking. If I'd still been drinking, I would have taken great glee in fleecing that guy for $100.

Many years later, I got a big kick out of something my buddy Chuck Chamberlain said. We were at his place in the hills of Laguna Beach, where he had a picture window overlooking the city. He gestured to the lights below and said, "You know, out there, there's murderers and robbers and every kind of person you can imagine, and they're all doing the best they can. If they knew better, they'd do better."

When I was drinking, that's all I knew. When I think about it, I had to be lying to myself, believing that my next drunk was somehow going to be different from my last, and maybe that made it easier to let everything else slip. All I know is that once you know different, things *are* different.

I only had three instances, all in my first eighteen months

of sobriety, when I thought it would be a pretty good idea to drink. When I talked to my buddies in AA about it, though, those urges just evaporated right away. After that I never had a notion to drink at all.

People wonder then why I still go to meetings so regularly, but there's something about the meetings that just takes you back to the times you were drinking and how screwed up you were. If you didn't do that, you'd forget all about it. Like everything else in life, the good memories stay with you, and the bad memories get erased. When you continue to go to the meetings, you see guys coming along who are having the same troubles you've had, which reminds you that you're still in recovery. That keeps it all fresh.

I suppose I've helped people a little there. But after a certain length of time, guys like me in AA get referred to as alligators, because we just sit around and don't say much. It's usually the guys in their first five years who become experts on alcoholism and have to tell you how it works, inside-out and backwards. But the longer you're on AA, the more you know that there isn't anything profound about it at all, nothing you can really say. It's something people just have to experience, and you can't tell them about it. All you can really do is sit there and be an example that the damn thing works.

Probably the most useful thing I did was publish a book by my buddy Chuck Chamberlain, called *A New Pair of Glasses*. Aside from the founder, Bill W., Chuck C. was about the most well-known and loved guy in AA, which is pretty good considering everyone's supposed to be anonymous.

One of Chuck's sons was the actor Richard Chamberlain, but Richard looked more like his mother. Chuck was part American Indian and had a distinctive look, with gray hair combed straight back, a Roman nose and wide-set eyes that lit up like Christmas.

He'd been a self-described "tongue-chewing, babbling idiot" on the bottle until he got with the program in 1946. From that point on, he became very successful in business and in life, but he always seemed to have endless time and energy to devote to helping others in the program. He was an entertaining speaker. I'd drive out of my way to hear him talk, though I usually didn't know what he was going on about.

Chuck made everything sound too easy. One of his main themes was saying that all alcoholics' problems, all of *everyone's* problems, was the ego. Nobody wants to hear how simple their problems are. I just figured he was some kind of nut, but a pleasant one. But after I got to know him, I developed a tremendous amount of respect for him. I also realized that he was very profound in such a simple way.

We'd be driving along and he'd see a bunch of cows in a pasture and say, "My cows are sure looking good this spring," and you'd wonder what the hell he was talking about. But his attitude was that everything he came in contact with was his, that it was just the old ego that made us feel separate from them.

Though he was a figure in AA, I actually got to know him through Donna, who had become friends with his wife after we bought the place in Monarch Bay in '69. We wound up becoming close friends.

A buddy who was visiting Chuck from Sacramento got the idea that there should be a book made of Chuck's lectures. Chuck thought he expressed his ideas best in a series of six one-hour sessions he'd done at a retreat at Pala Mesa.

It had been recorded, and the guy from Sacramento set about transcribing them. I then took them to my friend from the *Hammersmith* days, Milton Pickman, who had quite a bit of experience in book publishing. He read it and said it really needed to be edited, because it was all in Chuck's colloquial language. Milton's wife had recently passed away, and it had really hit him hard. He had time on his hands and volunteered to do the editing.

Milton spent a couple of months on it, and rewrote the entire thing twice. Then he re-read the original manuscript, and called me up, saying, "You know, I don't think we can change this. We've got to print it verbatim. It works best the way he said it."

He was right, and it took a big man to realize that, after the months of work Milton had put into changing it. The good part about that effort was that living with Chuck's words for those months brought Milton out of his funk. Ol' Chuck preached pretty good.

What Milton did best was negotiate, and he hammered a printer to get us the best deal on having 5000 copies printed. So, in 1984 we went into the publishing business, calling ourselves the New-Look Publishing Company.

At first I thought the book would excite only a bit of interest from friends. I gave away a thousand copies, mainly to people I knew who were in the program. There was information in the book for ordering additional copies, by sending $10 to a mail drop in Irvine.

In no time at all, the 5000 books were gone, so we did a second printing of 10,000. At that quantity we were able to bring the price down to $6. Those also sold right away, so we started doing printings of 50,000. *A New Pair of Glasses* is now in its 8th printing, with some 320,000 copies sold, and that's all by word of mouth, with no advertising and no distributor.

The New York office of AA failed to renew the copyright on the Alcoholics Anonymous book, so it fell into public domain. Since Chuck refers to it throughout his talks, our book now also has 164 pages of the AA book reprinted in it, and it's still $6, postpaid.*

The book wasn't done for profit, but it's been making money. We priced it to break even at $6 for a single copy. But people and groups have taken to buying cases of them—at $85 for a case of 20—which comes out to $4.25 per copy, but the

---

Available from New-Look Publishing Company, P.O. Box 17496, Irvine CA 92623, and, that's right, you send $6 (no cash, unless you want me to buy lunch with it) and we send you the book, postpaid.

postage on that is practically nothing, so we make money.

Before Elsa, Chuck's wife passed away, we sent her a check for $10,000, and the money has been accumulating ever since. Chuck didn't even want any agreement, but I told him I'd give him 90 percent of any profit if there was one, because I didn't want any of it.

At this writing, I'm going on 50 years of sobriety. I don't regret the years I spent drinking, but I'll tell you, I'm having as much of a ball now as I was then, and the difference is that now I get to remember it.

"But, Bob, we don't need any Viagra."

With Dan Quayle and this book's co-author Jim Washburn,
in a borrowed tie.

THE STATE OF THE UNION

I've met several US presidents over the years, and it was no big thing. They greet you, you shake their hand and that's about the extent of it, which doesn't thrill me much. You worry if that's all they ever see of normal people.

When you do talk to people in Washington, you get the impression that they think the United States is only Washington, New York, Los Angeles and Chicago. They don't have the foggiest idea what the United States is about. They'd all do well to hop in RVs and drive around the country for a couple of years. We could probably survive without any new laws for that long.

In my travels, it's seemed to me like the people in the big cities don't have much idea of what is going on outside their particular city. They're only up on the murders and the other local junk the TV news feeds them. Meanwhile, in the hinterlands, people are more up on national and world affairs. They're more attuned to what's really going on.

I wish the less populated parts of the country weren't draining out so. There's so much real estate out there, and people could get along so much better. But it's in people's nature to congregate, and they do that in cities on the coasts. If there were jobs and opportunity in the hinterlands, I think people would be there too. With Fleetwood, we purposely put our plants out there when we did our expansions, because the people are more anxious to work.

People in the city are much busier doing nothing, getting to and from where they're going. People in the country seem to have more time, to think and to learn things.

I worry a bit about the tradition of American know-how being lost. The baby boomers can't pour water out of a boot. Everything has to be made user-friendly for them. They understand computers, unless they ever have to open one up and try to actually figure out how it works.

There has been a lot said about the next great generation of American chefs being Hispanics, because they're all the helpers in the kitchens now. I think the next great generation of nearly *everything* will be Hispanic, because they're the ones working. All the white people are sitting around on their ass not doing anything.

My main guy in keeping Village Crean running is Manuel Najar, who has been with me for 25 years. No matter what you want done, Manuel can do it or knows someone who does.

I see people as individuals and don't understand jerks who are intolerant. Do these idiots even stop to think what this country would be like without the blacks and their contributions to our culture? We'd be like Germany, wearing leather shorts and dancing around to oom-pah music. It's the same with gays. It would be a pretty dull place without them.

When I travel across the US now, about the only place that still seems distinct to me is rural New England. It's probably changed less than other places. People are different there, while, everywhere else, everyone pretty much watches the same TV and reads the same papers.

When I first started traveling, the people in Texas were so different from Los Angeles it was like being in a foreign country, and Georgia and Idaho were more different yet. But nowadays, you go to those places and you can't tell one from the other. People talk, look and dress the same as they do in LA, and talk about the same things.

Walmarts are wiping out the old main street with all the little shops, and it's a shame because small towns were really special. Maybe they were doomed not to make it anyway, since all the young people light out from them to the cities. You see these towns that once had a textile mill, and now there's just a 7-11. We've really gone to hell in a hand basket.

I like to tell people that one of the reasons I made motor homes was so that we could burn up all our gasoline faster. As much as I've enjoyed and profited from things that run on gasoline, there's a part of me that would love to see us run out of it, so people would be forced to stay in one place and build a sense of community again. When I was growing up in Compton, it was a community and most of the country was that way: neighborhoods and small towns that meant something to the people there. I really miss that.

I see America becoming like the Soviet Union in a way. Unlike them, we'll have a lot of goodies, but, like them, we won't have much choice about it. There, the government decided whatever the hell cars it wanted to build and you were stuck with them. As much as our government might like to do that, conglomerates will beat them to it. We're going to have lots of whatever, but it will all be the same.

I like the idea of us trying to be more conscious of the ecology, but it's like trying to hold back the dawn. As long as people are going to want the standard of living they have, the ecology is going to take a dumping. And people aren't going to give up their standard of living. That's just the way it is.

I think it would be great if Orange County was still strictly orange trees with only 15,000 people living here, but that isn't to be. If a place is attractive, that's the very thing that ruins it, because everybody else wants that, and they pile in. Before long, because of everyone wanting to grab a piece of it, the qualities that attracted them to the place to begin with aren't there anymore.

That's like a natural law. When the Creans were living in North Dakota, it was letters from a friend in California about how nice it was that urged us out here. And when we got here, my folks sent letters out.

When I started going down to Cabo San Lucas in 1963, it was just like it was when Steinbeck wrote about it in 1941. There was a little cannery and the Chinaman's store, and no more than a couple of hundred people living in the village. It was really a nice place. Now it's a screaming madhouse. But there's a lot of kids there whooping it up who don't know what it was like in 1963, so they think it's a great spot. That's the way it happens, and having an opinion about it or trying to stop it is nonsense.

Maybe there'll be a plague, or a war or some huge catastrophe that will slice the human race down to a number that's more manageable. In 1918 there was a flu epidemic that killed 30 million people worldwide. Everything else in nature self-governs, and it makes sense that human population will too.

We think we're smarter than that, but we aren't. The silver lining is that, while we're going to screw up our own backyard, humans aren't using all that much of the world's real estate, and the environment has a great way of fixing itself. You can look at the place where Patton trained his troops in the California desert for World War II. They had a virtual war on that land for years, and now you can't find any evidence that anything ever happened out there.

I would just as soon never see another war in my lifetime. I've had enough of us being the cops of the world. I think we should pull all of our troops and aircraft carriers out of the Middle East and bring them home. The minute we do, France, Germany, the Saudis the Turks and everyone will all take a different look at things. As long as old Uncle Sugar is stupid enough to take care of their problems, they aren't going to do anything. If we do get involved anywhere, it should be like any other war, where we take the country over, replace the government that's there and then get the hell out. These half-assed wars accomplish nothing.

With the family, Mr. and Mrs. Donald O'Connor
and Mr. and Mrs. Buzz Aldrin.

A wealth of talent, and the three guys on the right
aren't too bad either. With Milton Berle,
Danny Thomas and Steve Allen.

Donna and her best friend Jane Withers
and Cesar Romero.

Donna with fellow tap dancers
Buddy Ebsen and Shirley Temple.

STILL MARRIED

On May 8, 1998, our 50th wedding anniversary, Donna and I renewed our wedding vows. It was just us, 500 guests and the Ray Conniff singers.

Our kids arranged the party, and threw it in a big hotel ballroom. It was the best party we've ever been to. Emily had snuck in our house and gone through all the photo albums, and made a great, hilarious slide show of our life together.

I had suggested to Donna that we should exchange rings again, and had her give me her ring. What she didn't know was that I took it to a jeweler and had it refit with a huge crow-choker of a diamond.

In all the excitement of reenacting our marriage vows, Donna didn't notice the switch. When I slipped the ring back on her finger, all she said was, "Gee, it looks bigger." She didn't get it. Meanwhile, this huge diamond was throwing shafts of light all over the hall like a disco's mirror ball.

People ask me how it is that Donna and I have been able to stay together for all these years. My answer to that is you've got to learn how to suffer. If you know how to suffer, you can stay married forever. What I mean is that there are always periods of time in a marriage when things aren't that great, but you have to suffer through them and things will get good again. Most people are spoiled little children who never get around to being adults, so the first time something doesn't go their way, they start snapping back and making things worse.

Another thing important to making a marriage last is that you not entertain any options. You see a lot of short-term marriages because the people figure that when things get rough they can just haul ass out of there and find somebody easier to get along with. As I went along in my marriage, I watched friends switch like that, and usually they were jumping from the frying pan to the fire. They seldom bettered themselves at all.

I've never had a problem being faithful, probably because I played the field in my early years before we married. I tested it all out, so I knew there were no mysteries out there. Maybe people who have had a more sheltered life get curious after ten or fifteen years of marriage, wondering what they're missing, and that causes problems.

During the day, Donna and I often go our separate ways. But our evenings are practically always spent together. We go to bed early, at nine or ten o'clock, but we'll watch TV and talk until midnight. After I quit drinking, I don't think there's anything I've felt or thought that I've kept from her.

I think what is important is not so much having shared interests as it is taking an interest in what each other does. From my side, the things I haven't always cared about are the social activities, the dinners and all that. Left to my own devices, I probably wouldn't go to them. But I do, because Donna has wanted to, and I usually have a great time. Meanwhile, some of the trips we've taken haven't particularly been things she wanted to do, but she'd go along, and also usually have a great time. I see so many couples where the guy says, "Gee, I'd like to go to Hawaii and go surfing," and the wife will just shut the whole thing down and go nowhere. Donna was never like that.

The thing that impressed me most when I first met her was that she wasn't critical of me. That was really unusual in my experience. Everyone was always dissatisfied with me, where Donna has never been critical about anything I do.

I think Donna's attitude was crucial to Fleetwood's success. She always supported me when I went out on a limb. She stood with me when I broke with Roy Clayton and went out on my own in 1951, and has at every point since then. So many people get a little bit comfortable in life and they're afraid to do anything else, curling up and saying, "Hey, we don't want to take any more chances." Instead, Donna and I have always

Donna with Lauren Bacall.

Donna with me. She gets around, doesn't she?

gone for it.

When people ask Donna what she loves about being with me, she has said it's the spontaneity and excitement of it, because she never knows what's going to happen next. It's always some ridiculous thing coming up, whether it's the Baja 1000 or meeting a president. We've packed a lot of stuff into 50 years, and most of it wasn't planned.

I guess we did alright as parents. We have four kids, fourteen grand-kids and two great-grandchildren, and not one of them is in prison.

Johnnie stayed clear of politics after his mud-splattered congressional run. He is still doing fine in the trailer manufacturing business with his company, Alfa Leisure, and, at this writing, is also going into motor home production.

After fighting off cancer and overseeing the building of Village Crean, Andy decided to go into the restaurant business. One of Newport Beach's oldest restaurants, the Villa Nova, went belly-up. Andy bought it out of bankruptcy, and, except for a brief period after a fire gutted the place, he has been going great guns with it ever since.

Remember how, instead of going to UCLA, Susie had taken off to be with a guy she met on the horse show circuit? Her instincts were pretty good: she's still with the guy, Steve Thomas, and they've done great in business and in raising their four sons and a daughter.

Steve's a real go-getter. He went to a trade school, then worked for a John Deere dealer. He saved his money and, every chance he got, would buy a piece of used equipment, that he'd fix up and rent out. Within a year he had his own business going full-time.

By the time he was done with it, his business was worth several million dollars. They sold it, moved out here, and set up a business supplying parts to the RV industry. I had designed a new motor home baggage door, because everyone's old designs were terrible. I showed it to Steve one day and told him

I needed to find someone who could manufacture it for us. He said, "I can do that." I already knew he could. He's since improved on the design, and makes all of Fleetwood's baggage doors now.

Emily didn't stay with the race car driver she married for very long. She wound up marrying *another* race car driver who lived next door to her. The difference between the new one and the old one was that the new one was always winning. He was Rich Vogler, and there wasn't another racer, outside of A.J. Foyt, who won more races than he did.

He was nuts about racing, with 170 USAC victories. He'd race in midgets, sprints, anything, on pavement or dirt. In 1987, he ran the Indy 500 and then went and competed in another race that night. Emily was just as hooked on racing as Rich was, and they had quite an adventure together, going everywhere. He was a good guy, but he was reckless as hell when he got behind a wheel.

Rich's father died in a race shortly after Rich and Emily married. Then Rich had a head injury in a crash, and had no memory for six months. Emily had to take care of him, because he was pretty much out of it. The only way she could calm him down was to put him in a car and take him for a ride. He bounced back from his injury, and went on winning races.

They were married for about ten years, and then, in July of 1990, he was competing in a sprint car race at Salem Speedway in Indiana, and had the race won. He was coming into the closing stretch, and there were two cars in front of him that he'd already lapped. He was the sort of guy who had to pass them again, though. He punched it, one of the cars moved a bit and Rich hit the wall, went off the track, hit a lamppost and was killed instantly. As she usually was, Emily had been there, watching the race.

Rich had talked about getting out of racing. In fact, he'd told the press that he didn't want to be a 40 year old sprint car driver. He was killed on a Saturday night, and on that

With my late son-in-law Rich Vogler at Indianapolis.

following Wednesday he was going to be 40 years old, so he made it.

Emily remarried, for a time, to a guy who also had been a race car driver, and whose father, coincidentally, had also died on the track. Emily bought my old boat, the Prowler '76, from the person I'd sold it to. At this writing, she's just returned from living on it for several seasons, touring the Caribbean, with five boys, two dogs and a school teacher. She is now engaged to marry the school teacher. He seems like a nice fellow.

Milton Berle checks to see if I'm ripe.

With my hands in Bob's pocket for once.
Frisking Rev. Bob Schuller as Uncle Miltie looks on.

SLY AND RETIRING

In the 1990s, Fleetwood soared far past any goals I could possibly have imagined in our early days. The same company that started in a Compton garage was now surpassing $3 billion in annual sales, and employing some 21,000 persons.

As well as most of the '90s went for Fleetwood, the decade wasn't without its screw-ups.

The first was our purchase in 1992 of a German RV company called Niesmann-Bischoff. We had done studies of the European market, and we saw a potential to do good business there. The Europeans buy nearly as many motor homes, and more trailers, than people do in the US (though traditionally their products are smaller).

Management came up with two motor home companies to consider buying. One built a low-end line, and the other was a high-end custom operation. They decided to negotiate with both parties and see which one panned out.

We wound up buying 80 percent of the high-end company, which was a horrible mistake. It was so far from Fleetwood's policy and way of doing things that it was ridiculous. I was in the midst of cardiac rehab at the time. When I finally flew over to observe their operation, I was amazed we'd bit it off.

In the first place, Niesmann-Bischoff built a custom product, not a manufactured one. Every unit was different, built to the specifications of the customer. Their units were really pigs—strange and not very user-friendly—because customers can't design motor homes. The company had few dealers, and chiefly sold their product direct to customers out of their own retail location. The firm was headed by a father (who retired when we bought in), son, son-in-law and daughter, and that sort of nepotism was not our policy at all.

It didn't take long to start losing tons of money. The regulations on business in Germany are killers. For example, if you hire people and they're on the payroll for over six months, you're practically married to them. You can't get rid of them. Niesmann-Bischoff used a lot of Fiat chassis, and when Fiat had a strike, our production came to a near-halt for two months. Meanwhile, we had to pay the employees full-time for sitting on their European asses.

Fleetwood had sent Nelson Potter, a guy we'd hired from one of the Wall Street brokerage houses, to straighten things out. The company used Nelson as a troubleshooter, though I can't recall any trouble that he ever shot. He spent a couple of years in Germany trying to run Niesmann-Bischoff, and it only went further downhill.

We couldn't even go out of business over there without giving the employees a gigantic severance pay-off. After losing money for four years, that's what it looked like we had to do. Nelson hired brokers to sell the company for us, but no one wanted to buy it. It was going to cost us $25 or $30 million just to close the company down.

That's when I involved myself in the proceedings. At a trade show in Essen, I had become friends with a German fellow named Erwin Hymer. He's the Fleetwood of Europe, with plants in several countries. He and I just hit it off, the way people sometimes mesh. Donna and I have stayed with him in his hometown in southern Germany, and he visited us here and went with us to President Nixon's funeral.

It occurred to me that Erwin might be willing to bail us out of Niesmann-Bischoff, because he could probably make it work. He had capable personnel and dealers all over Europe. I called him and said I wanted to come over and chat with him about business. He said that was fine, but that he was on holiday, and that he'd like Donna and me to join his family at their vacation home in the Swiss Alps.

We did, and just went around having a good time, not

even mentioning my reason for being there until the fourth day, when Erwin said, "John, what business did you want to talk about?"

I laid it out to him, "We've got this damn plant in which we're losing our shirt. We're really buried in it. We want to unload it, and I wanted to see if you could buy it."

He looked over the figures for only a few minutes before saying, "I think we can do something with it." The next day he called his office and had his guys meet with my guys at the plant. Within a week, Erwin had bought the thing, if that's what you call us paying him $4 million to take it over. That was a winner, though, compared to the $25 or $30 million it would have cost us to shut the plant down.

While we could only get the company to gulp down money for four years, Erwin has it running profitably now. I was pretty sure he could do that, because he liked the challenge. I'm sure if he'd had a failing factory in the US, I would have wanted the same challenge of builing it out.

But, you know, there just aren't many challenges like that when you get as big as Fleetwood. There used to be companies that were four times our size, and it was a tightly competitive situation, trying to surpass them. But we did pass them all, years ago, and have been Number One in everything we do. That takes a lot of the fun out of it for me.

I felt retirement had been on the back burner for three or four years. Doing the top management stuff when you get to be the size of Fleetwood is really dullsville. It's a lot of ceremony and bullshit that to me isn't that much fun. What I enjoy is building the prototypes, designing new product, working with the people in the plants, and conferring with dealers and owners in the field. Being in upper management, dealing with the financial world and the corporate politics, gets old quick.

Some people, like Nelson Potter, thrive on that sort of stuff, though. About a year before I retired, Glenn Kummer announced that Nelson was going to succeed him as the next president of Fleetwood. That mystified me, because I really felt Elden Smith or Jon Nord should have been in line for the job. Jon and Elden were equally deserving, each having done tremendous jobs heading up their divisions. They had often been at odds with Glenn, but they always prevailed in spite of him, because they were always acting in accord with Fleetwood's written policy. With our bonus system, they had both done well for themselves in their three decades with Fleetwood, and not long after Glenn made it known that Nelson was in line for the presidency, they both retired.

Granted, it would have been tough for Glenn to choose Elden over Jon or vice-versa. But they respected each other well enough that I don't think either would have felt too slighted. I don't know that they had that sort of respect for Nelson. I certainly didn't.

The thing that made me subsequently decide to take a hike was Fleetwood management's decision to go into retailing by buying scores of mobile home dealership lots. I've already written a bit about my opposition to that.

Dealer-manufacturers aren't anything new, but it used to mainly be smaller companies that were involved in it. In the past few years, though, some of our bigger competitors jumped into it.

As Fleetwood's president and chief operating officer, Glenn was bothered by this trend, because he could see that the manufacturers who were also making the retail profit on their units were commanding higher earnings per unit sold.

Meanwhile, Fleetwood remained the number one wholesale company by far. You would have to put the next two or three companies together to equal the business we were doing, so I wasn't alarmed by the other companies' retail move at all. I figured it was a trend that wouldn't get much further.

It started getting more serious when the consolidators came in, creating blocks of dealerships and then selling them to our competitors. We were starting to lose some shelf space around the country because of that. But in almost every case, the managers in the regional plants were able to pick up other dealers, so we really weren't losing any business.

I believed that the best thing Fleetwood could do would be to help support independent dealers, and concentrate on providing them with a competitive product with a lot of value. From that vantage, we could sit out the retail craze from the sidelines, since I think it's going to blow up in the manufacturers' faces. (As of mid-1999 it had, and it has only gotten worse since then.)

Some deals may look great on paper, but when you consider the day-to-day, ground-level realities of what you're getting into, it's an entirely different picture.

In Fleetwood's first twenty five years, I spent probably a quarter of my time calling on dealers at retail lots, to check out the product and see what the public wanted. Hence, I was well aware of what it took to run a retail establishment. It's a tough job that takes a lot of flexibility and savvy, and that's one of the reasons why I was so adamant against going into retail.

One of my favorite mobile home dealers, Pearl Murray in Palm Springs, once took in a snow plow as a down payment on a mobile home when business was slow. Palm Springs doesn't get snow very often, but she was able to sell that plow at a profit. There's no way a factory-owned store would have the savvy and guts to pull off deals like that, and that's not even a particularly extreme example of what dealers do to keep going.

My main concern was that each of the dealerships we'd be inheriting had several salesmen. Trailer salesmen will do anything to get a commission—and that's good; they're the kind of people you need to sell the merchandise—but they need to be monitored closely. Otherwise, they'll get a customer into a house by skirting around the down payment. When you do that, you're just begging for a repossession, and there's nothing worse than a repossessed mobile home. There's no place to store it. It's not good collateral. Nobody wants it. Our own Fleetwood

Finance company never financed mobile homes, because, unlike RVs, they're a high risk.

Mobile home dealerships are like auto dealerships, where it's the dealer's money at stake. The individual dealer has a vested interest in keeping a rein on his guys, and he can do it, because he comes from that school and knows all the tricks. But how is a big manufacturer like Fleetwood going to ride herd on them?

Our company policy had been very strict on the matter of selling to dealers exclusively, so our owning dealerships was a violation of long-standing, successful policy. The issue was also the first time in Fleetwood's history that the top management felt something I disagreed with was absolutely necessary to the company. Glenn and his people kept hammering me that the life or death of the company was riding on our getting into retail.

When I talked it over with Donna, I said, "These guys feel certain that they're right, that it's a good thing for the company, but I don't feel good about it, so I think I'll just get the fuck out."

And I did. I never told anyone at Fleetwood that's why I was leaving, but that was the reason.

So, in January of 1998, I retired from Fleetwood. I was named Chairman Emeritus, which meant I could attend board meetings and voice my opinion, though I couldn't vote on anything.

I wasn't at all tearful about my decision. Several months after I resigned, I attended the first Fleetwood shareholders' meeting that I didn't chair since we went public in 1965. I sat in the audience. And I have to say, it really felt good to be sitting there. I wasn't feeling un-empowered. I was thinking, "I'm so glad I'm not doing that shit anymore."

Fleetwood went into its first big retailing operation before I retired. We formed an outfit called Expression Homes in a partnership deal with a company called Pulte. The partnership was to market our mobile homes, and to develop housing subdivisions in which to put them.

I thought that was a sensible way for Glenn to go into retailing, because it was an arm's-length setup where we wouldn't be running the dealerships directly. That was good, because when I had seen manufacturers open company stores in the past, all the independent dealers were off of them like fleas off a dead dog. The dealers don't want their supplier competing with them down the block. They don't feel it's fair, and it isn't. That was one of my biggest objections.

But as soon as I retired and Glenn assumed the chairmanship, he became desperate to buy the 112 sales lots the consolidators had amassed in a package they called HomeUSA. Many of those dealerships had been good Fleetwood customers for years, and the consolidators told Glenn that if we didn't buy them, our biggest competitor, Champion, would. Champion was already nipping at our heels because it had merged with our next-largest competitor, Redman. Their combined sales made them nearly as big as us in mobile homes.

Fleetwood bought the package of dealerships in a cash and stock deal worth about $160 million. What the company got for about $1.5 million apiece were locations that consisted of some inexpensive, generally leased, real estate, each with an office and an inventory of floored mobile homes. The lots had hardly any real value to them at all.

Fleetwood had to post about three-quarters of the $160 million on the books as goodwill, and you can't write that off. Well, you can, but only amortized over 40 years, so you might as well have pushed the money down a garbage disposal.

If that wasn't bad enough, to complete the HomeUSA deal, Fleetwood had to get out of the partnership with Pulte, because they'd signed an exclusivity agreement with them. Fleetwood had to pay Pulte about $10 million to extricate themselves from that, with nothing to show for it.

Eventually, I see one of two things happening. The

Justice Department is going to wake up and see the manufacturer/dealerships for the scam and monopoly it is and make the industry divest. If that doesn't happen, the manufacturers will find that these dealerships are unmanageable. That latter possibility is more likely.

One of the other big mobile home companies that owns retail lots recently found that the credit contracts their dealerships had generated proved to be bad loans, and they had to repossess a huge number of units. In the meantime, they'd been posting the money from the unsold paper as profit. When the Securities and Exchange Commission investigated them and made them accurately report their numbers, their earnings over this period took a nose dive. When that news hit Wall Street, it tarred the entire industry, and all mobile home stocks took a dip.

It will be interesting to see how much, if any, of the Fleetwood policy the company retains over the coming years. It's been whittled from so many directions—owning dealerships, going into debt, not promoting from within the company, cutting the profit-sharing—that I scarcely recognize the thing.

I think a company loses a lot of its personality when the founder leaves. That's not necessarily bad, because I was ultraconservative over the years. Though in being conservative, I can't help noting that I did better than anybody else did by being aggressive, cutting corners or playing fast with other people's money.

Donna with "All My Children" star Susan Lucci.

With Bill Cosby.

RICH IS BETTER

The closest thing I ever had to a spiritual experience was a time as a kid when I almost drowned in the Kern River. It was during the first summer I was up there with my dad. I had just learned to swim, and most of the kids there were better at it. We usually swam at a spot where the river was wide and shallow, but there was another place down-river near some rapids, where kids had found that if they dived in at one particular place the current would carry them across the river. Then, you could hike upriver a ways and find a similar current that would carry you back.

I got up the nerve to try it one day, because all the other kids were already over on the other side. I caught the current, and was halfway across the river when I slipped out of the current and went tumbling downstream in a rushing torrent.

I remember catching a couple of breaths, and then I passed out. It was the most peaceful sensation. There was no panic or fear to it, just a slipping away, and a feeling that everything was all right. I don't even remember struggling or gagging.

I woke up lying across a rock with a naked guy pounding on my back. He was some kind of foreigner—Eastern European, I think—who had been sunbathing in the nude down-river when he saw me floating by. He happened to be a jock, a strong swimmer, and he jumped in and pulled me out. I've sometimes wondered if he was an angel, because he wasn't in the camp at all before or after that. The odds of someone like that being there, and of seeing me at that moment, were really slim. The guy should have received a medal, because people drowned in that river all the time. To this day, there is a sign mounted beside the river tallying all the lives it has taken.

He was beating the water out of me when I came to. The first thing I did was get up and piss like a horse. In about fifteen minutes I was fully recovered, and I went back to camp. I never told anyone about it, not my dad or anyone. By that afternoon I was back swimming in the river.

I don't know if that's what death feels like, just that peaceful slipping away. I hope so, because when you get to be my age, so many of the people you know have passed away. My lifetime friend Red died in the early '80s of cancer, and there's been a slew of friends going since then.

I think that there is a heaven, for a lot of reasons. For one thing, when you come out as a baby, you don't know anything about anything. You go through life, and when you die, you're the smartest you're going to be. I don't think that whoever put this whole universe together is going to waste that. There's a reason for all that experience. It all has to go somewhere.

I expect heaven is more of a spiritual place than here, where you're not tied to a physical body. Maybe it is something like a huge radio receiver and tape recorder, and, every second, your brain is sending off signals that are recorded there. It's not a physical thing, but, when you croak, the entire experience that makes up your being is recorded there. It's not the skin, meat and bone, but I think your individuality continues.

But I don't think about death that much, because it's beyond our comprehension. It's like the way standing outside and staring at a star-filled sky is beyond your comprehension.

Maybe that's one of the reasons why so many kids in the cities are screwed-up now: with all the light and smog, they never see any stars. They think everything's man-made. But, boy, if you get out in the desert on a starry night, you can see that there's a lot of stuff going on that you don't have any idea about.

I try to take the teachings of Jesus to heart, but almost all religions basically teach the same thing. We happen to have the Christian version. Generally, as I see it, you're supposed to have faith that the big radio receiver is working up there. And you're supposed to be good to your fellow man. It's pretty simple to me.

I think the purpose of life is that we're here to have a good time. Is that too simple? We're here to enjoy it.

When I was four years old, eating fried chicken was a good time; when I was a teenager, getting laid was a good time; and I always had a good time building things. And somewhere along the line doing unto others becomes a good time.

Maybe that's because you do better at things if you do them for someone else. We don't even get dressed nicely for our own sakes, but to please others.

Something in our Fleetwood company policy, at least as I wrote it, was that if you're in business to make money for yourself, chances are you won't succeed, but if you're in business to serve other people and do something for them that they can't do for themselves, you'll probably do well. And I believe that. If that's what motivates you, your whole life will be different.

On the housing side, over three-and-a-half million people have a Fleetwood roof over their heads, and something like 65,000 more families a year buy a Fleetwood home. Interviewers have occasionally asked me if I felt noble about having enabled so many people to buy their first home. I hear about people having such altruistic feelings, but I don't recognize that in myself.

I designed and built homes because it was fun, which is the same reason Donna and I assist charities the way we do. If you do it grudgingly, you're doing it for the wrong reason. If you do it because you like to do it, it's no skin off your nose, so I don't see why people make such a big deal about it.

I don't see the challenge in just making money. Donna and I played the stock market for about a year, and it was just plain boring. It was like watching the grass grow, or investing in real estate. I'd rather create something. Fleetwood stock was the only stock that interested me.

You might have to get old, but you don't have to get cranky. Donna says that sometimes she and the kids hold grudges for me, because I don't bother to. If somebody wrongs me—and nobody ever has in a way worth dwelling on—I just figure, "Well that's his problem," and forget it.

Perhaps that attitude is a backlash from the way my mother was when I was a child. You'd think grudges came with handles, she held them so well. She'd tell the same stories, over and over again, about how every bad thing that happened in her life was somebody else's fault. I heard her story of how she and her first husband had been cheated out of some laundry business over 100 times. And that didn't set well with me.

It made no sense. Friends and acquaintances are a pretty valuable asset, and you don't write some guy off because he deals you wrong once. There's hardly anybody you're ever going to meet who doesn't have a few warts or a bad day.

If I come across somebody who is a real snake, I just don't do business with him again. I learned that lesson in the Compton city jail. Don and I were in there for one of the usual reasons—it might have been grand theft—and I started talking with a guy who was in for receiving stolen property. I asked him how he came to be in jail, and he told me that the guy he'd sold the stuff to got popped and ratted on him.

I said, "Boy, when you get out of here, you've got somebody's ass to kick." He said, "No, no, what good will that do? I just won't do any more business with him." That made a lot of practical sense to me.

I had a heart attack in 1992 and didn't even know it. I was in the hospital at the time, having my carotid artery cleaned out. I was still blacked-out in the recovery room when the monitoring equipment flashed on the nurse's station. They came running in and threw the electricity to me and got me going. They put me in an ambulance, along with a cardiologist, and drove me to another hospital that was better set up to handle heart attacks. So I went to sleep in one hospital, woke up in another one, with no idea of what I'd been through. There was no emotional trauma attached to it at all.

I don't worry as much as I might when I go into surgery, because my family physician is always in there alongside the surgeon. Dr. Bob Roper is the sort of great, caring physician who looks after you 100 percent. And it isn't just because I'm stinking rich: any of his patients would tell you the same.

I called him once at 6 a.m. when Donna was having abdominal pains. By 6:30 he'd showed up at the house, checked her out and was driving her to the hospital. He called the surgeon on the way, and by 8:30 a.m. they had her appendix out.

Most of the family had split town when I had the heart attack. My daughter Susie was the first one on the scene, and she wanted to be able to be by my side, but she had a baby, my granddaughter Elizabeth, to look after. Dr. Roper offered to look after Elizabeth for a few days. When he was driving home, he called Jan, his wife, and said, "I've got a surprise for you."

When he got home, she saw the baby in the seat next to him, and asked, "Is there something you've been keeping from me?"

For the artery cleaning, they had put a balloon in me to get the artery opened up. They did that again a couple of months later. I figured if my carotids were that clogged up, my heart must be a real mess. Sure enough, that's what the cardiologist called for next. It was just before the Thanksgiving weekend in November of 1994, and he suggested waiting until after the holiday, because you don't want to be stuck in the hospital when they're short on personnel. I had a quadruple bypass done the Monday after the Thanksgiving weekend.

Two weeks after the surgery, the Mobile Home Association wanted to give me some big-ass award at a banquet near my home. I was feeling pretty good, so Manuel went to the hotel that afternoon to case the joint and have some ramps put in. At the appointed time, I put on my tux, got in my wheelchair, was wheeled in the hall's back entrance by Manuel, was announced, wheeled out on the stage, received the award, read a three page speech about all my friends who had helped me in life, was wheeled out, and was back home within exactly an hour.

I've had a few other surgeries over the years, for my back and other things, but none of it ever slowed me down for long. Even after I retired from Fleetwood, I continued to work on motor home designs with them, and I'm always tinkering on the home front, too. You know how those plastic bags from the supermarket are always flopping over in your trunk, with everything spilling out? I took a piece of wood, put five big cup hooks on it, and screwed it to the trunk ceiling on several of our cars. You hang your bags on the hooks, and they stay upright for the ride home. I think every car should have one. If I wasn't already rich, I'd manufacture them myself.

A couple of years ago I bought a 112-foot yacht, named the Donna C, and I've been fixing things on it ever since I got the pink slip.

One of the nice things about having money is that you don't have to worry much about the resale value when you want to modify something to suit you. The yacht's kitchen had some very stylish recessed lights, which were splendid for pointing at and saying, "My, aren't those some stylish lights?" Beyond that, they were useless. I was cooking in Braille, because I couldn't see a damn thing. I tore those out and installed some boxy plastic fluorescent fixtures like you see in RVs.

There were so many features on this yacht that could have been better that it gave me the urge to have one done right from scratch. That's what I'm doing now, having a 125-footer custom-made in Vancouver. I designed it, and it's going to be a beaut, with a walk-in freezer and refrigerator, a freezer/fish box that you can load up with a couple of tons of fish, and a Steinway grand piano in the salon.

The only reason I wound up where I am was that every job I ever had eventually became boring for me, up until I got into the trailer industry. That always challenged my creativity. It never did quit being fun.

There's a shop at Fleetwood's headquarters in Riverside where they invent folding tables and all sorts of fun gadgets for motor homes. They always have something different to do, and always have to employ their ingenuity. Every time I walk through there, I think that if I'd found a job like that 50 years ago, I'd still be punching a time card, and be just as happy.

That was the main motivation for me. I never did pay much attention to what I was getting paid. It had to be fun.

But, that said, money ain't bad. Sometimes, when newspaper writers have asked me what my greatest motivation in life was, I've told them it was poverty. Poverty is a great motivator. It's in many successful people's backgrounds. Most people in the younger generation have been raised with so many goodies that they never experience that kind of motivation.

Last year, we were heading out of Newport Bay on the Donna C, and we passed some teenagers in a dinghy, close enough to hear one girl on board comment to her friends, "Boy, it must suck to be rich."

As Joe E. Lewis said, "I've been poor and I've been rich. And I'll tell you one thing — rich is better."

I'm grateful for the way my life has gone. It's been good, like a fairy tale to me. And I think it has been that way because I never really expected any of it. I wasn't striving for wealth as a goal. It just came along. In the meantime, I've had a great family, wonderful friends and just one damn adventure after another. And I still get up every day fascinated to see what's next.

I think the book ends quite nicely right here, don't you? Unless you enjoy reading about backstabbing corporate shenanigans and the sorry decline of American business practices, I'd recommend you stop reading now. Call it a wrap. Your work is done. Go get a sandwich.

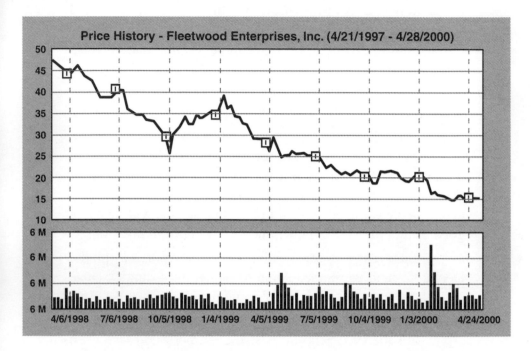

After I retired in 1998, leaving Fleetwood stock at an all-time high of $48-1/2, company policy went out the window, with dire results. At this writing, the stock price is below $13 and sinking. With a descent like this, maybe Fleetwood should be in the toboggan business.

BOW TO THE EAST —
WALL STREET WANTS YOU!

You couldn't take my advice, could you? There you were, with me happily retired, Donna and I riding off into the sunset in a Bounder, and Fleetwood nearing its 50th anniversary in capable hands.

Then you had to turn the page, to find that I am now calling that event Fleetwood's *second* anniversary, and that I am suddenly shut out of the Fleetwood boardroom. And why, you might wonder, am I starting out in business all over again at age 74?

Well, Donna and I *had* been sailing off into the sunset on the Donna C, on an extended trip to the Sea of Cortez with the also-now-retired Fleetwood VPs Elden Smith and Jon Nord and their wives. And I was really looking forward to getting away from it all and into my usual relaxing routine of fishing, cooking and jury-rigging every useless damn thing onboard. Believe me, that's relaxation compared to what I'd been doing.

Since I retired, I've needed to involve myself in more boardroom bullshit than I ever had before. As Chairman Emeritus, I didn't have a vote anymore, but I could still attend meetings and put my two cents in. At a special board meeting on the Monday three days before we sailed, I'd had to weigh in with those two cents like they were a roll of quarters.

As I've mentioned previously, I'd felt that Glenn had made a bad decision in buying the HomeUSA package of mobile home dealerships. I figured Glenn would try to make the retail lots work for a year or two, and then sell them off, probably losing a couple of hundred million dollars in the process.

C'est la vie. It's a bundle, but the company could survive that. The dust had hardly settled over the HomeUSA deal, though, when Glenn called this Monday morning special meeting of the board of directors.

These surprise meetings were becoming a habit with Glenn. Both the Pulte and HomeUSA deals had been put to the board the same way: Glenn would call an unscheduled meeting, giving the required 48-hour advance notice on a Friday, so there were no business days before Monday, when the board members would have to decide on these "urgent" deals using only the information Glenn and his people gave them.

This time, the agenda in the notice called for a proposed major merger with another manufactured housing competitor, one which was already heavily into retailing. My son Andy (who had been on the Fleetwood board since 1982) decided we should not be so trusting this time, and spent the weekend researching the competitor on the Internet.

I signed a confidentiality agreement that prevents me from mentioning the other manufacturer's actual name, so let's call it Deadwood. Andy found that the company was a disaster waiting to happen, except that it wasn't waiting. This was the same company I mentioned previously that had fudged so heavily on its earnings statements that the Securities and Exchange Commission had stepped in; the company whose shenanigans made the whole industry look suspect to investors, which drove down the value of all manufactured housing company stocks.

Deadwood's manufactured home sales were nearly the equal of ours, and its stock price had gone up to $42 at one point. But the SEC found that Deadwood was posting profits they were a long way from actually realizing. When their real position was reported the stock plunged to $12, and stockholders started suing. Meanwhile, Deadwood was further saddled with the principal and unbelievable 8% interest it owed on a $300 million loan.

Given these particulars, Deadwood did not strike Andy or me as being a particularly dynamic enterprise. I couldn't see anything but trouble in Fleetwood merging with them.

I called a meeting of my own, asking the directors whom I thought were trustworthy to join me on the Donna C in Newport Harbor on Sunday, the day before the board meeting.

The board had eight directors. Two of those were from Fleetwood's management: Glenn, who had become CEO when I retired, and Nelson Potter, whom Glenn had named president. Five of the remaining six members were ones I had named to the board.

Those five met me on the Donna C, and I went over how dangerous Andy and I thought the Deadwood merger was, and how far I believed Glenn and Nelson had moved Fleetwood away from the fundamental policies that had served the company so well. With the Pulte deal, HomeUSA and now Deadwood, it was obvious to me that I had made a terrible mistake in turning Fleetwood over to Glenn. He was in over his head, and couldn't manage properly. The company was in trouble, and he needed to be replaced. I told the board members on the boat that I wanted to be voted back in as chairman and that the first thing I'd do was fire Glenn and Nelson. Then I'd untangle the mess they'd created.

I'd contacted Elden Smith and Jon Nord, and they were willing to come back to the Fleetwood board. As relieved as I'd been to retire the year before, I didn't have any qualms about returning as chairman. With Elden and Jon back helping, there really wouldn't be much for the chairman to do, because they were so on top of things. While he was president, Glenn had presided over Fleetwood's best years, but Fleetwood's spectacular growth in his era was due to Jon and Elden running their divisions so well.

Neither of them were anxious to come back, but they would have done it to save the company. After we'd sorted things out, there were still enough good, policy-loyal plant managers in the company that we could have turned the reins over to them and gone confidently back into retirement.

At the board meeting that Monday, Glenn, his team,

and the guys from PaineWebber—who would be brokering the deal—all gave us their pitch.

A brokerage firm is legally required to weigh the fairness of a merger. It has to look at both companies and give their opinion that it's a square deal as far as the public and the stockholders are concerned. So the PaineWebber guys had a dog and pony show where they told how fine this merger was. Then they had a retail expert consultant give us a pitch about how wonderful the Deadwood retail lots would be for us, and how much money we could make selling pest control programs to the customers.

To hear them speak, it was a merger made in heaven, where all we'd have to do was count our money and spray bugs all day. But then Andy asked them what earnings we'd need to generate to pay the interest on Deadwood's debts and to cover the stock dividends the merger called for.

The answer was an amount equal to the combined earnings Fleetwood and Deadwood had generated in the past year, which had been their peak years. If there was ever a downturn in business, which there since has been, there not only would be no earnings or growth, but they'd have to siphon from the company's working capital to meet its new expenses. (Within a few months, this marvelous company PaineWebber was trying to saddle us with posted a staggering $63 million quarterly loss and its stock dropped to under $3!)

Finally, I asked, "Now PaineWebber has gone to a lot of trouble here, doing all this research and printing up these graphs. What's their fee for doing all this work?" And, of course, we were told they only get a fee if the deal goes through. That means they merely had about $10 million to gain by saying the merger looked solid!

I questioned their ability to be impartial in that circumstance. The senior PaineWebber man in attendance got all blustery over that, and he walked out of the meeting.

It was pretty obvious by then that the merger would

have been voted down, so Glenn didn't put it to a vote. He did manage to sidestep the motion to return me to the board, saying it was out of order and would be addressed at a future meeting.

When the meeting was over, both Andy and I asked Glenn, "Are you satisfied now? Can you settle down and go about running things in a less dangerous way?" And he said, "Oh, yes. Everything is fine."

The following morning I got a call from Glenn assuring me the Deadwood deal was off the table. It was looking more hopeful to me that things could work out with Glenn still running the company. I mentioned that I had some strategies I wanted to discuss with Fleetwood's manufactured homes head. Glenn put me off on that, saying the man wasn't available. I told Glenn I figured it could wait until I got back from Mexico.

So it was after all this Monday ruckus that we took off Thursday in the Donna C. We would have been irretrievably far down the Baja if rough weather hadn't caused us to lay up in Ensenada. That's where we got a call from Andy late Friday, saying he'd had *another* notice on his porch that day about *another* special Monday board meeting.

The agenda Andy read to me included a motion to pack the board with three new members, and a motion to create a five-man executive committee to sidestep any board members who might disagree with Glenn. There was a further motion to limit board meeting attendance to "actively-serving members," which was a nice, indirect way of saying they were going to toss my ass out of there.

I called Manuel at Village Crean and asked him to drive down to Ensenada to get me, and was home by 2 p.m. Saturday. I contacted a local law firm, and spent that afternoon and all day Sunday into the night with their lawyers, seeing if we could find some way to fend off this coup.

Of the five board members who had met with me on the boat before the last meeting, I was really only sure of three of them: Andy; Tom Fuentes, who is head of the Republican Party in Orange County; and Jim Doti, the president of Chapman University in Orange, CA.

From Glenn's new agenda, it was pretty obvious that what had been said on my boat the previous Sunday had been reported to him. The two other board members who had been on the boat were Walter Beran, who was the retired managing partner for Ernst and Ernst in the LA region (He'd known Glenn for decades, since Glenn's days at Ernst and Ernst), and Doug Lawson, a former minister who had been doing fund-raising for Bob Schuller when I met him.

On Monday morning, we showed up at the board meeting, and Glenn looked pretty damn surprised to see me. But we knew going in that there wasn't much we could do to stop him. All that our attorneys had discovered over the weekend was that Fleetwood's attorneys had their ducks in a row. Under Delaware law—where Fleetwood is incorporated—everything they were doing was legal.

Andy and my other son Johnnie had spent much of the weekend trying to sway the board members we were doubtful about back to our side. We had some small hope of their efforts prevailing, but the only thing we were certain our presence at the board meeting would accomplish was to make things more uncomfortable for Glenn. He'd have to stab me in my chest instead of the back.

With his years in the political arena, Tom Fuentes can be a feisty guy, and he got in Glenn's face right off the bat. Tom insisted upon seeing the minutes of the last meeting, and was told that the corporate secretaries didn't have them prepared yet. Then he just pressed on like a tank: "At the last meeting, I made a motion to bring Mr. Crean back on the board, and it was seconded by Dr. Doti, and you ruled it out of order and said we'd take that up at a later date. This is a later date."

Glenn said, "No, we're going to stick to the agenda. That's not on the agenda." Glenn next told me that I could make a statement if I liked, but then they would ask me to leave.

"I don't have a statement," I said, "but I had been invited to attend all board meetings, and it had been voted on by the board, and unless you want to vote again and make me not welcome, I'm going to stay right here."

Glenn then called for a vote on item number six on the agenda, which was the one to exclude me. Tom jumped up again and said, "Wait, you said you were going to stick with the agenda."

The Fleetwood corporate attorney then whispered something in Glenn's ear. Glenn asked for a motion to adjust the agenda, which was passed. Then they voted on item number six, which threw me out. Glenn and Nelson Potter voted against me, as did their man on the board, Tom Pitcher. Then Walter Beran raised his hand. Finally, down at the end of the table, Doug Lawson timidly raised his, too, as if he was hoping I wouldn't notice.

And that was that. I was ejected from the company I'd created and loved for nearly half a century!

After I left, the board voted in every item on the agenda, five to three, bing-bing-bing-bing-bing. Then they voted to give all the directors a $4000-a-year raise in salary, with an additional $6000 for those on the new executive committee.

During a break in the meeting, Tom Fuentes walked up to Doug Lawson, kissed the former minister on the cheek and said, "Judas Priest!" Tom figured that Doug had earned his thirty pieces of silver.

Aside from when I voiced my objection over being asked to leave, I hadn't said a thing in the meeting. When I get angry, I clam up, because that's not the time to speak. And I've never felt as angry and betrayed as I did then. I was astounded by what Glenn, Walter and Doug had done.

On my drive home, I was thinking, "Well, should I break these guys' legs or should I just *kill* them? What should I do with these sons of bitches?" Then all of a sudden I caught myself and said, "Hey, John, that ain't your modus operandi. You've never held any grudges or carried any resentments and you ain't gonna start now."

The next day, I called Glenn and told him I wasn't going to contest his moves. My family and I were Fleetwood's largest individual shareholders—we held 2.6 million shares, about 9% of the company—and we could have raised a pretty loud ruckus. But anything we did would only have hurt the company more, while also having no real chance of succeeding, because, under Delaware's incorporation laws, stockholders have no rights!

Back when hostile takeovers were all the rage, corporations lobbied Delaware lawmakers to shape the rules to help stave off such takeovers. But, as they are written, they also make it impossible for stockholders to regain control of a corporation once management has taken over. I have asked my local congressmen, Representatives Chris Cox, Dana Rohrabacher and Ed Royce, to have the SEC look into the fairness of Delaware's incorporation laws, because—I can't overemphasize this point—shareholders have no rights! Any action that might ensue won't effect me, as I've dumped my Fleetwood shares, but I'd like to see shareholders get some protections in the future.

In all the time I've known Glenn, I've always liked and trusted him. I thought he was a 100% square shooter. If someone had told me he was a weasel, I never would have believed it. Being sneaky with these last-minute board meetings wasn't like the Glenn I thought I knew. But I guess his actions showed his character, or lack of same. Power is a strong drug.

I've heard from people at Fleetwood that the party line in upper management now is that I'm old and senile and don't know what I'm doing. When some of the recent board actions spilled into the newspapers, Paul Bingham, Glenn's senior VP of finance, told reporters I was out of touch with the changing world of Fleetwood's business.

I guess that sounds better than admitting the real reason why I was thrown out: because I was a threat to Glenn's power.

And they've never said anything about the event that precipitated my ouster, my opposition to Glenn's plan to merge with Deadwood. As a few mere months have proved, that merger would have dragged Fleetwood right into the toilet. I was thrown out for saving Fleetwood from a disaster.

Looking at things from Glenn and Nelson's angle, I can see why they'd want to get rid of me. Nearly every other big business is playing Wall Street games and leveraging all over the place, gambling with borrowed money. They wanted to be at the gaming tables, while I was expecting them to work for a living.

When I retired, Fleetwood's 1998 annual report contained a letter signed by Glenn and Nelson praising "the basic management principals and business policies that John established" and assuring stockholders that they looked forward to "building upon Fleetwood's traditional management philosophy which he established."

But even long before I left they were chipping away at Fleetwood policy, and I acquiesced to it. Part of that was due to my usual belief in letting my management guys make their own decisions, including some wrong ones. But part, I have to admit, was me not just paying enough attention to the company. With my 1992 heart attack and other surgeries, I wasn't fully up to speed for several years, and it was pretty easy for me to be made to feel that I was out of touch.

Even so, I don't know how I let the company stray so far, because some of the things on which I'd allowed Fleetwood to slide were fundamental to me.

As I'd mentioned in the *How to Succeed...* chapter, my focus in running a business hadn't been to make a lot of money; it was to stay alive. If you make a lot of money along the way, great, but you don't do it by playing games that compromise the jobs you've created and the customers you serve. Fleetwood's whole game now is to impress Wall Street. What had mattered to me was giving the customers good value and treating the employees fairly. Our success was a natural result of that.

As I've mentioned previously, Glenn had sold off Fleetwood's credit corporation in 1996. In ten years, our credit corporation had proved to the finance industry that RV loans were good, solid business, and it had done that by being profitable. But Glenn wanted to unload it because it wasn't giving us quite the return on capital that our manufacturing was, and, hence, was bringing down the earnings average with which he hoped to impress Wall Street.

That kind of thinking made no sense at all to me. Whether it brought our average down or not, it was profit, and it was ours. The credit corporation also gave value to the consumer; our rates were lower than our competitors. And our selling it never did make the price of our stock go up.

If the money from the sale had been invested in boosting our manufacturing capability it wouldn't have been so bad. Instead it was used to finance a Dutch auction stock buy-back in mid-1996. One easy way to increase Fleetwood's earnings per share was to buy back shares: you have fewer pieces of pie out there, so everyone's piece gets a little bigger and, in theory, the value of the stock goes up. (It bears mentioning that PaineWebber was there to offer their sterling advice and pick up millions in commissions on several of these debilitating decisions.)

The company announced it would buy 11.4 million shares, and wound up buying 7.7 million shares from the public and then that September got me to sell them 2.4 million of my shares. Fleetwood's stock value did get a boost, though that was also a time when the industry was posting high earnings, and it might of had that boost anyway. Even Wall Street is starting to notice that the most valuable manufacturers are the ones who actually manufacture something.

The week before I was shut out of Fleetwood, a strategy I wanted to discuss with the manufactured homes head was focusing the division on making single-unit low-end homes—that's the young marrieds' first home, with mom and pop financing them. Fleetwood and the other retailer-manufacturers are all pushing fancier units with a big sales price and bigger profit.

If Fleetwood had gone into making low-end units in volume and cut its margins, the company could have claimed 95 percent of that low-end business and just sat there comfortably until the dealer-manufacturers killed themselves off, which is what I really think will happen.

In the fiscal year which ended in April 1999, Fleetwood had already lost $5.2 million on its retail efforts, not counting the $10 million they blew untangling the Pulte deal. At this writing, Fleetwood stock—which had excellent growth since 1965, until peaking at $48 $1/2$ a share by the time I announced my retirement—has dipped below $13 a share. So much for Glenn and Nelson's stock-enhancing moves.

Because Fleetwood's policy of constant growth has been replaced by one of constant trimming and money shuffling, it has been alienating employees and losing some of its best management people. With new plants, there was always a good chance for advancement, and the employees see that door closing.

At the same time, Fleetwood has been undercutting the bonus system that has been such an incentive for almost 50 years. The bonus percentage has been lowered, and, on top of that, the plants are now charged a "cost of capital" expense that comes out of the profit before the bonuses are figured. To have productive people, they have to be happy. Employees can't be giving their best if they feel they're getting screwed.

There was one grand exception to the bonus cuts: Glenn, Nelson, the board of directors and other top management are the beneficiaries of what they call a "dividend equivalent payout." They've been liberally awarded stock options over the years and even without exercising them—they'd be crazy to now, since they've driven the stock value to low—they're getting quarterly checks equivalent to the dividend paid to stockholders. So without showing any real faith in the company by actually having bought the stock, they get the full benefit. Tom Fuentes, who also benefits from the payouts, proposed that the board suspend them until the stock price improved, and was immediately shot down by Glenn's camp. They also recently voted in a nice golden parachute for Glenn.

At this writing, the company is gearing up to have a big wing-ding—and probably blow a couple of million more dollars—celebrating Fleetwood's 50th anniversary in 2000. But the Fleetwood that started in a Compton garage and grew for all those years doesn't exist anymore.

At a recent, scheduled board meeting Tom Fuentes asked Glenn, "How are you going to celebrate 50 years of the company when you're estranged from the founder?" And Glenn said, "There isn't anybody who knows of any estrangement."

I didn't advertise my ouster, but the word got around Fleetwood immediately anyway. I doubt my absence will mean much to the world at large, and I don't know that it should. What does matter is that they've abandoned the company policy. That policy *is* Fleetwood, and with it gone, the old Fleetwood is dead and it is now a new creature entirely.

So they can go celebrate their anniversary if they like, but it's truly their second anniversary, not their 50th. I won't be there, and I'll be surprised if Fleetwood's leadership will be around for too much longer either, the way they're going. In the meantime, they can celebrate their two-year history of taking the price of Fleetwood stock from $48 to below $13, of showing quarterly earnings that are 30 to 40 percent below estimates, of being de-listed by Standard & Poor's, of making one lousy decision after another, of alienating their best employees, of losing the company's leading place in manufactured home sales and of losing my beloved Bounder's long-held No. 1 sales position to Winnebago.

As for me, I thought for a couple of weeks that I'd settle into retirement. I turned 74 this past Fourth of July, I've done my bit, and I could keep busy enough enjoying my family, gallivanting around in my new boat and doing the cooking show until we manage to set the garage on fire.

I know people who look forward to retirement all their lives, but I've realized that's just not me. Not long after my ouster, I had lunch with my pal Dan Pocapalia, who is one of the real good guys in the business. His Kit Manufacturing Company is the only enterprise that's been around in the industry as long as I have. But Dan was 83 and he was considering selling his business. I made Dan an offer. Looking over his operation, I, of course, started thinking about ways to improve on it. I gave Dan such a rosy play-by-play of how I'd turn the place around that I think he got inspired to do it himself, and decided he wasn't quite ready to sell and retire yet.

Around the same time, I got a call informing me that Dale Skinner had died. He'd been in failing health, and Donna and I had been to see him just the week before. But his dying struck me pretty hard, both for the good man that he had been, and for the bulwark he had been to Fleetwood. He was so loyal to Fleetwood policy and such a stickler to it that he'd get on my case if I ever deviated from it. I'm sad to see him go, but I'm also glad he doesn't have to be around to see what Fleetwood is becoming.

As much as I thought I was ready to let it all go and retire, I found a fire had lit inside of me to go into business all over again. Nearly faster than it would take me to sit around and daydream about it, I designed a new low-end diesel motor home and started making plans to go into production. (Curiously, as soon as Fleetwood got wind of this, they went to work on a low-end diesel model.)

I still might make it someday, but that went on the back burner after Donna and I got to talking one night. Donna has a natural wisdom that can go right to the heart of something, and she said, "You've already been number one in motor homes, mobile homes and travel trailers. You don't have a heck of a lot to prove there. Why don't you do something new? It would be more fun for you."

She was right, as ever, and when I started thinking about what I might do that was of value to people, affordable housing immediately sprang to mind.

When I met with President Nixon back in 1974, I introduced myself and my industry by saying, "We make mobile homes, the only affordable housing available today." Aside from trailers, there was, and still is, no other affordable housing in the US. In California now, you can scarcely get into any kind of new house for under $150,000. In the cities, even a crappy condo often goes for twice that amount. That shuts an awful lot of people out of ever affording a home of their own.

I'm usually not big on awards, but one that I'm very proud of was when in 1999 *Builder* magazine—the home-building industry's trade publication—named me one of American housing's most influential leaders of the past century, alongside names like Franklin Roosevelt, William Levitt and Frank Lloyd Wright. *Builder* wrote: "One of the most prolific home builders in history, Crean built more than one million homes during his 50-year career. As founder and chairman of Fleetwood Enterprises, Crean professionalized and led the manufactured housing industry…In building Fleetwood, Crean helped to build the industry. Because of his leadership, his emphasis on customer satisfaction and high value permeated the entire industry. He was also a hands-on innovator, developing many advances in the manufactured housing industry himself."

I'll admit to all that, but mobile homes never provided as good an answer to the affordable housing problem as I would have liked. They've always been hard for prospective buyers to finance, because they haven't been tied to any real estate like a conventional home. No one wants to finance a mobile home because, if you have to repossess it, you have to store it somewhere, so it's like being stuck with a 65-foot maggot.

In March of 2000 I bought a tract of land in Hemet, California to build my first Crean Acres subdivision of 132 homes that working people and retirees can afford to buy. Long-time home builder Steve Carlin—who works for me now—and I came up with a house design that's stronger, safer, more fire-resistant, better-insulated and more cost effective, using different construction processes and newer technologies like steel studs and trusses instead of lumber, and block foam insulation. I'm planning for these homes, with three bedrooms, appliances, garage, landscaped front yards and fenced back yards, to sell for around $110,000. Once we've got past the learning curve, I'm hoping to get the price even lower in subsequent tracts.

The housing business is overdue for a revolution. Most of the changes in construction in recent years have been aimed at maximizing profits for developers, cramming as many people into as little space as possible. They aren't adapting the technology that's available to make a home that's more livable and of greater value to the homeowner.

I had tried to sell Fleetwood's management on a similar idea, and they just couldn't see it. That goes back to what I've said about vision being essential to an entrepreneur: you have to be able to see what isn't there yet, and Glenn and Co. just don't have that. These subdivisions also tie into another essential in my book: you find success by doing something for other people.

Along those lines, I'm also planning to provide the financing so the buyer won't get reamed. I've got the money. Thanks to Glenn's shenanigans, I sold off my remaining Fleetwood shares when I was ousted, and am sitting on a boodle of money instead of a bunch of sinking Fleetwood stock.

To be able to take a business to where you have it running right and growing, with satisfied customers, and satisfied, happy employees: that's almost a religion with me. Doing that is more of a kick than fishing or anything else I could think of.

I'm convinced that these housing tracts can be the next Levittowns. It will be a fun challenge to see if I can make John Crean Homes as successful as Fleetwood was by the time I reach my 84th birthday, but that will be a story for another book.

Right now, the future is an open highway for me. Donna and I couldn't feel more blessed when we think about the road we've traveled in our half-century together, but we still wake up each day excited to see what's around the next corner. It looks like it's going to be a while before we finally ride off into the sunset, and when we do now, it will probably be to host a block party in one of the new communities we're building. See you there!